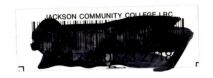

# PREPARE TO BOARD!

NC
Be
Pr
fea

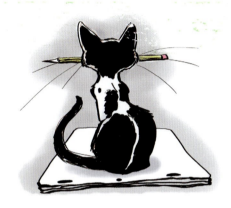

NANCY BEIMAN

# PREPARE TO BOARD!

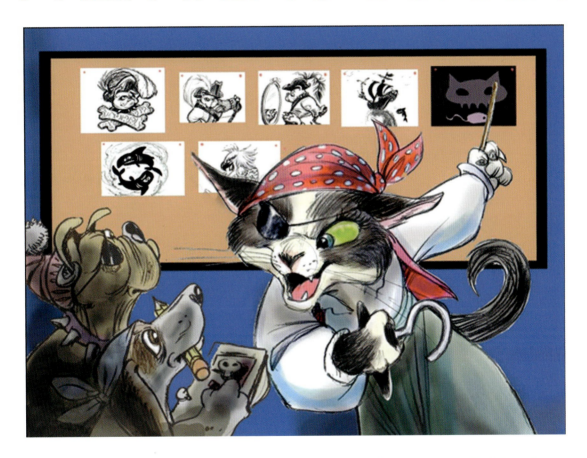

## CREATING STORY AND CHARACTERS
## FOR ANIMATED FEATURES AND SHORTS

ELSEVIER

Amsterdam · Boston · Heidelberg · London · New York · Oxford
Paris · San Diego ·San Francisco · Singapore · Sydney · Tokyo

Focal Press is an imprint of Elsevier

Focal
Press

| | |
|---|---|
| Senior Acquisitions Editor: | Paul Temme |
| Senior Project Manager: | Brandy Lilly |
| Associate Editor: | Georgia Kennedy |
| Assistant Editor: | Robin Weston |
| Marketing Manager: | Christine Degon Veroulis |
| Cover Design: | Nancy Beiman |
| Interior Design: | Detta Penna |

Focal Press is an imprint of Elsevier
30 Corporate Drive, Suite 400, Burlington, MA 01803, USA
Linacre House, Jordan Hill, Oxford OX2 8DP, UK

 Recognizing the importance of preserving what has been written, Elsevier prints its books on acid-free paper whenever possible.

**Library of Congress Cataloging-in-Publication Data**
Beiman, Nancy.
   Prepare to board! : creating story and characters for animation features and shorts / by Nancy Beiman.
      p. cm.
   Includes bibliographical references and index.
   ISBN-13: 978-0-240-80820-8 (pbk. : alk. paper)
   ISBN-10: 0-240-80820-7 (pbk. : alk. paper)    1. Animated films—Technique.    2. Animated films—Authorship.    3. Cartoon characters.    I. Title.
   NC1765.B38 2007
   791.43'34—dc22                                                        2006028112

**British Library Cataloguing-in-Publication Data**
A catalogue record for this book is available from the British Library.

ISBN 13: 978-0-240-80820-8

ISBN 10: 0-240-80820-7

For information on all Focal Press publications
visit our website at www.books.elsevier.com

07 08 09 10 11    10 9 8 7 6 5 4 3 2 1

Printed in China

# Contents

**Am I Blue? Creating Character Through Color  265**

 **Screen and Screen Again: Preparing for Production  277**

*Goodbye, Good Luck, and Have Fun!*

 **Further Reading:  Books, Discs, and Websites  279**

 **Appendices: Animated Interviews  283**

# Introduction

*"Just be sure you don't use the words 'old- fashioned!'"*

—Roy Disney in email to  author, 2005

This book describes visual storytelling and design methods developed during the "Golden Age of Animation" and still in use today, as Roy Disney pointed out to me. Some people say that story is the *only* thing that matters in animated film.  I agree. Good animation and good design never saved a bad story. Strong characters can make a weak story tolerable and a good story better, but characters develop within a story context. Each depends upon the other.

The first part of this book will concern itself with developing story *content. Technique* will be discussed in the second part, and the third part will deal with the *presentation* of the story and artwork before an audience.

Story works out of and depends on your experience and skill. There is no software that will draw good storyboards for you.

Memorable characters exist in every medium. The technology may vary but basic design principles remain constant. A well-drawn character will translate into a well-designed puppet or computer-generated imagery (CGI) character.  The principles described in the book's character design sections are intended for use in all media.

Eighty percent of an animated film's production time is spent in developing  the story, art direction, and designs for the characters. The other 20 percent is spent on the actual animation production and post-production.

Outlines, scripts, and storyboards for television, feature  length, and short animated films differ greatly from one another. Feature and short animated films are more popular than ever before. Yet their production differs from that of a television show. Most films and television shows start with a script. While scripts are important on longer animated films, they are not necessarily written at the start of the production. Animated short films may be created without any script at all.

This book will concentrate on visual scriptwriting.

There is a danger of concentrating solely on technique—the 'how'—of animation (squash and stretch, how to turn a head, how to do a walk, how to run a program) and considering story and context—the 'why'—almost an afterthought.

This is putting the cart before the horse.

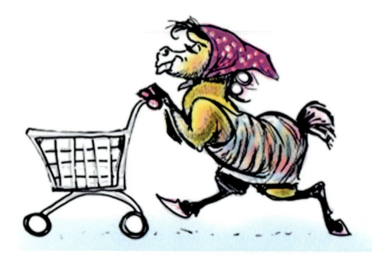

Animation and story are not mutually exclusive. Good stories and appealing characters will transcend their technology. Professional animators and hardcore fans will notice minor inconsistencies in a film. If the story is good, and the characters appealing, the audience will overlook these same inconsistencies.

Animated characters are often able to defy the laws of gravity and physics, but animated stories cannot defy the laws of common sense. The animated film must create its own reality. We must immediately comprehend the power of the poisoned apple, or the character weakness of a lion cub or a "Beast." Boredom and frustration results if a character's properties change mid-picture solely to accommodate weak storytelling.

It is not enough to rely on the soundtrack to carry the story. Ideally, dialogue in an animated film complements the visuals and not vice versa. The very best character animation can still tell the story with the soundtrack turned off. It should illustrate a story that is worth telling.

Good writing leaves a lot to the reader's imagination. Each reader creates their individual pictures of the settings and the characters' appearances based on information that the author provides. Author and reader collaborate to create the story. An animated film distributes a few artists' fantasies to large masses of people. We should try to make them good ones.

Animated actors are harder to watch than human actors. The animator must convince the audience to suspend disbelief and accept imaginary characters as living beings with real problems. Most live actors don't have this problem since we accept them as 'real' from the start. Animation *brings the inanimate to life*—the life is not there to begin with.

A good character can be developed from a story. A good character can *inspire* the story. Story is the most important thing in animation, but creating appealing characters to tell it—*animated* characters—is the *other* most important thing. Which element should the animator develop first?

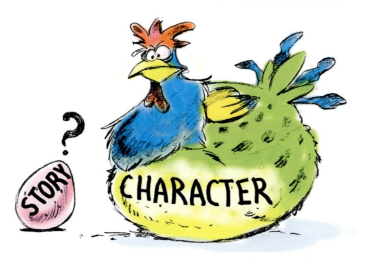

**Which comes first?**

Character and story reinforce one another and are created concurrently during preproduction. They will be discussed in all three parts of this book since developing one in
the absence of the other is like making an omelet without eggs.

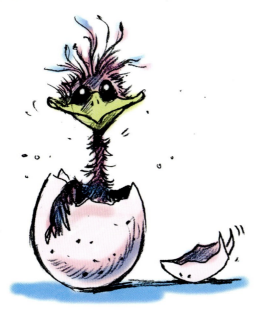

**Character and story develop simultaneously!**

Development is a marvelous creative process in which the journey is as important as
the destination. It's what you do, *and* also how you do it!

I've always felt that animators are not merely "actors with pencils," as the cliché goes.
That term does not begin to cover what an animator really does.

We bring the inanimate to life.

We create universes.

We are *magicians*.

Nancy Beiman
Rochester, New York
August, 2006

# Dedication and Thanks

Jack Hannah, T. Hee, Ken O'Connor, Bill Moore, and Elmer Plummer taught at the California Institute of the Arts' Character Animation Program so that their knowledge of animation, learned from the ground up during its Golden Age, would not die with them. My notes from their classes, written between 1975 and 1979, are the backbone of this book. It was a real privilege to learn from these talented artists.

A new generation of students from the Rochester Institute of Technology generously permitted me to print some of their class exercises and senior project materials. I thank Brittney Lee, Nathaniel Hubbell, William Robinson, Jim Downer, Sarah Kropiewnicki, Kimberly Miner, Jeremy Galante, Rui Jin, David Suroviec, Joseph Daniels, and Jedidiah Mitchell, my students in the School of Film and Animation, and Alycia Yee from the School of Photography, for their outstanding work.

I thank Margaret Adamic of Walt Disney Publishing Worldwide for permission to reprint artwork from Disney Enterprises, Inc., and Howard Green, Vice President, Studio Communications, Buena Vista Pictures Marketing, for his valuable assistance.

Thanks to David Fulp for his photo of T. Hee posing in front of Ralph Eggleston's caricature portrait, to John Van Vliet for the T. Hee 'ranch' portrait, and to Cyndy Bohanovsky for the Ken Anderson photo. I also thank Patricia Bernard for permission to use my illustrations from her books *Basil Bigboots the Pirate* and *Duffy and the Invisible Crocodile*, and Daniel Schechter and Globalvision Inc. for two illustrations I drew for the documentary film IN DEBT WE TRUST.

I owe special thanks to Floyd Norman, Nina Paley, John Van Vliet, David Celsi, Dean Yeagle, Nina L. Haley, J. Adam Fox, Nelson Rhodes, Doug Crane, John McCartney, Brian P. McEntee, and Mark Newgarden for permission to use some of their illustration work so that this did not become a one-woman show.

This book and its author are indebted to many key people. Art director/author Brian P. McEntee provided terms for the Glossary and, along with Sheridan College instructor Mark Mayerson, proofread the entire manuscript and suggested improvements to the text and illustrations. Greg Ford and Ronnie Scheib read early drafts of the book and fact-checked my Looney Tunes history. My parents, Melvyn and Frances Beiman, provided 'lay perspective' on the book's readability. Yvette Kaplan, Tom Sito, and Tony White offered excellent suggestions for the book's format and contents at the beginning of the project. Jud Hurd published my interviews with animators in *CARTOONIST PROfiles* magazine for 13 years and encouraged me to write interviews and articles on animation. Editors Paul Temme, Amy Jollymore, and Georgia Kennedy at Elsevier/Focal Press were a pleasure to work with. I also thank my friends and mentors Shamus Culhane, Selby Daley Kelly, T. Hee, Mary Alice O'Connor, Ken O'Connor, Alice Davis, Frank Thomas, Ollie Johnston, and Joe Grant for their friendship and advice over the years. Last, but not least, I would like to extend my heartfelt thanks to Roy Disney for his continuing support for the art and artists of animation.

This book is dedicated to A. Kendall (Ken) O'Connor—a brilliant layout man, designer, draftsman, story man, art director, and teacher who was able to explain everything from how a caterpillar's muscles move to why a 1926 trash can silhouette differs from that of a modern one. In story, these things matter! So this is for you, Ken.

*Circumstances alter cases!*

Nancy Beiman

# Part One

# Getting Started

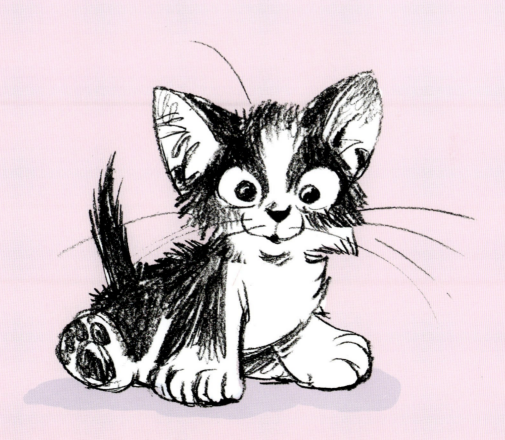

# First Catch Your Rabbit: Creating Concepts and Characters

There is a famous old cookbook recipe for stewed rabbit. The first sentence of the recipe gets right to the point. It reads: "First, catch your rabbit."

How do you "catch the rabbit" and create original characters and stories? Where do ideas for original stories and characters come from?

A story recipe depends on the freshness of the ingredients, the quality of the preparation, and the skills of the creator.

The first two ingredients— *Character* and *Conflict*—develop simultaneously. Both must be established at the beginning of your story and, like well-written newspaper headlines, they will immediately grab the reader's attention. A quick search through several online news sites yielded the following unusual "human interest" stories:

- Robot Runs On Flies and Sewage
- Berlin Bear Steals Bicycle, Attempts Breakout From Zoo
- Boozy Bear Plunders Camper's Beer
- Zombie Worms Found Off Sweden

These actual news items already sound like story lines for animated cartoons. All of the stories have one thing in common: they convey a visual image.

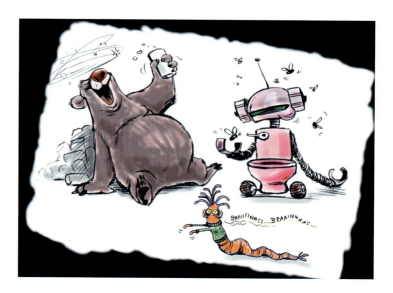

**[Fig. 1-2] Sketches based on online news reports from the BBC, the Australian Broadcasting Corporation, and Reuters News Service.**

Some of these headlines leave the reader wanting to know what happened next— (Where was the bear going to *go* with the bicycle?)—or empathizing with a character's situation—(What kind of self-esteem does a fly-eating robot have?). An animated story line may grow from a grain of truth.

Animation pre-production is called *development* for a reason. One definition of development is "the act of improving by expanding or enlarging or refining." The story and characters grow and change during pre-production from simple ideas to the complex, structured, *visual* story.

The next ingredient in the story stew is imagination. Animation is not reality and it is at its best when it portrays things that could *possibly* happen. The seed of reality provides the viewer with a point of identification and then germinates into a fantastic story.

Feature animation often does not start with a written script. The germ of the story can be conveyed in a short *outline* or *treatment*. The characters and plot twists are then developed visually. Stories can change dramatically when they are boarded. Scripts are not finalized until the latter stages of preproduction so that they may incorporate new material created on the storyboard.

Old-time animation story men referred to a story as the "clothesline" on which they would "hang" gags and character development. The shorter film develops more quickly than a feature since it has less time to tell the story. You should be able to convey a story idea in a few short, direct sentences. If you are unable to do this, the idea needs work.

Here are some stories from existing animated films retold as newspaper headlines. Can you identify the films?

- Flying Elephant Rescues Mother, Saves Circus
- Rabbit Takes Revenge on Hunter
- Dalmatian Puppies Missing, Possible Victims of Fur Coat Ring
- Heroic Ogre Saves Princess from Dragon, Removes Tyrannical King

**Exercise:** Write three more 'headlines' based on existing animated films. Does each headline convey a visual image of the story?

This technique is actually used in animation and live-action pre-production under another name.

The *log line* (a brief description of the story and conflict) is the foundation for the story edifice. Walt Disney said that an animated film's story was constructed "like building a building with building blocks. Our building blocks would be 'personalities'" (Ken Anderson interviewed by Nancy Beiman, 1979.) The entire interview appears in Appendix 3. Log Lines are discussed in Chapter 4.

# Linear and Non-linear Storytelling

A linear story progresses from A (beginning) to B (middle) to C (resolution) in sequential time. A situation is established at the start, a complication arises in the middle section, and resolution of some kind comes at the end. Most feature-length animation works in linear format.

Linear stories can also work in reverse, as seen in Piet Kroon's short film *T.R.A.N.S.I.T.* The film opens as a man is immigrating to Argentina after a murder. It progresses into the past to show how the characters' relationships made this outcome inevitable.

Non-linear animation concentrates on creating an effect or mood rather than telling a carefully plotted story. Many short experimental films fall into this category. WAKING LIFE is a rare example of a feature-length non-linear story. It follows dreamlike logic that evolves over time instead of proceeding toward a specific goal.

Linear and non-linear stories will both require extensive preproduction work, though non-linear stories might not rely as much on character development to achieve their effect. If you are planning to make a non-linear film conveying moods or emotions, research different artistic styles, color, sound, music, and effects that will create the desired impressions in the viewer's mind.

You may not wish to make an autobiographical film, but elements from your life can add a dash of reality that strengthens the situation and characters. True-life adventures will be discussed in detail in Chapter 2.

# Setting Limitations and Finding Liberation

"Do anything you like" is the hardest assignment I ever had. Limitations must be set so that the story doesn't run off in all directions.

My students' first character design assignment is to assemble a "found character" based on a series of words pulled out of an envelope. They are provided with a character name, sex, species, age, and time period, but no story context. Their second assignment has them changing a human character into an animal in three drawings. The midpoint is sometimes more interesting than the final!

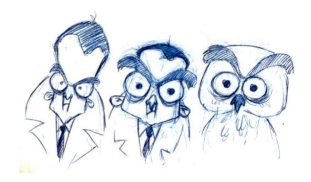

**[Fig. 1-3] A 1900's gangster turns into an owl. Character design assignment reproduced by permission of William Robinson.**

For their third assignment students create a pair of characters that contrast Large with Small. No other information is provided. The fourth assignment provides their first story context: characters must illustrate a simple story line taken from a nursery rhyme.

My students invariably find the 'found character' and 'large versus small' assignments more difficult than the nursery rhyme . The creation of the nursery rhyme characters is considered easier since the story context provides a guideline for the character's appearance and personality. By narrowing the focus (using a pre-existing story, names, and descriptions as a framework), a set of limitations are created that become "liberations." Characters are easier to design when placed within a story context.

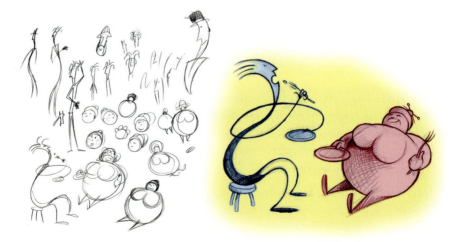

**[Fig. 1-4] "Jack and Mrs. Sprat" (nursery rhyme). Character design assignment reproduced by permission of Jim Downer.**

A character created in isolation as in the other three exercises is just a design. It is not a personality. The human-to-animal assignment infuses some of the human's quality into the animal, which is the beginning of personality development. The story context in the fourth assignment is the crucial ingredient in our recipe. The story will influence the character's personality and appearance and the character's personality will influence the story development. Which comes first, the chicken or the egg, character or story? Both elements are equally important.

Figure 1-5 shows designs for (a) an ordinary dog and (b) the dog from this old nursery rhyme:

*Old Mother Hubbard went to the cupboard, to get her poor dog a bone.*

*But when she got there, the cupboard was bare, and so the poor dog had none.*

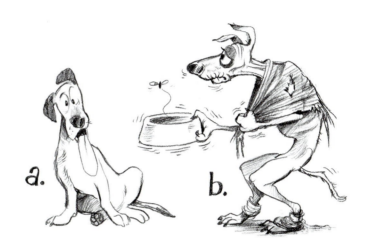

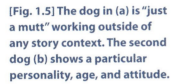

**[Fig. 1.5] The dog in (a) is "just a mutt" working outside of any story context. The second dog (b) shows a particular personality, age, and attitude.**

The second illustration portrays a stronger character than the first since there is more visual information to set the animal's personality and appearance. The words "old" and "poor" in the nursery rhyme lead to a visual interpretation so that we *see* that the dog is old and poor before we *hear* it. Dialogue should support the visual elements of an animated film.

# Shopping for Story: Creating Lists

A story can be created by chance or by deliberation, or you can write a shopping list for the ingredients!

Free association can get the creative juices flowing. Use words that create visual images. Draw four columns on a sheet of lined paper and begin. It helps to do this exercise with another person since you can "bounce" ideas off one another and build on each other's word associations.

The first column is a list of *characters*. Can they be animal, vegetable, or mineral? Are they organic or inorganic? You are not restricted by what exists in the real world. Put that animation magic to work. Any one or any thing is a possible animated character. Describe them in one or two words. Do not write lengthy biographies or back stories.

Can they be human or animal? Are they four legged or two legged? Could a character be a combination of organic and inorganic objects? Imaginary creatures are the hardest ones to do, and so if you wish to design one make separate lists of words that describe the creature's abilities and appearance. (1) Can it fly and swim? Does it tap dance and sing opera? (2) Does it have feathers, fur, scales, or all of the above? Write down as many variations as you can think of. At this point, everything is possible. The words "no" and "can't" are not in your vocabulary.

List all of your ideas no matter how odd they may seem. Do not throw anything out at this stage. Build on earlier suggestions by free-association. Be creative and have fun. But characters do not work well in isolation. They must be put into some sort of context.

*Where does this story take place?*

Write a list of possible *locations* in Column Two. These can be fanciful and vary greatly in scale. One major feature film, OSMOSIS JONES, was staged entirely on the molecular level inside a human body.

Can you place your characters inside a refrigerator, in France, on a dog's back, inside a sock drawer, under the bed, on the moon, or under the ocean? See if one location leads you to think of another, or of characters that might populate it.

Make a list of *situations and occupations* in the third column. Birthdays, weddings, funerals, jail breaks, alien abductions, trips to the dentist, preparation of a meal, a dance, a wedding, thieves, shepherds, and insurance salesmen are all fair game.

Next, list possible *conflicts* in the fourth column. What weaknesses do these characters have? Do their parents approve of what they are doing? Is one character in danger? Is it searching for something? Now, mix and match words from the character, location, situation, and conflict lists to form short sentences. See which combinations suggest images or stories. You may be inspired by a single word or use material from all four lists. As you do this, a story may start to build itself. Draw rough sketches and *thumbnails* to illustrate ideas suggested by the word combinations. The following story outline was assembled from the four sample lists:

Characters: Vegetables (tomatoes, onions, corn, and melons).

Location: The refrigerator.

Occupation: Thief.

Situation: A group of vegetable criminals decide to make a jail break from the refrigerator before they are put into a stew.

Conflict: They are on Death Row (in the fridge) since they have all gone "bad." The cook is their executioner. Figure 1-6 depicts possible "bad vegetable" characters.

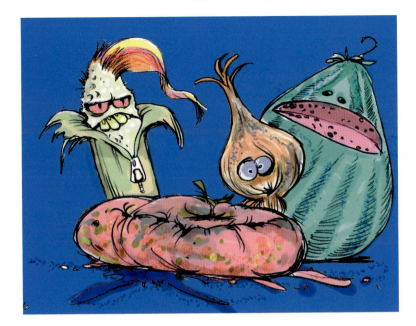

[Fig. 1-6] When vegetables
go bad.

Draw thumbnails of characters and situations on a yellow-lined pad. Do not use an eraser and do not throw away any of the drawings. Work rough and don't worry about design details at this time. Final character design is created at a later stage.  Don't just use one character or explore one story avenue; we're in *blue sky* territory so anything goes. It is okay to use color when thumbnailing rough character designs, but keep the story sketches in black and white for now.

"Normal" characters can become very interesting when placed in unfamiliar context. This time we will work with the word "wedding" from the 'situation' list. What if the groom and bride are a shepherd and shepherdess? Perhaps the wedding guests could be sheep and sheepdogs as shown in Figure 1-7.

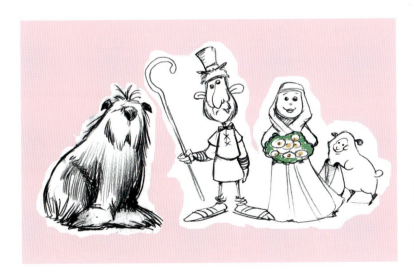

[Fig. 1-7] What is right with
this picture? The shepherds
are not as interesting as
the animals. The most
interesting characters
should tell your stories.

Some comic potential is lost since the shepherds do not seem to be as out of place in this setting as the animals do. The animals are, frankly, more interesting than the people.

*A story should always be told by the most interesting characters.* The animals are more interesting than the shepherds in this story since they appear outside their usual context. What if the animals became the main characters? That's an improvement since humanized animal characters play to the strong points of the animation medium. Could the sheep get married instead of the shepherds? What sort of characters might interact with them? Could the wedding guests be shepherds, sheepdogs, and wolves? Do the animals behave like humans? How does this story point affect the design of the film and the characters? Can sheep and wolves be used to represent certain kinds of human personalities? Might the animals be caricatures of human relatives and character types? Recognizable human traits create sympathy for fantastic characters. It is important to make your main characters more interesting than the secondary characters. If the hero's story does not attract and maintain your interest, perhaps you are working with the wrong character. Figure 1-8 shows a more novel staging of the wedding.

**[Fig. 1-8] Using animal characters to suggest human traits and foibles is as old as Aesop.**

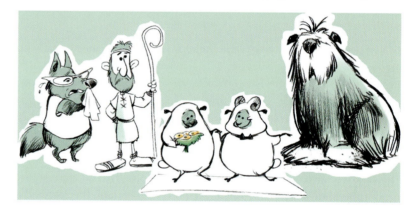

The wedding story may still not be working with the most interesting characters.

I call the next part of the questionnaire the "What Ifs?" What if the loving couple is from two different species? What if they are a star-crossed sheep and a wolf? What if a sheep married a sheepdog? What stories and conflicts might be created by these contrasting characters?

The characters' appearances are just the beginning. Their actions and personalities will develop from your observations and caricatures of real life.

**[Fig 1-9] Contrasts between characters can create a story. Try different combinations of scale and species and work with the most interesting one.**

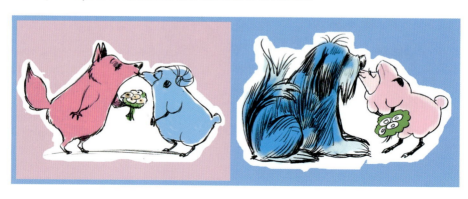

# Nothing Is Normal: Researching Action

Your most important research tool is a sketchbook. You should draw in the sketchbook every day. Visit zoos, playgrounds, basketball games, even the laundromat. Draw *rough impressions of moving figures*, not portraits or immobile poses. Write notes next to the drawing that describe the subject's attitude.  Sketch quick poses that express characters in motion. Figure 1-10 shows a page of gesture drawings from my sketchbooks with some explanatory notes.

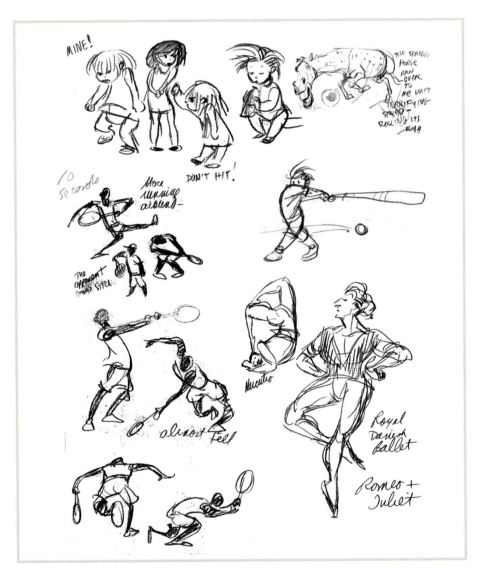

[Fig. 1-10] A page assembled from my sketchbooks. Notes are sometimes added to describe the subject's emotional state. Some of these sketches were used as reference for later character designs.

Think of gesture drawing as reference material for acting, character, and story.

Gesture drawings of humans and animals in action will help you create stronger poses for your animated characters and make you a better actor. Working from life is recommended but dance and music videos or action films can also be used as 'models' since these films portray action that is more intense than normal. Run the tapes or discs in slow motion, watch the actors' progressive movements, and draw as if the model was in the room instead of onscreen. The films of Charlie Chaplin and Buster Keaton provide particularly good comic and dramatic action reference. Avoid drawing from photographs since this will usually make your drawing appear "flat." Your subject should be moving in the third and fourth dimensions.

Once you start observing people and animals you will see that no one and nothing is ever 'ordinary'. Everyone moves slightly differently from one another. People and animals also move differently when they are in different moods. These varying attitudes should be taken into account when creating model sheets and storyboards for your characters since they will influence the animation that comes afterward.

Pets are great subjects for gesture drawing because they never stand still! Don't try to draw formal portraits. Draw them while they are playing or moving around. You will know their characteristic gestures and attitudes from experience. Work quickly and never scratch out a drawing—just draw another sketch on the same page if you are not satisfied with the first one. You'll soon be able to do it from memory.

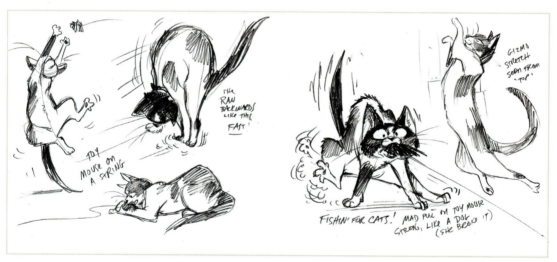

**[Fig. 1-11] My cat Gizmo, drawn from memory. She moved far too fast to 'pose' for any of the pictures. I drew rough sketches of her movements after she finished them. Gesture drawing is an impression of movement, not actuality.**

# All Thumbs: Quick Sketches And Thumbnails

Character designs and storyboards both start out as rough and simple *thumbnails*.

Thumbnails are drawn thoughts. These small sketches, combined with brief notes, capture ideas for a story or character so that the memory is not lost. Thumbnails can be worked up into a finished drawing at a later time.

Always work *rough* before going *clean*. Do not render or model final drawings at this stage of development. Draw a new thumbnail if you think you can stage something better. Thumbnails allow you to change the drawings and your mind.

Figure 1-12 shows two versions of a simple action originally described by animator Frank Thomas. The first sketch (a) only shows the basic action, but (b) is a series of *thumbnails* that convey the character's attitude and personality along with the action. The thumbnails also tell a story. Is it possible to depict the action in (b) with only one sketch? (Try it for yourself using this character or one of your own designs.)

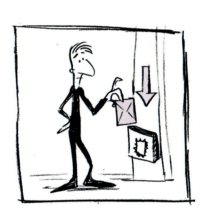

A.    just mailing a letter

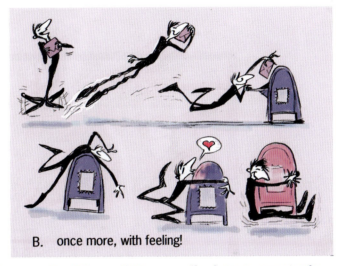

B.    once more, with feeling!

[Fig. 1-12] Frank Thomas' example: (a) A man mails a letter, or (b) A man mails a letter to someone he loves. The emotional state of the character affects every move he makes. Thumbnail drawings portray different stages of the animated action.

# Reality Is Overrated

Use reality as inspiration when creating animated characters and stories but adapt it, don't copy it. Real life provides basic reference material. Animation improves on it.

Animated characters should be believable, not realistic. The laws of gravity and physics may change in animation. A character can float on a cushion of emotional bliss as shown in Figure 1-12b, or change its physical shape, color, or size when its mood varies. Visual hyperbole, caricature, and stylized action are much more interesting than literal renditions of natural motion.

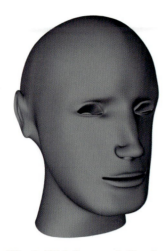

[Fig. 1-13] A Cryogenic Head.

Human characters are the hardest ones to do. It is difficult to portray "realistic" humans convincingly in animation because everyone sees a human face every day in the bathroom mirror and knows how to make it move. Inaccuracies and deviations from the norm will be obvious. (There's more "wiggle room" in animal design since you don't see a lion in the bathroom mirror every day.) Computer-generated imagery (CGI) animation sometimes tries too hard for literalism, which can lead to the creation of human characters with staring eyes and doll-like features that (ironically) appear to lack all life and animation. This is known as the *'cryogenic effect'*. Let us compare the design of two human heads. The CGI head in Figure 1-13 was an isolated exercise created outside of a story context. One drawing of a front view and one side view was imported into a computer program. The artist did not first analyze and sketch its planes or expressions or base the design on caricatured reality. The resulting head is neither realistic nor believable.

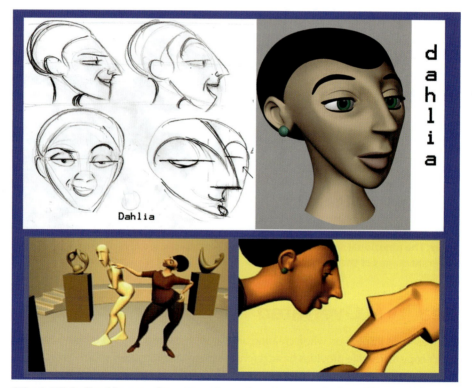

[Fig. 1-14] Stylized human characters. Reproduced by permission of Nathaniel Hubbell.

The stylized CGI character in Figure 1-14 was based on caricatures by the Mexican artist Miguel Covarrubias rather than photorealistic references. The story required human characters with expressive features and mobile bodies. Dahlia's caricatured and stylized features create appeal and interest in her design. Rough *construction models* of her head and body were drawn after the design was finalized and before computer modeling began. Action sketches of Dahlia's facial expressions and body movements served as guidelines when she was modeled, rigged, and textured.

The action took place in an art museum where human characters interacted with living artwork. Each proportion of Dahlia's face and body was carefully planned. She and her cubist dance partner were designed at the same time so that they worked well together. Animation is hyper-reality. It has to go a little farther than live action to create the illusion of life.

# Past and Present: Researching Settings and Costumes

"Back in the day," animation designers and cartoonists kept a "morgue" of reference pictures. Mine was an enormous black filing cabinet stuffed with files labeled, "Fashion," "Celebrities," "Wild Animals, Africa," "Pets," "Children," and so on.

The Internet is the world's greatest reference library if you already know what you are looking for. It is a good idea to familiarize yourself with the art and mores of other times and places if you are serious about working as a story artist or character designer. Knowledge and research will help you to find the right reference materials for a film set in a particular period. This is the way to avoid anachronisms (items used out of their context in time) unless they are necessary for your story. Figure 1-15 is an example of an anachronism.

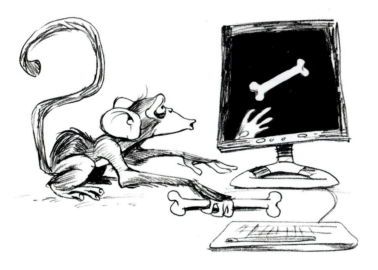

[Fig. 1-15] A computer is an anachronism in the Stone Age.

Production development incorporates all of the arts and a good chunk of life into its matrix. Each project presents you with an opportunity to learn about different cultures, historic eras, and characters. The development artist has the enviable task of being paid to learn. Researching a film is a fascinating and educational experience.

A story artist or character designer will want to learn a little bit about a lot of things, including, but not limited to: dance; history (world and national); popular and high-culture music, art, film, and literature; geography; anatomy (human and animal); zoology and biology; theatre; color theory; industrial and product design; astronomy; acting; sports; botany; fashion design and fashion history by decade and by country; child behavior; national customs and landmarks; fantasy in art and literature; caricature; architecture; archaeology; folktales; psychology; and any hobbies you might care to add. As we shall see in Chapter 3, it also helps to know something about yourself.

The aspiring story artist should understand film language, learn how signature styles of filmmaking evolved over time, and be familiar with live-action and animated films from many countries and eras. Most importantly: the story artist must know the difference between feature and short animation storyboards and the boards used for comic strips, television, and live-action films. These differences are discussed in Chapter 3.

# Vive la Difference! Animation and Live-action Storyboards

"While directing short (animated) subjects, I soon discovered that the original planning of the overall picture, where the director had complete control of the project, was where the picture was actually made good … having OK'd the picture and taken delivery of it from the story department … the final result was assured."

—David Hand, director of SNOW WHITE AND THE SEVEN DWARFS

Live-action and animation storyboards differ dramatically from one another. Live-action storyboards provide notes for camera angles, rough blocking for the actors, and the general setup for each shot. The figures on the storyboards do not represent specific actors since the casting may not yet be set. The board artist will roughly block the characters' performances without making detailed breakdowns of the action. Arrows are used to indicate a character's motion in the shot. A lengthy description of the action within the scene often appears beneath each panel. One or two panels suffice for each shot unless the camera is in motion. Live-action storyboards are used by directors, art directors, and cinematographers as a rough guide for the film's staging.

Animation storyboard *creates the characters along with the settings*. The storyboard *IS* the animated actors' performance. Every part of the film is planned in storyboard stage—character designs, acting, action, pacing, story, dialogue, effects, camera moves, and editing.

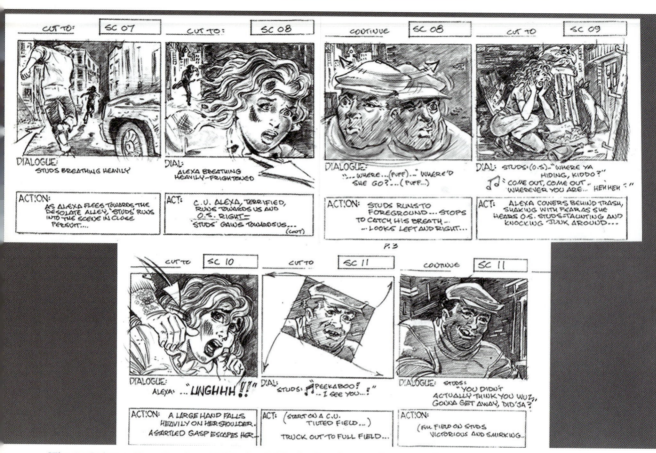

[Fig. 2-1] Live-action storyboard. Staging is blocked and extensive notes describe the action in the scene. Reproduced by permission of Doug Crane.

[Fig. 2-2] Storyboards from my theatrical short film YOUR FEET'S TOO BIG. Dialogue and brief descriptions of action are written on separate slips of paper beneath individual panels. The characters' emotions are portrayed in detail.

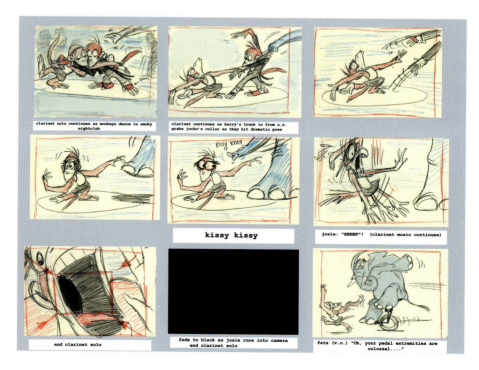

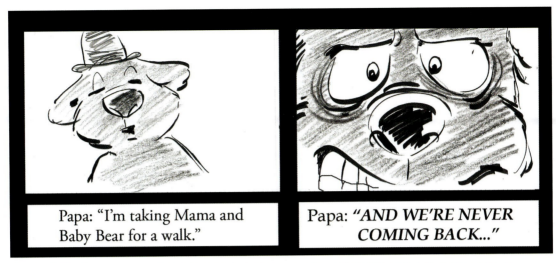

[Fig. 2-3] The feature animation artist depicts camera moves as individual drawings on separate panels. Here is a cut from a medium close-up to an extreme close-up.

Each scene of an animated film has its action and acting depicted on a series of individual storyboards. All actions and camera moves that will appear in the film are drawn on the boards since *an animated film is edited on the storyboards and in story reel before it is actually animated or shot.* Although animation "pencil tests" and trial renders will be made during the production process, the final camera work is not done until all of the creative work is completed. Animation camera work is a technical process recording performances and camera moves that were planned in story and layout at the beginning of production. Animation storyboard and layout artists are the equivalent of live-action cinematographers and editors.

An animation editor creates the *story reel* or *animatic* with the director. These are composed of digitized storyboards that are edited to the length of each scene so that the pace of the film is established before the animation begins. The editor replaces the storyboards with animated scenes as they are completed and assembles and breaks down synchronization for voice tracks, music, and sound effects for the final soundtrack. Animation is so labor intensive and expensive that it is important to eliminate wasted footage before it is created. Figure 2-4 is a rough comparison of live-action and animated film-production methods.

**[Fig. 2-4] Comparison of Live-action and Animated Film-production Methods**

| Phase | Animation | Live Action |
|---|---|---|
| **Script** | A script may exist at the start but will undergo significant change as it is translated to storyboards. It may be rewritten numerous times as a result of board changes. New characters and situations created by storyboard artists can support or supplant the script. | The script will exist prior to shooting. The characters and plot twists are created by writers. Rewrites are completed before shooting starts. Actors and directors may add new material to the script. |
| **Storyboard** | Storyboard artists design all shots and camera moves and create the character performances. The animated film is edited on the storyboards before production animation begins. | Storyboards are used only for rough action and camera blocking. They will illustrate the script, not change it. The actors create their performances. Representations of actors on live-action boards are deliberately kept vague. |
| **Inspirational art and settings** | Required. Inspirational artists create settings and characters for the film. Any location is possible. Time is the only limitation. | May be created for film but is not required. Filming locations are scouted or built as sets. Locations may be limited by time and budget. |
| **Characters and performance** | Characters are designed by artists. Voice artists are recorded before the animator's performance is created. The characters may or may not resemble the voice actor. The animator creates the visual performance using the voice track as a guide. | Characters are developed by writers, actors, and the director. Actors create visuals and audio for their performances. They are recognizable and can have a strong creative influence on the performance. |
| **Color and art direction** | Rough animation is created in black-and-white pencil tests or low-resolution graphics. Color is added late in the production process. The art direction, color, props, and settings are created by art directors and development artists during preproduction. | Color styling and lighting are designed by the art director and the cameraman during the film shoot. The art director will set color palettes and set dressers will arrange props on set. |

| Phase | Animation | Live Action |
|-------|-----------|-------------|
| **Camera** | *Camera is part of post-production in animation,* recording materials that have been created in storyboard, layout, background, and animation. In CGI films, rendering replaces camera work. The footage shot will be close to the preplanned length of the animated scenes. There are no cover scenes. | Camera is part of *production* in live action. Live action typically shoots at a 15:1 ratio, animation at 1.25:1 or less. The live-action cameraman has a strong creative influence on the staging and lighting of the shots. Multiple camera setups may be used to cover shots. |
| **Editing** | *Editing is part of pre-production* in animation. Storyboards depict all camera and character action. The Director times filmed storyboard panels and the Editor cuts in rough or final soundtrack to create a story reel before animation begins. Final animation is cut into pre-existing story reels. | *Editing is part of post-production* in live action. Shot footage is edited to form final film. The Editor has a strong creative influence on the timing and pacing of the finished film. Special effects are also added at this time. |

The most obvious difference between the two media is that live-action films are edited in post-production. *Animation is edited in pre-production.* The animation storyboard *is* the film, as director David Hand (BAMBI and SNOW WHITE AND THE SEVEN DWARFS) stated at the beginning of this chapter.

Live-action storyboard artists function as assistant directors and assistant cinematographers. They draw blueprints for the composition and lighting of the shots. The final composition is determined by the director and cinematographer. Live-action storyboards do not depict or influence the actor's performance. A good rule of thumb is that animation is produced *backwards from live action*. A flow chart describing the anatomy of animation appears in Figure 2-5.

# THE ANATOMY OF ANIMATION

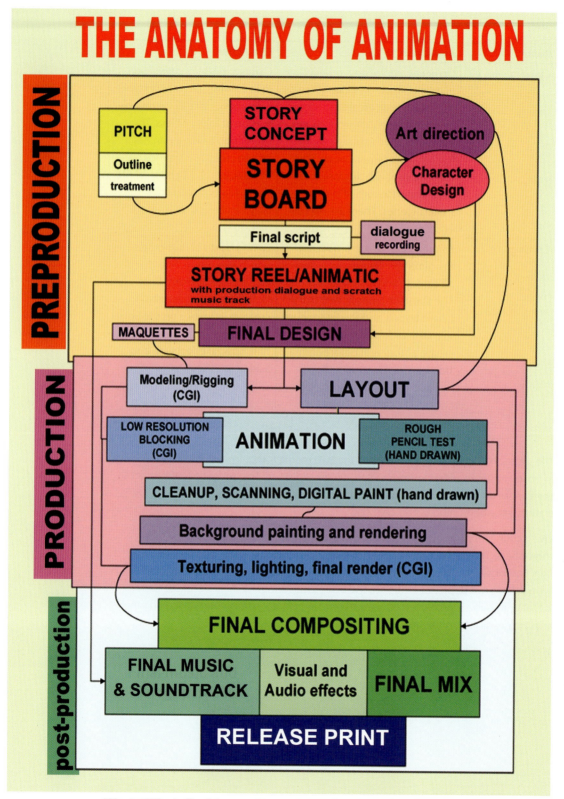

[Fig. 2-5] The bulk of the creative work in animation is done in preproduction. Animation production takes longer and costs more if story or design changes are made after animation and modeling have started. Postproduction will generally take the least time, although this will vary depending on the project.

*Stop-motion animation* is a notable exception to the animation production chart depicted in Figure 2-5. Stop-motion characters are actual three-dimensional objects. Animators work in (very slow) real time on miniature sets. Stop-motion productions will use detailed storyboards and animatics (usually done as a "pop-through" using the actual puppets), but otherwise their production resembles that of a live-action film. Puppets and sets are constructed during pre-production as the storyboard is completed. The camera work is continuous during production and the cameraman contributes creatively to the look of the film. A stop-motion film is partially edited in post-production. Time must also be budgeted to digitally "*clean up*" or mask out the supports and rigs behind the puppets so that they do not show in the finished film.

# Comic Boards and Animation Boards

Comic and graphic novel artists also use storyboards to rough out their projects before creating the finished artwork. There is, however, a major difference between film and comic storyboards. The comic artist has complete freedom to design frames and panels on the page. Panels may be vertical or irregularly shaped. Effects can be added to the panel borders, or characters can burst right through them.

Figure 2-6 is a page from the graphic novel *David Chelsea in Love* by David Chelsea. The shattered, jagged shape and varying size of the panels suggest the cramped conditions in the building's stairwell and the emotional attitude of some of the characters. The action in some frames overlaps others. A cinematic quality is conveyed by the characters' movement through numerous panels that depict progressive action. A close-up shot inserted at the end draws attention to one character. The page can be viewed as one work of art and as a series of small frames that create an elaborate design.

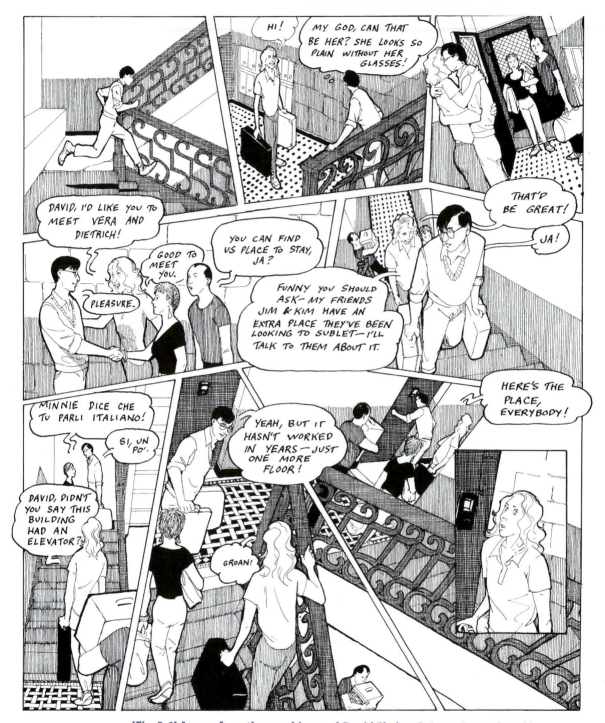

[Fig. 2-6] A page from the graphic novel *David Chelsea in Love.* Reproduced by permission of David Chelsea.

Motion pictures and computer graphics are more restricted in their staging. *The motion picture screen or computer monitor is an unchanging 'frame'.* The animator creates variety in staging by moving the camera, animating the characters within the frame, or cutting to a new camera angle. *The borders of the screen/frame are a standard size that cannot be modified by the filmmaker. All storyboard panels will have the same proportions as the screen. Wider boards are used for widescreen films. The frame is* **always** *horizontal. Some standard screen ratios are shown in* Figure 2-7.

Academy
Standard
1.33:1

Wide Screen
can be up to
2 : 1

**[Fig. 2-7] Academy Standard and Wide Screen ratios. There are many other variations but all film and new media frames are horizontal rectangles.**

The animation storyboard artist must first and foremost be an excellent actor. While it is true that the voice actor gives 50 percent of the character's performance, it is the storyboard artist's work that determines the acting that we see on screen. The animated characters are developed on the storyboard before the voices are recorded. The animation storyboard artist performs all the character parts during *pitches*, whether they are male, female, animal, human, or inorganic; he or she creates dramatic pacing and cutting and indicates the settings and emotional moods that layout artists and animators will develop in the final film. In addition, storyboard drawings are frequently used as acting and design reference for character designers who may be working on the production at the same time that the boards are created. So the animation storyboard artist is also a bit of a casting director! (Pitches are discussed in Chapter 18.)

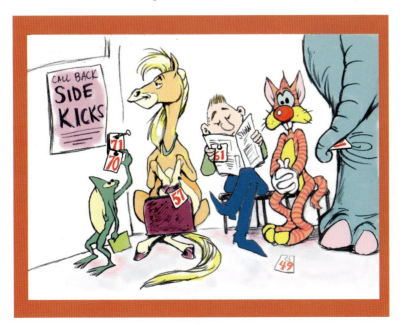

**[Fig. 2-8] The Animated Character Casting Call involves working up a variety of character design suggestions and deciding which ones work best in the story. Storyboard drawings are often used as reference for the designs. Some animated walk-ons become "stars" after appearing in supporting roles for other characters. (Donald Duck, Goofy, and Porky Pig are former "bit" players!)**

# Television Boards and Feature Boards

Animated features and short films will have all sections of the pre-production—character, story, production design—in development simultaneously. There can be a great deal of 'wiggle room' and reworking of character designs and story points during the comparatively long production time. It is not unusual for entire sequences to be dropped or character designs completely reworked during production because of a story change. The feature and short-film storyboard artist's main concern is telling the story. The character model is of secondary importance since the designs might not be finalized before the storyboards begin. A feature or short-film storyboard will depict camera moves on several panels. Field guides will usually not be included since individual drawings may be replaced or revised later.

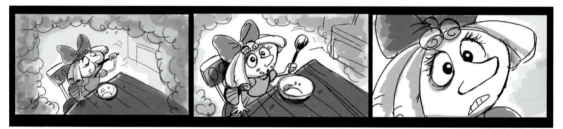

[Fig. 2-9] A feature-film storyboard will draw out camera moves on several panels. Modular board construction makes revisions on one or more panels easier.

A storyboard for an animated series is produced very differently since character designs and finished scripts will nearly always exist before the storyboards are drawn. Sometimes the protagonist will be an established character with designs that may not be changed. Whether old or new, a *"Bible"* of final character, prop, and set designs will be handed to the storyboard artist and the character and prop models must be strictly followed when boards are drawn. Television storyboards contain detailed camera moves and are very *clean* and *tight*, as shown in Figure 2-10.

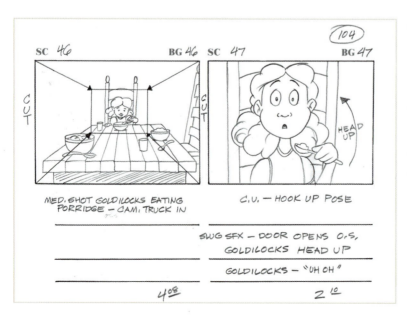

[Fig. 2-10] Animation boards for television series differ considerably from feature boards. The television board will include field guide (camera) moves and sometimes lengthy descriptions of the action. Reproduced by permission of Nelson Rhodes.

The television storyboard must illustrate the script as written using characters, backgrounds, and props drawn *'on model'* or exactly the way they will look in the finished film, in every panel. Precise descriptions of the action are written in special panels below the drawings and all camera moves are drawn on the storyboards.  These types of boards are technically much more difficult to draw than feature boards, since they usually do not allow for variations in design or reworking of the story. The board artist must follow rules of perspective and include background detail since television storyboards are frequently enlarged and used as layouts in *production*. The character drawings on the boards may also be enlarged and used as animation keys. Acting is important but all props, characters, and backgrounds must be *tight cleanups*.

All animated action and editing is preplanned before the animation begins. It is crucial to avoid wasting time as well as money since feature animation can take years to finish. Television animation has a tight production schedule with little time allocated for change and revision. Commercial deadlines are written in stone. A commercial *must* be finished before its air date. There will not be an opportunity to 'make it up.'

*How long is a short film?* Will the principles used in constructing a feature apply to a short film or student production? Yes, but with one difference. The budget for a student film is measured *in time*. An incomplete film may result in a failing grade.

I expect my students to have their characters and settings designed and their storyboards  *up on reels* with final dialogue track approximately one-third of the way through the project's schedule. The middle third is devoted to layout, animation, and other production matters such as modeling and rigging, and the final third is spent *tweaking* the animation, scanning and coloring drawings, lighting and rendering computer films, and completing *post-production*. Animation post-production takes much less time than it does in live action unless the animation is combined with live action or special effects. (Stop-motion animation needs time for digital cleanup as discussed earlier in this chapter.) Sufficient post-production time must be budgeted for compositing and rendering the final images and mixing the soundtrack.

The computer has made animation much easier and cheaper to produce than previously. Computer scanning and testing programs appreciably shorten the production time of drawn and stop-motion animation. Computer graphics gave animators virtual tools for a new digital branch of the art.

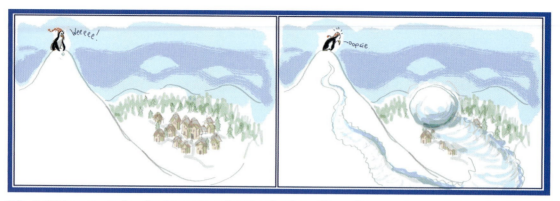

[Fig. 2-11] Improper planning in story and preproduction will result in ever-increasing trouble down the line.  Reproduced by permission of Brian P. McEntee.

But computer graphics won't save a weak story or a poorly planned production. Errors and omissions in preproduction will snowball into major problems for all types of animation as production gets under way. It's essential to know what your film is about before you start animating since it's very hard to 'fix it in the editing' at the end of the production.

# Putting Yourself Into Your Work

3

"Would anyone other than mother care to look at this?"

—Frank Thomas and Ollie Johnston, *The Fourteen Points of Animation*, 1975

Your experiences and adventures can be grist for an animated character or story. An experience that you *would like to have* can also provide rich material for an animated story. Did you ever fantasize about being an animal, or being able to fly? Animation makes it possible for you to do both.

Animation means "creation of life." Life is the animator's reference book. You've met literally thousands of people in your lifetime. You have had adventures in your own home and at school, perhaps with a sister or a brother. You have had parents and real or imaginary friends. Maybe you owned a pet cat or dog. You have lived in a house, a town, a country. A story viewed through the prism of your own life experience is far more interesting than a generic construction based on formulaic relationships. "Write what you know," the saying goes. You know yourself and your friends and family. Their personalities and qualities can be used as inspiration to bring characters to life whether the story is contemporary or set in a distant time or place.

Robert Louis Stevenson based the character of Long John Silver in *Treasure Island* on one of his friends. Stevenson gave the pirate character traits that opposed every one of the friend's virtues but retained his energetic and ingratiating manner—and his wooden leg. Sir Arthur Conan Doyle based Sherlock Holmes on Joseph Bell, an acerbic and observant professor at the University of Edinburgh medical school.

Biographical elements provide a "human touch" that enables the audience to identify with and sympathize with exotic or outlandish characters. They transform simple designs into living and breathing creatures with believable problems and aspirations.

Consider the following figure of two penguins and an egg. (Figure 3-1)

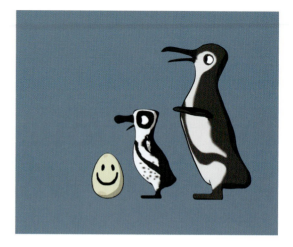

**[Fig. 3-1] Two penguins and an egg. Reproduced by permission of Kimberly Miner.**

Now let us consider the same characters within a story context. Mama Penguin has charged Big Brother Penguin with the care of his (very) little brother. Big Brother would much rather go play with his friends, as shown in Figure 3-2

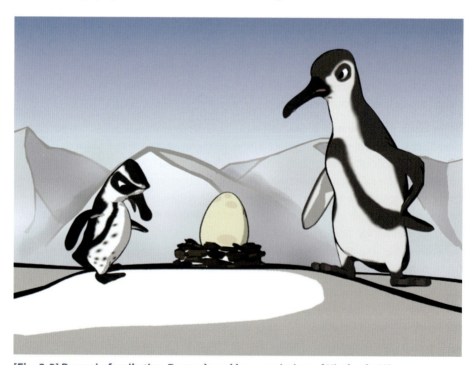

**[Fig. 3-2] Penguin family ties. Reproduced by permission of Kimberly Miner.**

Figure 3-1 shows a pair of penguins and an egg. Figure 3-2 depicts characters that relate to one another on an emotional level. The artist based the penguin children on herself and her siblings.

A good story artist utilizes life experience to give a character or story a base that an audience identifies with emotionally. This is the quality in animation that communicates across time and culture. It is not necessary to literally recreate the real-life event that inspired the story. The suggestion of humanity is what creates human interest.

Of course there are exceptions to this rule. You may want to leave out all human references to create a totally alien character or alienating environment. All stories, whether based on worldly or otherworldly rules, must sustain the interest of an audience. Even a monstrous character can inspire audience sympathy and, occasionally, empathy.

The Seven Dwarfs were not major characters in the Grimm Brothers' original story of SNOW WHITE AND THE SEVEN DWARFS. They were only plot motivators and did not have names. In the Disney film, the Dwarfs were each given a name that described a particular type of character. Each Dwarf reflected a different aspect of a complete human personality—not all of them good ones. Grumpy, Dopey, and Doc were more developed characters than the other four, with Grumpy being the most interesting of them all. Under the gruff exterior was a heart of gold, which he did his best to hide.

It was thought that audiences would not be able to sit for an hour to watch a feature-length cartoon. The critics would have been correct if SNOW WHITE AND THE SEVEN DWARFS had the same story construction as many short cartoons of the period. Cartoons in the 1930s frequently resolved a simple problem with music and dance in six minutes, emphasized lovely visuals over story and characterization, or were manic outpourings of creativity and "screwy" gags relying on neither plot nor logic.

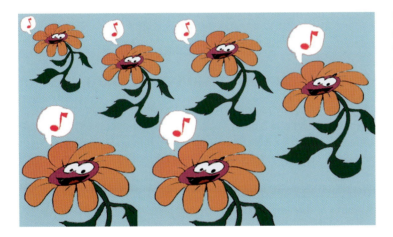

[Fig. 3-3] **Many early cartoons were structured around music. Some were "moving paintings" that emphasized pretty visuals over plot.**

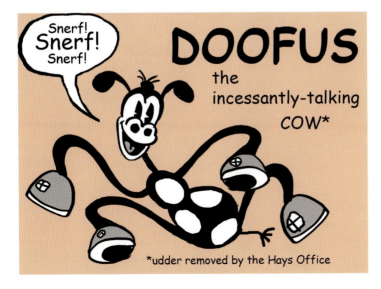

[Fig. 3-4] **The "screwball" humor of the 1930s produced manic cartoons with characters that were entertaining for six minutes but did not have the emotional range to carry a feature-length film.**

Short films are vignettes. A feature film is a mural. Feature stories must hold the audience's interest for ten times the length of a short film. It is necessary to pace the story well and alternate manic moments with sequences that allow the story to advance, and the audience to rest. We must care about what happens to the characters.

SNOW WHITE AND THE SEVEN DWARFS is about a murder. The villainous Witch/Queen wants Snow White dead and succeeds in killing her through a trick. Fortunately, a flaw in the magic enables Snow White's Prince to break the spell. This is the bare bones of the story.

SNOW WHITE AND THE SEVEN DWARFS is also a love story, but the love interest—the Prince—is off screen for most of the picture. Originally he had a much larger role, but the more interesting Dwarfs and animals carry the bulk of the film's action. Sequences in the film are well-paced and evenly divided between comedy and drama. The famous dance party at the Dwarfs' cottage immediately follows the Witch's creation of the poisoned apple that will kill Snow White. After the dance Snow White sings *Some Day My Prince Will Come*" as the Dwarfs and animals listen. We see and hear what the girl has to live for and know that all is about to be taken away from her. This knowledge adds poignancy to the song. The three consecutive sequences neatly encapsulate the film's entire plot and show the characters' personalities and relationships even when viewed separately from the rest of the film.

# The Use of Symbolic Animals and Objects

Animals have been used for millennia to symbolize human foibles. Most animal symbols in Western culture come from the fables of Aesop and La Fontaine and from medieval morality plays. Animal characters may be designed with human traits (Figure 3-5a). Human characters may display animal characteristics (Figure 3-5b).

**[Fig. 3-5] (a) Grace Drayton's dreaming kitten from 1921 has babyish features common to infant humans and animals. (Nancy Beiman collection) The girl in Figure (b) has a distinctly cat-like air. Reproduced by permission of John McCartney.**

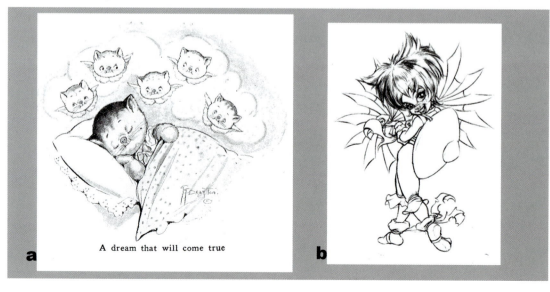

A dream that will come true

a

b

"The Great Roe is a mythological beast with the head of a lion and the body of a lion, but not the same lion."

—Woody Allen

Here is a list of animals and their symbolic meanings. Some animals have been used to represent more than one human trait and opposing traits are sometimes represented by the same animal.

- Lion (brave, dignified, the King of the Beasts)
- Lamb (meek, mild, innocent)
- Mouse (timid and defenseless)
- Rabbit (clever and resourceful *or* timid and defenseless)
- Bear (brute strength, brawn without brain)
- Cow and sheep (unintelligent, docile, a follower)
- Cat (sly, cruel, deceptive, and self-centered)
- Dog (loyal and brave *or* a fawning servant)

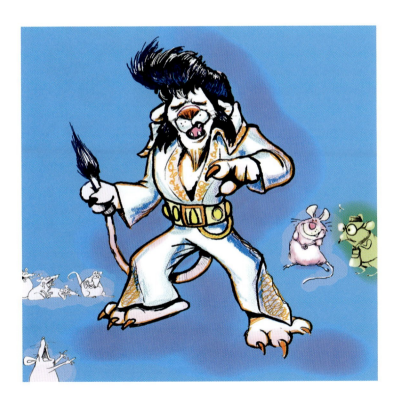

[Fig. 3-6] Symbolic Beasts. The viewer responds subconsciously to these cultural references, presuming that the lion is brave and the mouse is timid. What if roles were reversed so that the lion was timid and the mouse brave? The lion's outfit also displays symbolic meaning. The use of contrasting symbols creates a visual pun.

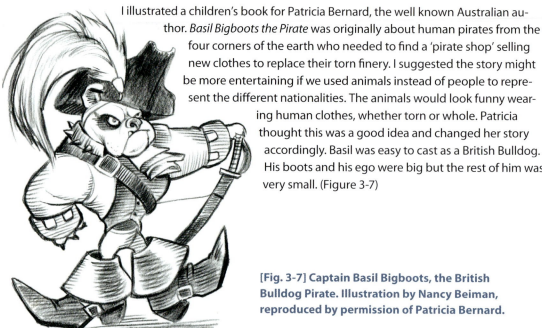

I illustrated a children's book for Patricia Bernard, the well known Australian author. *Basil Bigboots the Pirate* was originally about human pirates from the four corners of the earth who needed to find a 'pirate shop' selling new clothes to replace their torn finery. I suggested the story might be more entertaining if we used animals instead of people to represent the different nationalities. The animals would look funny wearing human clothes, whether torn or whole. Patricia thought this was a good idea and changed her story accordingly. Basil was easy to cast as a British Bulldog. His boots and his ego were big but the rest of him was very small. (Figure 3-7)

[Fig. 3-7] Captain Basil Bigboots, the British Bulldog Pirate. Illustration by Nancy Beiman, reproduced by permission of Patricia Bernard.

Which creatures would best represent pirates from South America, Africa, and China? We quickly settled on a parrot and a gorilla for the first two countries' symbolic animals. I then drew thumbnails of a Chinese dragon pirate. Patricia suggested that a panda would be a much better choice, and she was right. The panda has black circles around its eyes that suggest eye patches. This creates a *visual pun*.

Patricia added an American character after I drew up this sketch of Boston Bertie, the 'wildcat' dealer in secondhand pirate ships. (Figure 3-9)

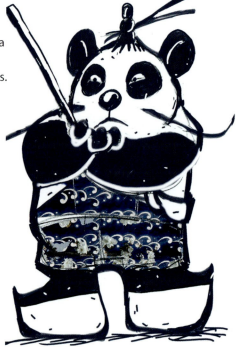

[Fig. 3-8] Chinese pirate from *Basil Bigboots the Pirate.* Illustration by Nancy Beiman, reproduced by permission of Patricia Bernard.

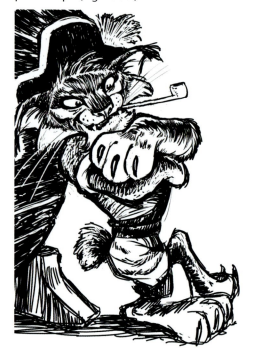

[Fig. 3-9] Would you buy a used pirate ship from Boston Bertie? Illustration by Nancy Beiman, reproduced by permission of Patricia Bernard.

A "story map" was created for the book before it was written. Story maps can be of a town or country or of an entire planet. These need not be complex drawings. A simple square with circles or boxes labeled with the elements of the story is quite sufficient. Everything on the story map should be relevant to the story and should be *used* in the story. In *Basil*'s case, the map was a very literal one. The pirates travel to the four quarters of the compass in search of their shop. North America was not originally on the story map and so it only existed in *Basil*'s universe after Patricia added Boston Bertie to the story. The final tale was completely different from the one we started out with, and we had a lot of fun changing it!

It's much easier to change things at the beginning of the production than when you are halfway through. Be open to alternative views when developing a story idea and characters. It is fun, it's creative, and it leads to better storytelling.

**"I AM A ROCK, I AM AN ISLAND."**

—Paul Simon and Art Garfunkel, *I Am a Rock*

One definition of animation is "the act of infusing life." Objects that are inanimate in the real world can come to life in your imaginary one and become symbolic or actual personalities. For example, a rock can be used to portray strength, solidity, or immobility. It conveys a different meaning altogether when it shatters through stress or is worn down into sand by the actions of wind and water.

The animation medium superbly conveys abstract concepts and emotions through symbolic objects and colors with the added dimension of movement over time. An "invulnerable" rock may be emotionally fragile. Water and rivers symbolize life, yet they become menacing when they flood. A cloud can be a fleecy impermanent thing or a terrifying storm. In animation, a tree is never just a tree—it may be your leading lady!

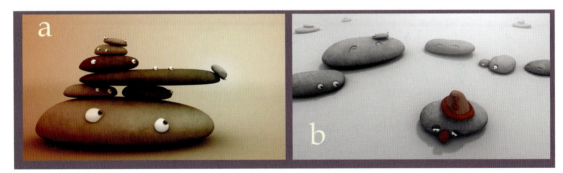

[Fig. 3-10] The abstract concept of danger (a) and humor (b) is illustrated graphically with rocks contrasting physical permanence with emotional variability. Animation brings life to allegorical symbols and colors. Reproduced by permission of Joseph Daniels.

A man holding a club conveys a very different meaning than a man holding a baseball bat even though the two objects are roughly the same size and shape and are used to hit things. An object's meaning varies with its context.

Suitable props will add dimension and depth to your character animation. Symbolic shapes also convey meaning to your audience. These are discussed in Chapter 6. The emotional use of color is discussed in Chapter 17.

# The Newsman's Story Guide: Who, What, When, Where, and Why

**Exercise:** *Design four cats.*

Do not start drawing right away. Think about the assignment carefully. What information have you been given? What information is missing? A story artist or character designer will ask for more background about these cats before working on designs.

Who are they? What are they? Where do they live? When does the action take place? Why do they do what they do and who or what do they interact with?

If you do not ask these questions, you may still design good cats, but they will be designs, not characters.

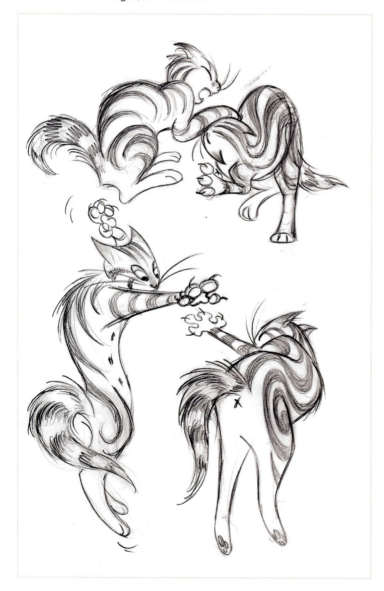

[Fig. 3-11] Four cats. The designs are graphically interesting but individual characters have not been defined. Reproduced by permission of Nina L. Haley.

Now try the assignment again, using the following information: Mama, a very proper and dignified cat, has three kittens. A story begins when you flesh out the original description of "four cats."

Now explore the characters. Are they "real" cats? Do they have human qualities or are they pure animal? Make a list of props that they could interact with. Where do they live? Which locations and props offer the best possibilities for animation? You can experiment with the scale of the mother cat to her kittens, as shown in Figure 3-12.

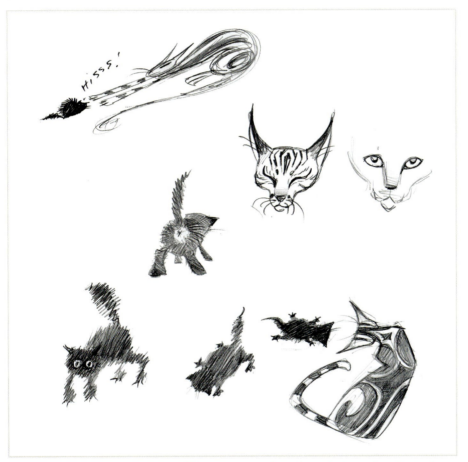

[Fig. 3-12] Kittens will have very different proportions from their mother. Body shape and agility will vary with age. Reproduced by permission of Nina L. Haley.

Now do a few small drawings (thumbnails) of the cats working with some of the props and write short sentences under the drawings describing how the situation might develop. Do not cross out any of the drawings and do not throw any of them away. At this stage, you should be open to all suggestions, no matter how crazy they may sound. You may sketch new ideas that will create a story, or take an existing story in a different direction.

How do you turn generic cats, rocks, or trees into individual characters? You could use human beings as a reference for their personalities. Start with the basics. Here's where your life experience literally comes into the picture.

**Exercise:** Sketch two human characters based on yourself and a friend at five years of age. Change the two humans into cats, translating the humans' attitudes and expressions to the cats' faces and bodies. Next, turn the humans into objects that portray their personality types. Experiment with the shape and scale of three different objects.

You know your own personality and that of your friend. How do you translate this quality into a character design, especially a nonhuman one? You can base the designs on caricatures but that is not always necessary.

By just *thinking about the pets, friends, and people you have met* while you are working, you will subconsciously start to incorporate some of their mannerisms and appearances into your design and story. This will make the characters uniquely yours and not a mere imitation of a style. No two people have precisely the same experiences in life. Referring to your own memory bank will keep your designs and stories fresh.

"You see, but you do not observe."

—Sir Arthur Conan Doyle (Sherlock Holmes), *A Scandal in Bohemia*

Observe life with the artist's eye. Notice everything. Draw it in your sketchbook. You will not only have an endless source of reference for animation, you will never be bored!

Interesting drawings of human relationships and motion can be done while waiting in an airport or train station or launderette. Attend horse, cat, and dog shows and county fairs. Visit zoos and children's playgrounds. Draw in your sketchbook every day. Any situation or location becomes interesting if you observe and analyze how living crea-

**[Fig. 3-13]** There is no such thing as an ordinary location. Interesting gesture drawings can be done at home, a supermarket, or a playground.

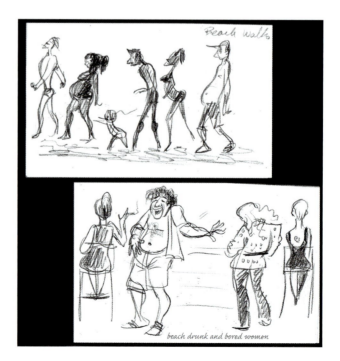

tures move and react. There is no such thing as a dull location—there is only the lack of perception of the extraordinary variety in life. Everything becomes interesting when you view it with the artist's eye.

Do not copy other animated films. It is too easy to be caught up in a style and imitate it so that the style is emphasized over the substance of your project. You will be looking through another animator's eyes and creating a pale imitation of *their* references and experiences.

Familiarize yourself with the work of the great artists and cartoonists of earlier times. Am I contradicting myself? No, because there are so many more cartoonists and illustrators than there are animators. Animation is a little more than a century old.  Cartoon art is 500 years old and graphic art is over 40,000 years old. Drawing inspiration from

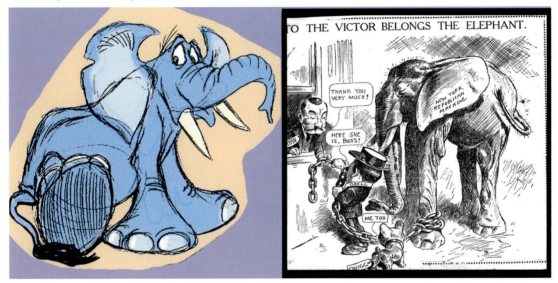

[Fig. 3-14] "Harry" from the film Your Feet's Too Big (1984) by Nancy Beiman, and Republican Elephant by T. S. Sullivant (1904). I based my character design on Sullivant's cartoons such as the one shown here. (Nancy Beiman collection.)

unusual source materials will help you design characters that are graphically interesting and original. Figure 3-14 shows how I used a classic cartoonist's work as inspiration for one of my own characters.

Be sure to always put a bit of yourself into your work. It is true that there are no new stories. There are only stories and characters that *you* have not done before. Your interpretations of the material will make it your own. Never copy anything outright. Put your source aside after a while and use your imagination to elaborate on it. The resultant mix will lead to original creation.

Do not forget to consider character relationships from the very start. Emotional relationships can develop over time, but their base remains consistent. (The penguin mama and children in Figure 3-2 will always have the same relationship to one another.)

You've now considered themes from a variety of sources and are ready to start developing situations and characters. Two approaches to story development are discussed in Chapter 4.

# 4

# Situation and Character Driven Stories

> "Comedy and fantasy are the two most difficult things in the world to do, because your audience is not educated exactly to what, for example, a rabbit six feet high will do. You have to make him believable to yourself.…That's the basic business of the whole matter."
>
> —Chuck Jones

There are two basic types of character animation films: situational film and character-driven film. In a character-driven film, the story works out of the character's personality. For example, a rabbit innocently occupies a rabbit hole on the exact spot where a prospector wishes to dig for gold. The prospector attacks the rabbit.

If I rename the rabbit hero of this story "Bugs Bunny," we instantly know how the plot will develop. Bugs' code of honor allows him to take justified revenge on the prospector since he has been attacked. The story develops out of Bugs' personality. An unknown rabbit might react differently and there would be no guidelines as there are with an established character.

A classic story formula goes something like this: "Act One: Get your hero up a tree. Act Two: Throw rocks at him. Act Three: Get him down out of the tree."

Stories based on "situation" often put ordinary characters in extraordinary predicaments.

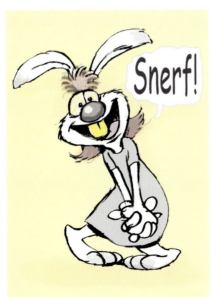

**[Fig. 4-1] An unknown character needs to establish its "rules of engagement" with its adversaries, while a familiar character may react in a familiar way.**

In Gene Deitch's adaptation of Jules Feiffer's MUNRO, the titular hero is a normal four-year-old boy who is drafted into the American army through a bureaucratic oversight. The little boy "gets up a tree" when he is placed in an adult situation. The "rocks" in the story come when Munro's attempts to tell the truth about his age are ignored by the military brass. His confessions are considered unmanly. The adults refuse to see that he is just a boy. Munro attempts to adapt but only "gets down from the tree" when he throws a tantrum and his childishness becomes obvious to everyone. At the end of the story Munro is once again a normal, unremarkable four-year-old boy.

Messages can be conveyed in an entertaining fashion by appealing characters. MUNRO used humor to contrast the child's mature behavior with the military characters' immature minds. War is likened to a children's game. The message—war is absurd; the 'cause' the army fights for is childish—could easily have become formulaic and didactic if stated more obviously.

Stories become interesting when the heroes use their virtues and skills to overcome obstacles and character flaws and reach a clearly defined goal. This does not mean that you need a violent conflict, or even a villain, to make a story work.

A character's conflict can be within himself, or against nature—perhaps a stubborn weed is growing in the flower bed. There are no dull stories. There are only stories that aren't well told. You can MAKE something interesting. It's your job.

Characters that react off one another and show us an unfamiliar view of this or another world can be quite as interesting as characters who fight one another. Conflict in a story does NOT mean violence or fighting. It can be something as simple as waiting for a kettle to boil.

The hero is affected by his or her experience. At the end of the story the hero will have undergone a change of habit, personality, or even physical appearance (think of Cinderella's magical transformation). The process of change, also known as a *character arc*, brings animated characters to life. The character arc is roughly similar to the story arc which will be discussed later in this book. Both arcs start on one level and develop through conflict to end on a higher plane than the one on which they started.

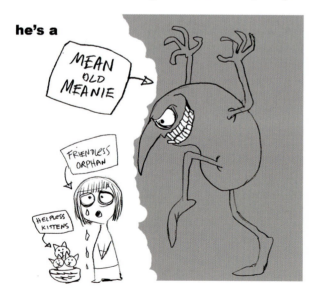

he's a

MEAN OLD MEANIE

FRIENDLESS ORPHAN

HELPLESS KITTENS

**...and he wants to TAKE OVER THE WORLD!**

[Fig. 4-2] Simplistic story formulas with stock or formulaic characters lead to predictable conclusions.

The Ugly Duckling literally changes into a new character. Many animated characters go through a physical and emotional transformation during the course of their stories. But Munro remains the same small boy at the end of his army adventure because MUNRO is really a story about foolish bureaucracy. The titular character is only a catalyst that precipitates the action.

Clichéd characters never create the illusion of life since their personalities and actions are completely predictable.

Stock heroes may overcome some obvious personal weakness or external obstacle By Working Together or Going on a Journey or By Just Being Themselves instead of *thinking* for themselves. All their problems are resolved by the fadeout because the stock story formula guarantees a happy ending. The audience knows exactly what to expect.

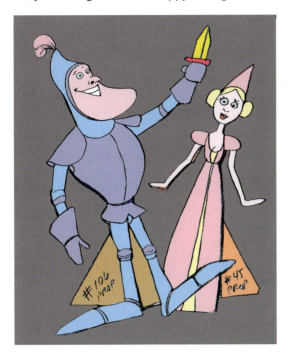

**[Fig. 4-3] A Stock Story. Pick one letter from each category. "I must find the (a) ring, (b)Princess, (c) kingdom, (d) golden fleece, and rescue the (a) Princess, (b) ring, (c) golden fleece, (d) kingdom, to win the (a) kingdom, (b) golden fleece, (c) Princess, (d) ring, but first must overcome my (a) enemy, (b) lack of self-esteem, (c) father, or (d) all of the above."**

Formulaic plotting without real conflict or character development produces dull and predictable stories. This is where your personal experience comes in. An appealing *character* with human virtues and failings will create more interest than a standard-issue *character type* that has appeared in many other animated films. Unusual characters will solve problems in an unusual way, so that even when the story is "stock," the interpretation is not.

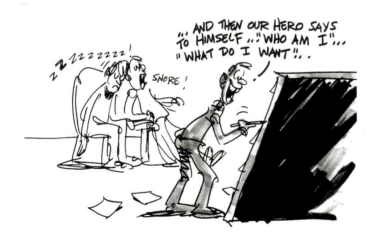

**[Fig. 4-4] A hero's goal must be clearly defined at the start. Illustration from SON OF FASTER CHEAPER, reproduced by permission of Floyd Norman.**

[Fig. 4-5] Count Dracula Goes to Bermuda. Pass the moon block!

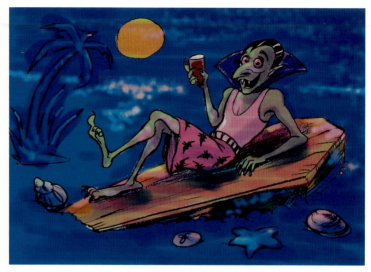

Movie or comic-inspired vampires, monsters, and mad doctors can easily become cli-chéd. Consider placing them in unfamiliar locations and varying their costumes and props accordingly, as shown in Figure 4-5. This approach can create new stories with old characters.

## Stop If You've Heard This One

*A man falls into his computer/television set and finds himself in a new world. A woman turns out to be a vampire and bites her date's neck. A man dies and his possessions are packed in a box. A hunter's prey catches the hunter instead. A man cannot distinguish be-tween dreams and reality.*

These situations have been used in hundreds of films. They are not stories, but gim-micks. Gimmicky films impose their stories on the characters. There are no character arcs; only interchangeable puppets moving toward the foregone conclusion of a card-board ballet.

Gimmicks like the ones listed above should be avoided when constructing stories for animated films—unless you can make them seem new and different from all the other versions of the story or character.

Why did the preview audience for SNOW WHITE AND THE SEVEN DWARFS cry when the princess died? The ending of the story was well known at the time. SNOW WHITE AND THE SEVEN DWARFS created characters with believable personalities and desires that aroused audience sympathy so that cartoon drawings were seen as living beings. The Dwarfs in the original Grimm Brothers story were nameless 'little men'. In the film, each Dwarf is a distinct character that represents one aspect of a human personality. Snow White's interaction with the Dwarfs and animals adds depth to her character and makes us care about what happens to her. Snow White's relationship with the Dwarfs is that of a mother to little children. The Dwarfs are both adult and childish, with rec-ognizable human flaws and virtues. But the Wicked Queen is a one-dimensional villain with no redeeming qualities. Her hatred of Snow White is the conflict that motivates the story.

A fairy-tale story's ending is predictable—they all live happily ever after—but the journey need not be. A well-paced story with sympathetic characters will hold our attention even when we already know the ending. So if you can find a new twist on gimmicky situations such as the ones listed at the beginning of this section, by all means try it. Develop the characters and don't construct story-by-numbers. Strong characters will make an old and familiar story new and interesting.

# Defining Conflict

Many classic animated films are based on simple conflicts. An internal or external obstacle must be overcome. The stories of CINDERELLA, SNOW WHITE AND THE SEVEN DWARFS, and SLEEPING BEAUTY all contain conflicts between the heroine of each story and jealous characters who wish to displace or kill her. This conflict may be described as: '*I want something* that you have.'

Some characters are victims of circumstance. DUMBO must save his mother from jail and be accepted in the circus world. PINOCCHIO, an innocent led astray, must rescue his father from the whale by his own initiative. Beauty must rescue her father and also save Beast's life. Nemo's father must find his son who is lost somewhere in the Pacific Ocean. These conflicts are life-or-death situations. The characters '*must do it.*'

Simba in THE LION KING must overcome his character weakness and accept his responsibilities. This conflict may be described as '*I don't want to do it.*' Characters may prevail despite early setbacks. (This is a common device in animation storytelling.) They '*will do it.*'

Good characters make these simple conflicts interesting. It has been said that there are only a certain set number of basic plots in literature. If your characters are appealing and believable you will avoid the been-there-done-that feeling that comes when stock characters are placed in predictable situations.

> **Exercise:** Design and thumbnail two characters illustrating the following conflicts. You may use several sketches per example and include props.
>
> 1.  I can't do it.
> 2.  I must do it.
> 3.  I want something that you have.

An example is shown in Figure 4-6. This elementary conflict creates the germ of a story.

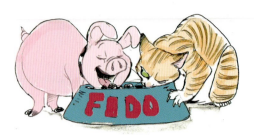

[Fig. 4-6] I don't want to do it.
Which character displays the
conflict?

# Log Lines

A brief description distills the essence of the story and makes a concept easy to understand. This description is sometimes called a *log line*. Here are some hypothetical log
lines from animated features:

- Surface appearance can be deceptive. People come in layers, like onions. —SHREK
- A freak turns his defect into an asset, redeeming himself and his mother. —DUMBO
- Magic comes from personal initiative and the working of conscience. —PINOCCHIO
- A callow youth learns to accept his responsibilities. —THE LION KING
- There is some good in every character. —LILO & STITCH

Short films can also have log lines:

- A large opponent menaces a peace-loving rabbit, who takes appropriate revenge.
  —nearly every Bugs Bunny cartoon ever made
- One sister wants the other sister dead. —ANNA AND BELLA (this is the actual log
  line for Børge Ring's film)
- A bulldog wishes to adopt a small kitten but his owner won't let him bring any
  more things into the house. —FEED THE KITTY  (Chuck Jones)
- An eccentric inventor's dog is much cleverer than he is. —all of Nick Park's *Wallace
  and Gromit* films

Write a few brief sentences describing your basic story ideas and characters. You will
have time to elaborate the gags and plot twists later. Create several log lines and
thumbnail the more interesting ones. The sky is the limit at this point—this is why this
phase of development is called *'blue sky'*. Work with ideas that interest and intrigue
you—don't create stories that you think a studio or audience *expects to see*. The best
animation is made by artists who project their enthusiasm and spontaneity into their
work.

# Stealing The Show

The story should be told by the *most interesting* characters. Secondary characters are often used to help tell the hero's story. We often identify more with them than we do with the hero. For example, the rather ordinary Doctor Watson writes about the adventures of his extraordinary and unpredictable friend Mr. Sherlock Holmes. We see a great part of Snow White's story through the eyes of the Seven Dwarfs and the forest animals in the animated SNOW WHITE AND THE SEVEN DWARFS.  These likable characters find her appealing, so we do too. We do not learn about the Seven Dwarfs' background since this material is not relevant to Snow White's story.

Subplots that distract from the main story idea should be avoided, or the film will break up into a series of disconnected threads. All subplots and secondary characters must support the main story. If the sidekick is more interesting than the hero, maybe you are telling the wrong character's story!

Heroes should have recognizable goals to achieve, obstacles to overcome, and a few flaws that make them imperfect and therefore interesting to us. If your hero easily solves every problem and never makes a mistake, they will never encounter conflict. There will be no surprise or suspense in their story since the outcome will be a foregone conclusion. Your hero will become a bore and secondary characters that *do* have obstacles to overcome will easily distract us from the main story.

There should be a piece of Kryptonite for every Superman.

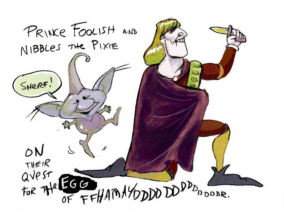

**[Fig. 4-7] Secondary characters may become more interesting than "perfect" heroes.**

Animated characters often use catch phrases from popular culture to get a laugh. The Warner Brothers Studio's cartoons immortalized many phrases that originated on radio shows.

Pop culture references can become a cliché that dates the film to a specific time.

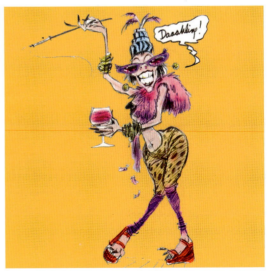

**[Fig. 4-8] Disco Fever! Nothing dates faster than 'hipness' and 'edginess'.**

Topical references should be avoided unless they help advance the story, and even then, the story should not depend on them. Most topical jokes need to be explained to anyone born after the date the film was released. Some work without explanation. The Genie's caricature transformations in ALADDIN'S *"A Friend Like Me"* song are funny even though most five-year-olds did not know who William F. Buckley or Ed Sullivan was when the film was originally released. The story point reads well regardless. The comedy comes from the Genie's quick-change artistry and the wildly different speech patterns and movements of the caricatures. It is easy to understand that the Genie is transforming into different people and the cultural references are a bonus joke. The quick changes are a feature of the Genie's personality and are not simply a gimmick.

Good animation is perennial: if the stories and characters are appealing enough, they will connect with their audience long after contemporary references in the film are forgotten.

# Parodies and Pastiches

*Parodies* are mockeries of preexisting material. They will use the same plot elements and characters as the original staged as farce. Figure 4-9 shows a new staging of *Romeo and Juliet*. The characters may be taking themselves seriously, but their ludicrous appearance and the falling balcony makes the scene comic. Parodies may or may not be affectionate, but you must be familiar with the original material to accurately mock it.

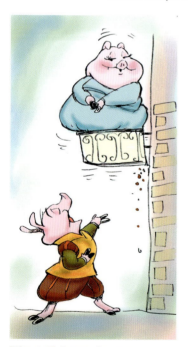

[Fig. 4-9] A parody uses absurd characters and over-the-top interpretations to affectionately or sarcastically mock its source material.

Parodies tend to work best in short formats. If the raucous mood continues for too long a time the mocking tone can become wearying. Parodying another movie or story essentially allows someone else to write the story for you. Your film is a reflection of another work and its success will depend on whether audiences are familiar with the original material.

A *pastiche* takes the elements of the source's style and affectionately reworks the material into something new. It can contain parody but it is a distillation of a genre. Chuck Jones directed a brilliant series of pastiche cartoons including WHAT'S OPERA DOC? which distilled the 16-hour Wagnerian Ring cycle into a six-minute cartoon. SHREK's leads were characters from classic fairy tales, except that the roles were changed and fairy-tale clichés were turned on their heads—the "bad ogre" was the hero, the "beautiful princess" was the monster, and the "noble king" was the villain. Pastiches allow you to create original characters that have more depth and personality than a story that parodies a specific role or film.

When targeting a genre rather than a specific film, the animator takes cultural references that are familiar to the audience and reinterprets them to create something new. It's not what you do—it really *is* how you do it.

# 5

# What If? Contrasting the Possible and the Fanciful

The film medium is literally fantastic.

Film takes you outside the limits of time and space. Animation can take you outside the limits of your own body. There is a type of film that deals with the 'here and now'. It is called *documentary filmmaking* since it documents something that already exists.

Animation creates new worlds and fantastic characters who think and feel and live. Animation doesn't need sets, location shoots, or actors. The only limit on your setting or characters is your imagination.

Animation is at its best when it depicts something that could *possibly* exist. It is counterproductive to duplicate reality in animation unless you are doing special effects that must blend in with live action. If you enjoy 'realism' you may want to work in this field or in live action.

An animated film's weakness is usually the story. There is a fallacious belief that since animation is "just a cartoon" the story does not need to have the same dramatic structure as that of a live-action film. In truth, animation needs *more* structure so that we identify with the imaginary characters and their problems. Limitations need to be set. A story where 'anything can happen' or where characters 'can do anything' will lack suspense since your characters will easily solve any conflict that might arise. Supposedly anarchic stories like *Alice in Wonderland* and *Through the Looking Glass* take place in lands with their own set of rules. The odd characters in both of the *Alice in Wonderland* books always have an explanation for their behavior, which only Alice considers odd. We perceive Wonderland through 'normal' Alice's eyes as she attempts to impose the laws of the real world on the fantastic characters.

Some stories reverse accepted realities. Jonathan Swift did this in *Gulliver's Travels* when he had horses behaving like civilized people and manlike "Yahoos" acting like brute beasts.

**[Fig. 5-1] Houyhnhnms were the equine rulers and Yahoos were manlike beasts in Jonathan Swift's *Gulliver's Travels*.**

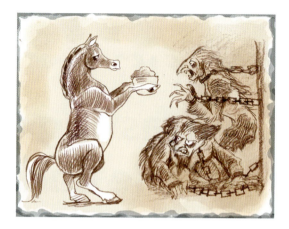

Reversals can apply to character types as well as situations. Characters that work against type can create amusing story conflicts. What if bulls were peaceful, bank robbers were childlike, and dragons were timid poets? These characters have all appeared in memorable animated cartoons (FERDINAND THE BULL, BABY BUGGY BUNNY, and THE RELUCTANT DRAGON).

Consider things that *could* possibly happen to the characters and the story as well as those that *can*. Remember that animation is not restricted by the laws of physics or gravity! *Believability is more important to an animated film than realism*. We are able to accept an animated world where fish and rabbits talk, or where people travel to other planets without space suits. The secret is consistency. Each project has its own set of rules that guide the action of the characters and the development of the story.

What if insects ran the world and exterminated people? What if fish were able to live on dry land? You can start with a normal story situation and develop it in an unusual way. Try contrasting the ordinary with the extraordinary. Here is a simple example: A hound dog, a family pet, chases rabbits around the back yard of a suburban house. If this is as far as you go with the story, you can create an amusing story showing the dog's interactions with little woodland creatures as depicted in Figure 5-2.

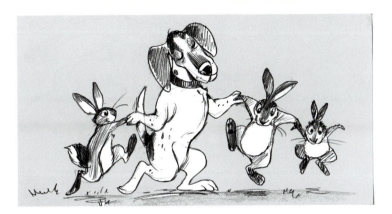

**[Fig. 5-2] A very cute cartoon situation with very cute animals doing very cute things.**

These characters can be fun to animate, but the setting and story have been used many times before. So it is once again time to ask "What if?" What if the story develops in an unexpected fashion? What if an alien spaceship lands near the doghouse? It *could* happen. But why stop there? Add more "what ifs," developing what might result from this contrast between the normal and the unusual. Will this be a comic story? Try using extreme scale contrasts in your characters and prop designs. If the alien appears to be small and ineffectual, it may be totally harmless, or it might be a serious threat in a small package. Is this a dramatic story? Perhaps the alien will have a fearsome appearance. It can be larger and designed in a different style than the dog and the rabbits. Sketch several rough ideas for each character and draw thumbnails of some interactions between them.

I've decided to make this a comic story. Here are some ways that the alien's appearance might influence the situation.

■    What if the alien looks like a rabbit?

■    What if it looks like another dog? What if it was a very small dog?

■    What if the dog thinks the alien is a toy?

■    What if the alien's weapons resembled cookies or dog food and actually attracted the dog?

■    What if the rabbits were very aggressive toward the alien?

■    What if the alien's other weapons resembled carrots and attracted the rabbits?

■    Some exploratory illustrations appear in Figure 5-3.

The new situation has the poor alien continually bedeviled by a dog and woodland creatures that lack the proper respect for its mission and/or person. Its defenses are useless. This leads us, and it, to the logical question: *How does this story end?*

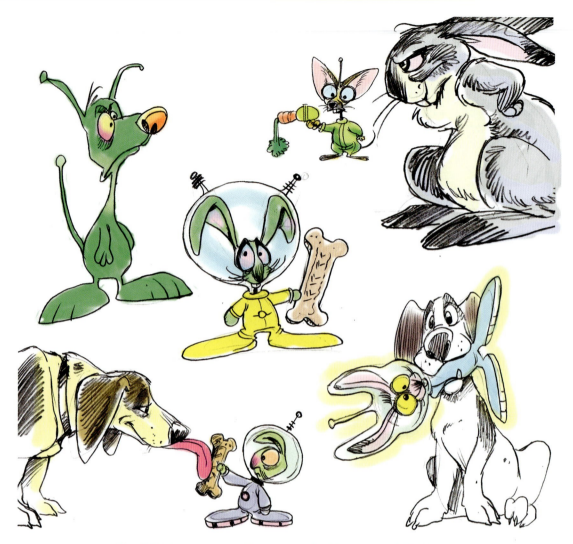

[Fig. 5-3] **Here are some aliens: some doglike, some rabbitlike, all completely ineffectual.**

Draw rough on lined yellow sketch pads while you are experimenting with story ideas and character designs. The lines on the pads provide built-in "rulers" that help set the characters' scale and room for the notes you take during story meetings.

Your final designs should be in color and drawn on white unlined paper or card. Draw variations in scale as well as design and see which characters work best together. Designs may use tone or color (recommended). Work rough and don't cross anything out. How would the plot develop if the alien was large and threatening? What if it looked like a different animal? The different physical and emotional properties of the aliens and the Earthlings will change the story.

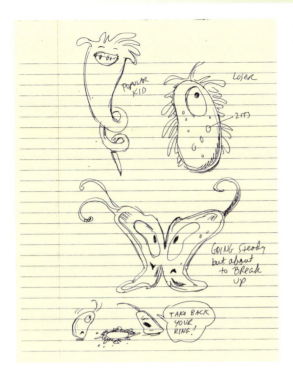

[Fig. 5-4] Yellow sketch pads provide construction lines and are cheap and easy to obtain. They are very useful during the development period when the character design and story are still in flux.

# Beginning at the Ending: The Tex Avery 'Twist'

Remember this Golden Rule of Animation Pre-production: *ALWAYS know where, and how, your picture is going to end, before you start production.*

The ending and beginning of the story should be determined before you work on the middle section. The middle of the story can be expanded or contracted as time and budget allows. You have to start somewhere, and your ending *must* be there.

Some films are constructed on the "moving train" pattern where the action is already under way when the story begins. Cat chases mouse, dog chases cat. Little time is needed for establishing shots since the characters' situation is evident from the start of the film. These films typically build a series of gags, each one stronger than the other, with the most spectacular one at the finish. The Road Runner and Coyote cartoons are good examples of the "moving train" story.

Director Tex Avery delighted in creating meticulously plotted hyperbolic stories that broke all the rules of animation, but he once found himself stumped for an ending.

I interviewed Tex Avery about story construction in 1978, and we discussed this exceptional film.

TEX AVERY: When analyzing a cartoon situation you should consider these three points: Is it a *good* situation? What can you do to develop it, and how are you going to finish it? Can you "switch" the story or do it in a new way?

Don't use dialogue unless it is absolutely necessary. You shouldn't tell what is happening on the screen.

NANCY BEIMAN: Would you have an idea of the total picture, beginning and end, from the start? Or would you build a film from a basic gag or situation and do the beginning and end last?

TEX AVERY: We'd generally start with the beginning and ending first. This leaves you room to 'fill in'. You should have a definite finish. A switch or surprise ending is good; a "tag." You can build up one situation to a ridiculous extent … and when the audience feels that you can't go any farther, you "top" it, thereby surprising them.

When constructing a story, you should start listing gags, not necessarily in order. Don't throw any of them out yet. Dovetail them until the gags become stronger and stronger. The gags don't have to be related to one another, but each should top the previous one.

One picture we didn't know how to end was BAD LUCK BLACKIE. [Author's note: This study in superstition is the story of a black cat that assists a small white kitten by repeatedly crossing a bullying bulldog's path; each time Blackie does this, ever-larger objects immediately fall in from offscreen and hit the dog on the head.] We built that picture so that it went from the bulldog getting hit by a flowerpot to the kitchen sink to a battleship. To sort of get a little humor into the thing we had Blackie run across the dog's path differently each time—once on tiptoe, once like a Russian dancer. This was a gag within a gag. Finally we couldn't think of anything else to drop on [the bulldog]. How do you end it? Well, you're obliged to come back to the hero at the end of a cartoon. So you pull a switch—the kitten [now painted black] turns nasty and laughs like the dog did all through the picture.

NANCY BEIMAN: You didn't have that ending from the start?

TEX AVERY: No. We didn't know where we were going to end up.

Interview with Tex Avery © 1978, 2005 by Nancy Beiman.

Although Tex refers to gags for short Hollywood cartoons, this manner of story construction is standard for plot points in feature films as well. An animation story is not an uncharted journey. Everything must be planned beforehand.

Tex mentions the "obligation" to show the hero at the end of a cartoon. This device is not used in all animated stories. DUMBO, PINOCCHIO, and DUCK AMUCK are examples that break this 'rule'. In the case of the alien-versus-dog-and-rabbits story described earlier in this chapter, you may have more than one hero to consider! The story may have no heroes at all. As story and layout man Ken O'Connor stated, "Circumstances alter cases."

**Exercise:** Draw two or three thumbnails for a comic ending and two or three more for a dramatic ending to the alien-versus-dog-and-rabbits scenario discussed in this chapter. You may use different character designs for the two stories. Work on lined yellow paper and keep your early drawings rough. Add color to your final designs.

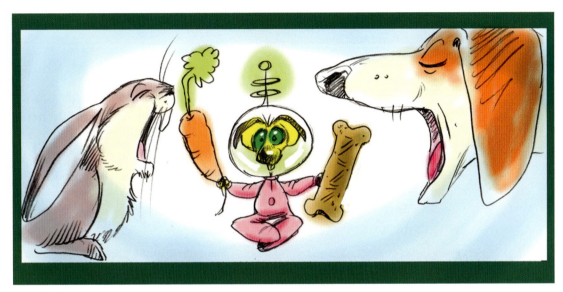

**[Fig. 5-5] The end or a new beginning?**

*"I can't believe that!" said Alice.*

*"Can't you?" the queen said in a pitying tone. "Try again, draw a long breath, and shut your eyes."*

*Alice laughed. "There's no use trying," she said. "One can't believe impossible things."*

*"I dare say you haven't had much practice," said the queen. "When I was your age, I always did it for half an hour a day. Why, sometimes I've believed as many as six impossible things before breakfast."*

—Lewis Carroll, *Alice in Wonderland*

# Establishing Rules

The hardest assignment I have ever received was to "do whatever I liked." You can run off in all directions if you don't set the rules for your project at the start. Rules allow your new animated world and your characters to function with their own set of natural laws, which might not be those of the real world.

Here are some Rules created for the "Road Runner" cartoons by Chuck Jones and story man Mike Maltese:

1. The Road Runner never leaves the Road.

2. The action always takes place in the American Southwest.

3. The Coyote's clever traps invariably backfire on him.

It ultimately does not matter that the Coyote does not catch the Road Runner. Jones defined the Coyote's mindset and the point of the series by quoting George Santayana: "Fanaticism consists in redoubling your efforts when you have forgotten your aim."

Be sure to follow your own rules. If you have created a world where characters can breathe underwater without special equipment, it is disturbing to have one character suddenly find it impossible to breathe unless there is a need (and an explanation) for it in the story.

Every detail of character and setting should contribute to getting the story across as clearly as possible. If your story takes place in ancient Greece, but characters can 'pop' forward to modern times, be sure to explain the rules of your new world so that we understand how and why this time shift happens. If your character must go *against* a rule—say, by befriending a character that we, and it, see as an enemy—establish your rules first before they are broken. For example, everyone knows cartoon dogs and cats hate each other. Or do they? In Chuck Jones' FEED THE KITTY, this rule is reversed when a tough bulldog falls in love with a cute kitten. Conflict arises when the dog tries to hide his new friend from his mistress, who has told him that he may not have any more "things" in the house. The kitten is placed in situations of extreme danger, but when all is revealed to the mistress, she lets the dog keep the kitten.

Exercise: Sketch some simple characters for the following four situations. Next, list some rules that might affect the character relationships and the story. Illustrate each rule with a thumbnail of the characters in a recognizable setting. Work on lined yellow pads to help you scale the size of the characters. Keep the sketches very rough and do not cross anything out. After you have drawn a few characters sketch possible conflicts and endings for each situation.

1. A difficult mother-in-law is visiting her daughter and son-in-law. The mother-in-law is a Witch.

2. Children on the first day of school. The characters are all single-celled organisms.

4. A hunter chases a small animal. Consider different animals and locations that might influence the story. Is the hunter a human or an animal?

5. Your story takes place inside and on top of a dresser. All of your characters are made from different articles of clothing.

Remember, your first idea may not be the best one. Keep an open mind about story and characters at this point. Experiment with different situations and don't take the obvious way out. The rule in some story sessions is to 'never say "No"' at this point in development. An idea that seems odd at first may become 'right' later on. In story as with animation, it is better to go 'too far' and pull back than to not act strongly enough.

You are now refining your characters' appearance and investigating how they act and interact with one another. Do your designs have appeal? We will define this essential quality in the next chapter.

# Appealing or Appalling? Beginning Character Design

6

You do not have to like a character to find it appealing. You need only care to know about what happens to it. Appeal in animation may be defined in the phrase, "Do I, the viewer, want to spend a few minutes or hours of my life with this character and this story? Am I willing to suspend disbelief and accept the character as a sentient being? Are its problems of interest to me?"

An appealing character is interesting to look at. Appeal does *not* mean that it is 'cute', lovable, infantile, or cuddly. Monster movies contain good examples of appealing 'negative' characters. We want to know about the monster *and* the victims. Victims are often disposable props who never develop as personalities. We are horrified by what happens to them, but we sometimes identify more with the monster!

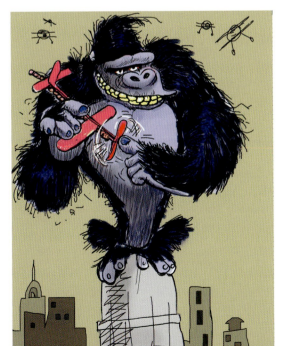

**[Fig. 6-1] Giant Ape attacks city! Do we identify with the city or the ape? We may feel empathy for the human victims and sympathy for the monster.**

An appealing character will have a design that is interesting, but not so complex that it is unable to perform actions required by the story. The design of the character and the production must never prevent the character's actions from being clearly perceived by the audience.

Form follows function in animation. The story and its action will affect your character's design. For example, if Character A has to hug Character B, it is very important to make Character A's arms long enough to fit around Character B's body!  (Figure 6-2)

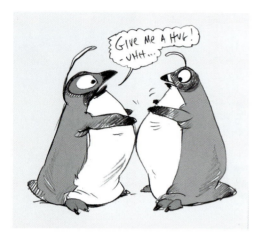

**[Fig. 6-2] Know what the character has to do before you model it. The design should help, not hinder, character motion.**

 If character A is designed in isolation and not concurrently with Character B, such accidents can easily occur. Make your mistakes on paper. It is an easy matter to adjust the length of Character A's arms before you start animating, but not so easy once you have already built the puppet on a set or on the computer.

The storyboard artists should be made aware of a character's scale, strength, and physical limitations at the start of production so that they do not board actions that are impossible for the 'actors' to perform. Characters without fingers and thumbs such as the penguins in Figure 6-2 would have to play piano by some other method. Dealing with a physical limitation can produce very entertaining animated solutions.

Drawn characters can stretch their arms if necessary, but we must consider this stretchiness a conscious design on the part of the creator, not an attempt to repair a design mistake. We now are dealing with a chicken-or-egg theory. If we haven't yet set our story, but want to design an appealing character, where do we start?

# Reading the Design: Silhouette Value

A good animated character, in any medium, will have a recognizable shape. When we can identify it instantly in silhouette, we say that it *reads* well.

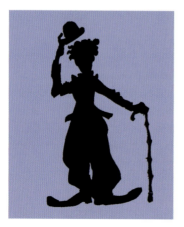

**[Fig. 6-3] A famous silhouette.**

A common design failing is to add details to the character without first working on underlying construction. This results in a weak, unconvincing design as shown in  Figure 6-4.

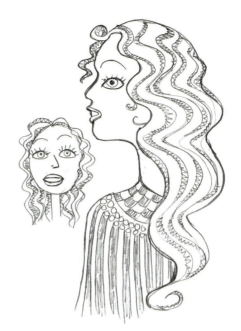

[Fig. 6-4] A weak design, with most of the effort spent on the surface details.

# Construction Sights

Create a rough silhouette for each character at the start of the project. Work loosely and experiment with a variety of shapes. When you have found one that you like, shade the silhouette in to test the readability. If you have more than one character, work on them simultaneously and vary the size and shapes of the silhouettes as shown in Figure 6-5.

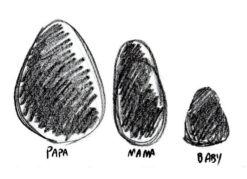

[Fig. 6-5] The Three Bears' rough silhouettes are ovals with no two the same size and shape. This creates a contrast in scale before the characters are designed.

After you have your basic silhouettes, *design your characters from the inside out*. Break each silhouette into sections to indicate the size of the head and length of the legs. Do not divide the shape evenly since this leads to uninteresting design. The bears' heads and torsos are designed within the oval shapes in Figure 6-6. Simple graphic shapes are used to construct the head, body, and limbs. Legs and arms are 'drawn through' the torso so that they attach on opposite sides of the body and create a feeling of volume in the design. Ears and hair are added as separate shapes after the underlying head and body shapes are constructed. Surface details (clothing, textures, and patterns) are added last.

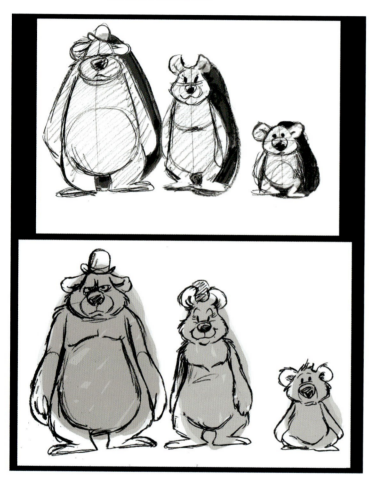

**[Fig. 6-6] The Three Bears' construction works within the oval silhouettes. The second drawing refines the body shapes and adds texture (hair). Separate shapes for hair and ears are added after the body is constructed.**

Body shapes can impart subconscious meaning to the viewer. For example, two figures in an animated story represent Youth and Old Age. I designed the younger figure in Figure 6-7 as a column of coltish long legs topped by a large ellipse of a head that suggests childish inexperience. The older figure is entirely contained in a circle that symbolizes her self-sufficiency and age. The shapes tell us something about their characters before they have even begun to move.

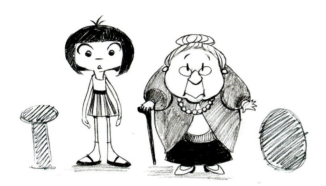

[Fig. 6-7] Characters portray their age in their silhouettes. The older figure contains some infantile features such as small extremities scaling against a larger body.

The bony structure of the human skeleton, particularly the jaw and spine, shrinks as a person ages. This loss of bone mass and a heavier body causes an old person's hands and feet to appear proportionately smaller than those of younger people. Babies also have large, heavy bodies that contrast with small, rounded arms and legs. Some elderly character designs may share these infantile proportions, as shown in figure 6-7. Young animals tend to have large feet and longer legs than adults, depending on the species. The girl in Figure 6-7 has long legs that resemble those of a young horse or deer.

Conversely, the cartilaginous tissue in the nose and ears never stops growing and joints become gnarled with arthritis as a person ages. Elderly people appear to have larger noses and ears because they really do, as illustrated by the troll family in Figure 6-8. The troll parent's hands have enlarged finger joints and her nose and ears are enormous. The young troll's skeletal definition is hidden under a layer of baby fat.

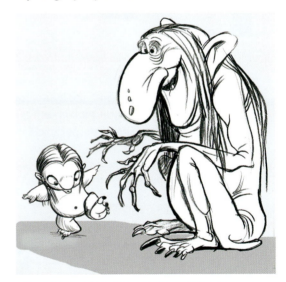

[Fig. 6-8] Youth and age also exhibit significant physical differences. The old troll has a huge nose and ears that keep growing throughout life. Its hands are gnarled but are relatively small in relation to its large body. The baby troll's infantile proportions are shared by the older character in Figure 6-7.

*Always consider silhouette value when designing a character.* The standard method of testing a design is to black in the entire shape. If you can still understand the meaning of the design or pose after you have done this, the character or pose is said to 'read' well. Some characters read more strongly than others. Here are silhouette figures of two Chinese monks that represent enthusiasm and experience. The younger character is unbalanced and top-heavy. His form was based on the shape of a long-necked vase. This character's motions are strong but ineffective, since he does not think before he acts. The Master is weightier due to his age and experience. His form is based on that of a rock; he is grounded, stable, and his moves are deliberate and decisive. (Figure 6-9)

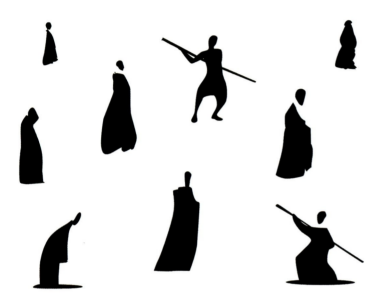

**[Fig. 6-9] These silhouettes read well and depict typical attitudes of two characters. Reproduced by permission of Joseph Daniels and Jedidiah Mitchell.**

Even 'ordinary' characters can become interesting if props and appropriate costume are designed with the figure. Tools and uniforms symbolizing specific occupations can create variety in background or crowd character designs. Never just draw 'a man' or 'a woman'. Simple props can create a personality.

**[Fig. 6-10] Design props along with a character's body shape. This will help establish their character and create interest in your design. Shading in the silhouette tests the design's readability.**

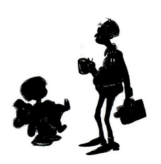
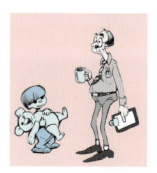

Analyze the design of a graphic character to determine how it moves. Does its shape *morph* (distort) or will it remain unaffected while surface details animate across it? All of these questions must be answered before your character design is put into production.

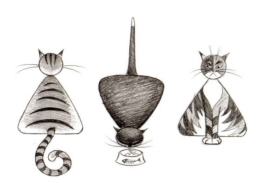

[Fig. 6-11] A graphic character may not deform or move in three dimensions when animating. Standardized models ensure that its features do not morph constantly. This technique should be used sparingly since it can become distracting. Reproduced by permission of Nina L. Haley.

# Foundation Shapes and Their Meaning

I will refer to some shapes as "foundation" shapes since they form the basis for complex designs in the art of many cultures. The four foundation shapes are *circles and ovals*, which are easiest to draw and distort, *squares, triangles*, and *cylinders*. These shapes translate into 'primitives' in CGI programs. The graphic animated symbol and the more rounded, dimensional character will both be created from the interplay of these foundation shapes. A graphically-styled film may use the shapes with little modification, as shown in Figure 6-12. A dimensional character's design will seem more complex but will still use graphic foundation shapes for its basic construction.

[Fig. 6-12] A simple character may consist only of foundation shapes. EM! ® from *We All Die Alone* by Mark Newgarden. Reproduced by permission of Mark Newgarden.

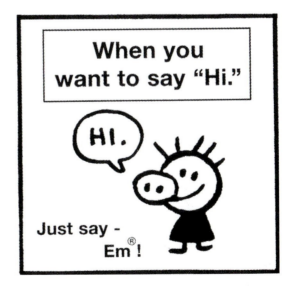

Human faces display the same variant on a simple pattern. Figure 6-13 shows different face shapes with the features at differing levels. One is round, one square, and two are oval. The size of the eyes, mouth, and nose vary to create even greater differences. The shape of the hair complements and emphasizes the facial design.

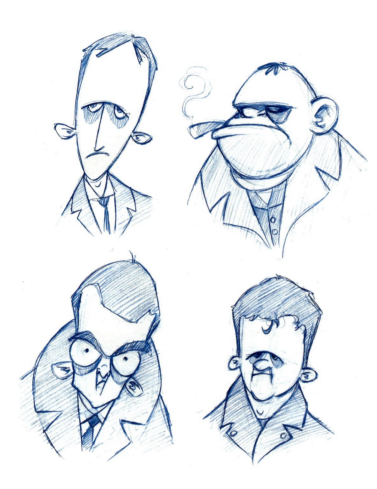

[Fig. 6-13] Varied proportions on basic shapes will create new characters. Faces with even proportions will often seem less lifelike than caricatures. These Gangster Studies were based on antique photographs. Reproduced by permission of William Robinson.

Caricatures of famous or infamous people may provide inspiration for a character design. This gives it more depth than one created from whole cloth. Figure 6-14 shows variations on one woman's face. If you use a caricature of a person as a basis for your character, determine which foundation shapes and proportions suggest their likeness. Use these shapes as a starting point for construction and "push" the design so that it becomes something new. You may combine features from more than one person and even add a few animal traits to create an original character. Use sketchbook drawings as reference for typical poses and features. Vary the proportions and try several different designs where some features are emphasized more than the others—but make sure that all of them work together as part of an organic whole. A good design features *repetition with variation and exaggeration*. The least interesting proportions are closest to reality.

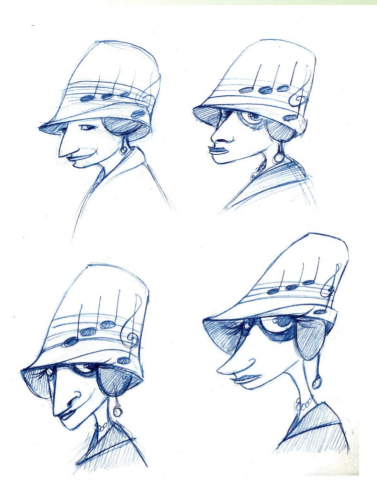

**[Fig. 6-14] Different characters are created by varying facial and body proportions. These caricatures were all based on the same historic photograph. Reproduced by permission of William Robinson.**

**Exercise:** Take drawings from your sketchbook and one photograph or illustration of a person from a specific historical era. Design a new character wearing period clothing standing in the sketchbook pose. Then "push" the proportions in several drawings as shown in Figure 6-14.

# The Shape of Things

Certain shapes have taken on symbolic meaning over the centuries. Circular characters are seen as cute or non-threatening. A character constructed primarily from triangular shapes will seem proactive or aggressive. Sherlock Holmes is a perfect example of this character type: he has a pointed nose, pointed fingers, wears a triangular cape, and even his name sounds 'sharp'. Watson, the steadfast friend who narrates the stories, sounds like a 'square'. Generations of illustrators have portrayed him as a square-jawed, square-bodied, heavyset figure as a contrast to Holmes' thinness (Figure 6-15).

**[Fig. 6-15] Sherlock Holmes and Doctor Watson, a triangle and a square. I've accentuated Watson's 'squareness' by adding a checkered pattern to his clothing.**

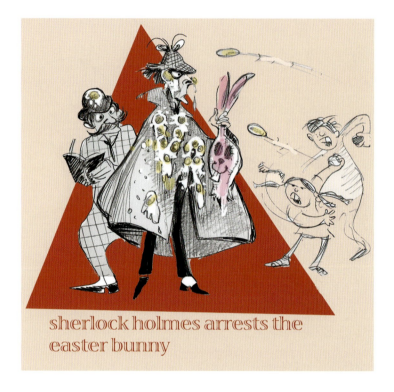

It is very amusing to turn these stereotypes upside down and work against type. An adorable round little character could have a nasty personality, a triangular design can be used for a reactive or passive character, and a square can be a real blockhead. Variations on the basic shapes are used in character construction in all media. The shapes have, over time, taken on specific meanings in certain contexts. Sometimes the same shape can be used to portray diametrically opposing characteristics. A circle is open and trusting or a babyish nonentity (Fig. 6-16). A square is trustworthy, dependable, and centered or it can be a real blockhead (Fig. 6-17). A triangle is quick, sharp, aggressive, and insightful. Triangular characters precipitate the action and get things done. They may be either heroes or villains, but they are always active (Fig. 6-18). Yet a triangle, when used point uppermost as the foundation shape for a head, indicates a character of low intelligence (Fig. 6-19). These stereotypical shapes can help the character's appearance convey its personality.

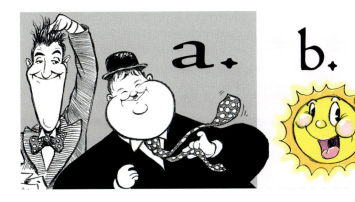

[Fig. 6-16] CIRCLE/OVAL: (a) reassuring, trusting, non-aggressive, OR (b) bland, saccharine, infantile.

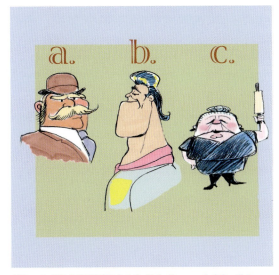

[Fig. 6-17] SQUARE: (a) Solid, dependable, (b) strong, balanced, OR: (c) unyielding, inflexible.

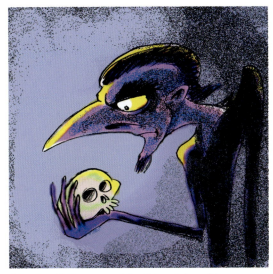

[Fig. 6-18] Alas, poor Hamlet… I drew him, Horatio.

[Fig. 6-19] A pointy-headed gangster. Reproduced by permission of William Robinson.

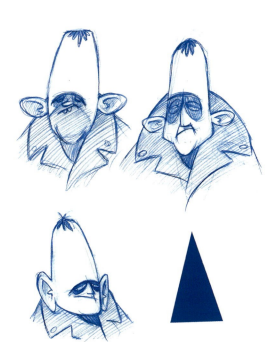

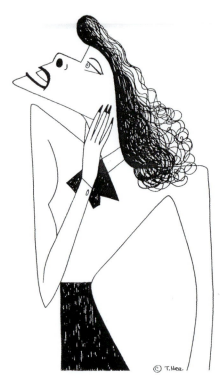

**[Fig. 6-20] The opposition of curved and straight forms and positive and negative space creates interest in the design. Caricature of Katherine Hepburn by T. Hee (Nancy Beiman collection).**

Stereotyped characters are very common: 'Fat people are jolly, thin people with glasses are nerds, villains are huge and menacing'. This is not true at all times but it will be useful to you *sometimes*. Stereotypical elements may appear in the design to render characters' personalities instantly recognizable. It is more interesting to avoid using them and instead create personality through the character's body language and movement. The creation of character through movement will be discussed in Chapter 8.

Stereotypes are shortcuts: everything is familiar to your audience, so you don't have to work to establish anything new. If you must work with stereotypical characters, think of personality quirks that will differentiate them from the hundreds of similar stereotypes that have been done before. Always remember: there is never 'only one way' to do anything. The 'right' way is the one that works for the story.

You will find that you can create more variety in the design by playing forms against one another. Work for a pleasing variety of shapes and good silhouette value. Figure 6-20's negative space is as important to the design as the drawing itself.

# Going Organic

Good design is a continuing process of simplification and communication. Inanimate objects may be 'organic' in the sense that animation brings them to life, but the meaning of the word differs when used in a design sense. Organic designs have shapes that flow into one another. They are not simply stuck together like a snowman. Remember that your designs describe a volume, not merely the outline of a shape. Think in the third dimension, not in line. Design the whole character, not a series of discrete components.

Identically-sized foundation shapes can create a repetitive and uninteresting design as shown in Figure 6-21. A flat and symmetrically-constructed character is in danger of illustrating what I call the cookie-cutter or "Gingerbread Man" effect. This symmetry is generally avoided unless you are actually *designing* a Gingerbread Man.

**[Fig. 6-21] Each part of the cat's form is a discrete shape with no blending. The shapes are roughly the same size, which gives the design a cookie-cutter appearance.**

The figure in 6-22 is slightly more organic but could use improvement. The head is roughly the same size as the body, and the length of the legs is about equal to the height of the cat's head.

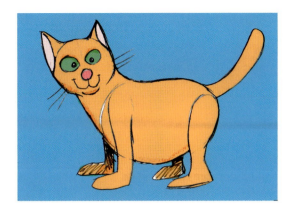

[Fig. 6-22] Another cat. The character is still symmetrical, but the separate parts of the design have now blended to make an organic whole.

Let us try varying the proportions of the cat. Perhaps the chest area might be smaller and flow more into the body shape, creating a softly triangular body. The head could be distinctly separated from the body by a thinner neck. The legs might be long and slender for an exotic look, or we might shorten the body and create a heavier character with simple shapes that suggest long fur. The entire cat might be contained in a triangular shape, or it might be a large oval with pinpoint legs and thin tail. Tiny extremities will make the body look larger and heavier. Construct the cat's body along a "line of action" and then draw the legs through the body shape. The placement of joints and volumes can vary but the character must be able to animate.

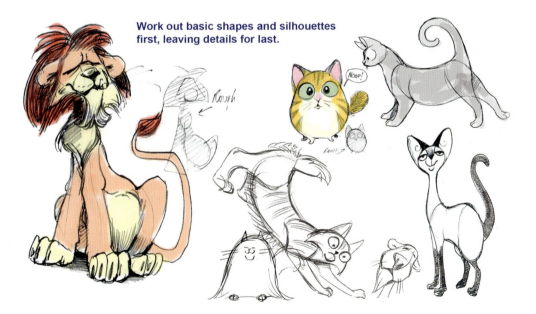

[Fig. 6-23] These cats are variations on a theme. Note how the leg and body proportions change in the sketches. The final design may consist of a head taken from one sketch with the body and feet taken from another. Rough constructions, lines of action, and foundation shapes are indicated in gray tone.

Study human and animal anatomy to learn how a character's external shape and range of motion are both determined by its underlying muscle and bone structure. Mammalian, avian, or reptilian skeletons can be adapted or combined to give naturally occurring or fantastic creatures a solid structure that helps you design, draw, and rig believable characters. Figure 6-24 shows a simple skeleton with muscle masses that can be modified and used for many four-legged characters. Some artistic anatomy books are listed in Chapter 24 for further reading.

**[Fig. 6-24] Here is a simple four-legged skeleton with overlaid muscle masses. It is important to design your character from the inside out since muscle and bone structure influence its surface appearance and its range of motions.**

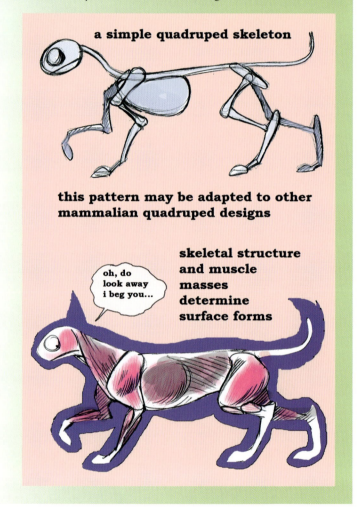

# Creating a Character from Inanimate Objects

Thus far we have only discussed organic shapes and creatures. Animation allows you to bring inorganic or inanimate objects to life. Inanimate objects have frequently been used to suggest human personality types. Their construction is similar to that used for organic characters. The only difference may be that the primary or 'foundation' shapes may appear more obviously in the final design, which may not permit the elastic movement commonly found in an organic character.

Use visual puns when working with inanimate objects. Silhouettes can suggest other creatures. Do a chair's proportions suggest a child or an adult character? Does a musical instrument resemble a bird?

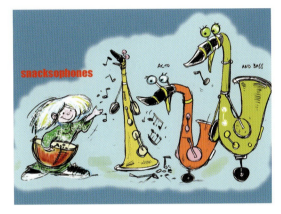

**[Fig. 6-25] Three saxophones turn into goose bodies and the mouthpieces became the beaks. The silhouette creates a 'visual pun' but the design resembles the musical instrument more than the bird.**

Try to avoid simply slapping a face on top of the object. Work with elements in the original design. See which ones suggest facial features or limbs. A good way to work is to start with an unmodified picture of the object and do repeated drawings, each more exaggerated, to *evolve* the features from it. Think of how the object's shape can suggest other creatures. Materials can also influence character motion, as shown in Figure 6-26. This technique may also be used when turning a human character into an object or an animal.

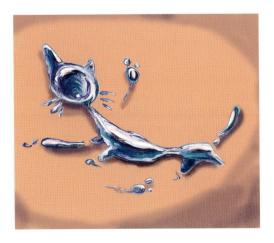

**[Fig. 6-26] The fluidly flexible cat's movement is caricatured in quicksilver. The inorganic and the organic blend in this visual pun.**

**Exercise:** Blend a human or animal design with an inanimate object in three drawings. Show the human or animal character in drawing A, then draw the object that you wish to combine it with as drawing C. Blend the features in drawing B. You may add more blend drawings if necessary. An example is shown in Figure 6-27. You may find that the midpoint drawing is more interesting than the final. Each design will vary. Try changing your original character into several different objects. Then try the exercise in reverse, starting with the inanimate object and translating it into a human or animal.

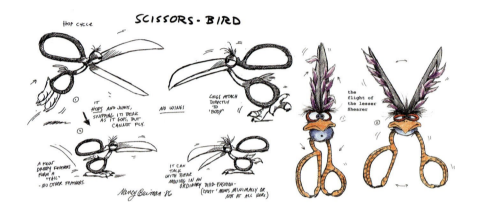

[Fig. 6-27] **Inanimate objects can suggest human or animal characteristics and be brought to life in animation. The secret is to combine organic and inorganic elements in a way that does not completely lose the characteristics of the original object.** *Evolve* **the design in a series of sketches to see which features work best.**

Inorganic designs may have different sections appear as discrete forms (wheels and headlights on a truck body, for example). Or you may combine the organic and the inorganic in one design (a talking truck with lips in its grille). Care should be taken in this instance not to lose the quality that reads as "truck." The degree of organic input to the inorganic original will vary depending on the type of *universe* you create for your characters.

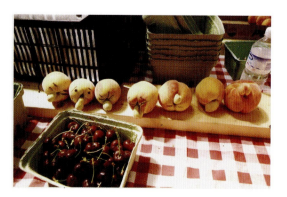

[Fig. 6-28] **Character inspiration can come from organic or inorganic sources. These peaches from a Vancouver farmers' market resemble human faces. Photo by Nancy Beiman.**

# Across the Universe

"In the beginning the Universe was created. This has made a lot of people very angry and has been widely regarded as a bad move."

—Douglas Adams, *The Hitchhiker's Guide to the Galaxy*

Characters, backgrounds, and props that share a common context by their design are said to be from the same *universe*. Design standards may be derived from inspirational artwork, or they can be set by the lead designer on the production. HERCULES was a film that used both of these tools to create its universe. Illustrator Gerald Scarfe interpreted ancient Greek vase paintings and sculpture in his inspirational sketches. The final character designs merged elements of Scarfe's style with hallmarks of Greek design.

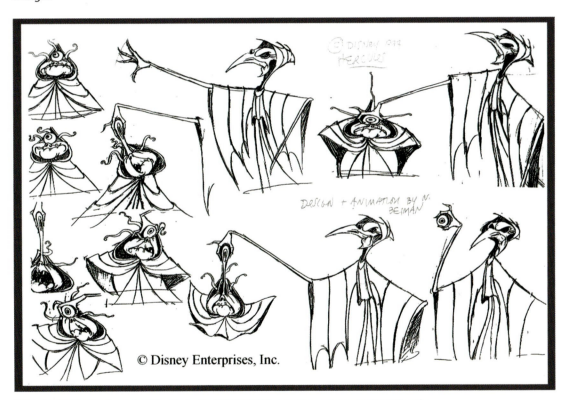

© Disney Enterprises, Inc.

[Fig. 6-29] My designs for The Fates in HERCULES were based on ancient Greek sculpture and character sketches drawn by designer Gerald Scarfe. Reproduced by permission of Disney Enterprises, Inc.

Establishing a 'universe' is very important when a large crew is working on one project. Individual styles are incorporated into the universal matrix. The 'universal' design principle, like all the other rules of design, can be broken if your story requires it. An alien being may literally be 'from another universe'.

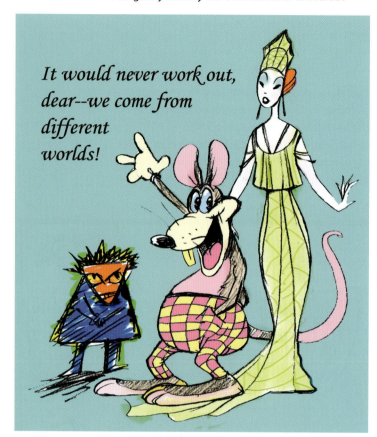

*It would never work out, dear--we come from different worlds!*

[Fig. 6-30] Characters that work together usually exist in a universe where their props, backgrounds, and character designs are unified by design. Characters can be from different universes if an explanation is provided in the story. Too much variation can cause confusion.

WHO FRAMED ROGER RABBIT? featured animated characters from very different universes performing together (Betty Boop, Donald Duck, and Daffy Duck) and even marrying one another (Jessica and Roger Rabbit). The "toons" work in 1940s Hollywood but live in Toontown, a parallel cartoon universe that contains characters from all of animation history including some that appeared in films made later than WHO FRAMED ROGER RABBIT's time period. (The apparent anachronism was intentional: some characters had to wait for their big "break.") The TOY STORY movies are also exceptions to the 'unified-universe' theory of character design. The toys were designed in a variety of sizes and styles. A cartoon dinosaur, a troop of plastic Marines, a china piggy bank, a spaceman, and a rag-doll cowboy each existed in its individual 'universe' while sharing the common world of Andy's room. The toys ventured out into yet another universe, the 'real world' outside their house, where they were all out of place. These are exceptions that prove the rule. In most cases there will be a stylistic device—the shape of the eyes or the heads, the lightness or heaviness of the outlines, a common rendering style—that sets a film's characters, backgrounds, and props into the same universe.

Not all animated characters have a family resemblance. How many cartoon families have children who look nothing at all like their parents? The Inappropriates in Figure 6-31 may be deliberately designed that way for comic purposes. The characters in Figure 6-32 all exist in the same universe.

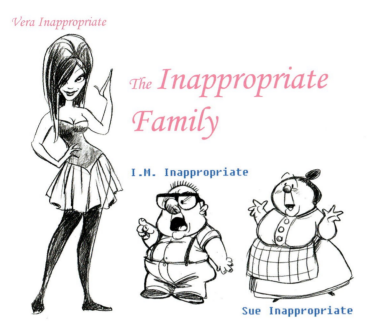

*Vera Inappropriate*

The *Inappropriate Family*

I.M. Inappropriate

Sue Inappropriate

**[Fig. 6-31] Contrasting styles will call attention to themselves. Or they may make a comic point. The daughter of these two grotesques is designed in a completely different style from her parents.**

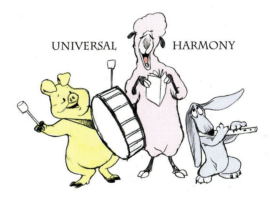

UNIVERSAL    HARMONY

**[Fig. 6-32] Unification of design creates believability in your characters and settings. Each animated film creates its own reality.**

Exercise: Design three dogs using the principles discussed in this chapter. Base one on circles, another on squares, and another on triangles. Are there certain breeds whose body types suggest these basic shapes?

Next, design three characters based on inanimate objects. Will you be able to use 'foundation shapes' to delineate different character types? Are these characters from the same *universe*?

Once you have rough designs worked out and a universe established, the next step is to scale the characters to each other and to the backgrounds and props in your project. You might say that *Size Matters*.

# Size Matters: The Importance of Scale

A character's scale can vary from sequence to sequence. If you are designing "Jack and the Beanstalk," your hero will have two size relationships. The first one will be to the objects in his home, and the second to objects in the Giant's castle. Scale is established by designing the props with the character, but insufficient information can cause confusion.

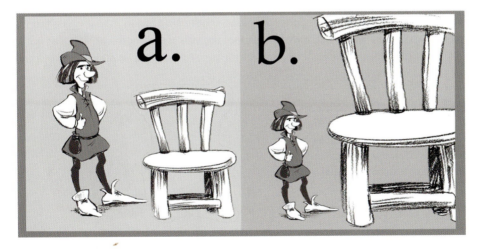

[Fig. 7-1] Jack and two chairs. The scale is ambiguous in (b).

In Figure 7-1(a) we can accept that Jack is a normal-sized man with a normal-sized chair since they appear to work to the same scale. Example (b) is more ambiguous. It is not really clear in the second drawing whether Jack is a normal man with a very large chair, or a tiny man standing next to a normal-sized chair. He is put into proper context in Figure 7-2 by the addition of a background that shares the same scale as the chair.

[Fig. 7-2] The characters' scale relative to the setting must be worked out at the start of the production. New scales are worked out for different settings, if required.

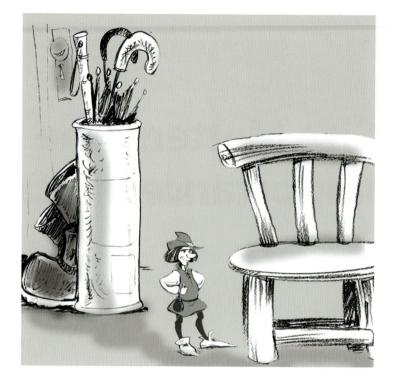

Scale must be determined at the start of the project. It's particularly important to get this right when working with CGI characters. In one instance, a student designed and modeled two characters independently of one another and found that when he put them together, the passive character was twice the size of the aggressor. This was not 'realistic' but it was extremely funny, and fortunately for him this "mistake" worked out well in the context of his film.

[Fig. 7-3] A very large rabbit chased by a very small fox. The fox was originally planned to be larger than the rabbit. The mistake produced a funnier film. Most scale accidents won't end this happily.

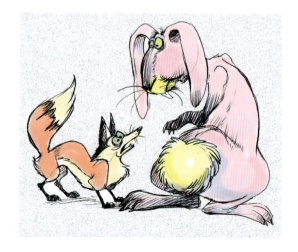

Designers and story artists create a character 'lineup' similar to the one in Figure 7-4 at the start of the production to indicate variations in character size and scale. Many different scale combinations are tried to see which ones work best. Once rough size differences are agreed on, storyboard artists use the rough character sketches as *"placeholder"* characters on rough boards. The boards may be redrawn when the final character designs are created.

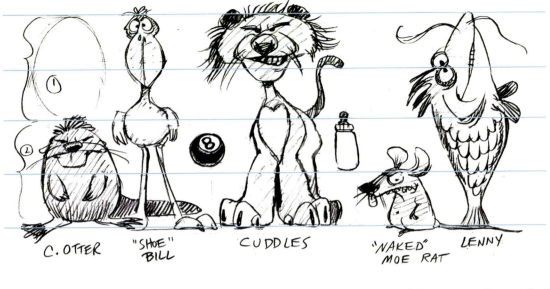

C. OTTER          "SHOE"          CUDDLES          "NAKED"          LENNY
                   BILL                            MOE RAT

LENNY, SHOE + CUDDLES = 2X OTTER
        MOE = ½ OTTER

*"When Nature Calls"*
Main Character Lineup

[Fig. 7-4] A 'lineup' of characters and typical props is drawn up at the start of the production to provide size and silhouette reference for storyboard artists. The character designs may not be finalized until much later.

## Practicing Your Scales

Characters will display scale variations relative to *each other*, as in the lineup shown in Figure 7-4. Scale is additionally determined by backgrounds and props, as shown in Figures 7-2 and 7-5.

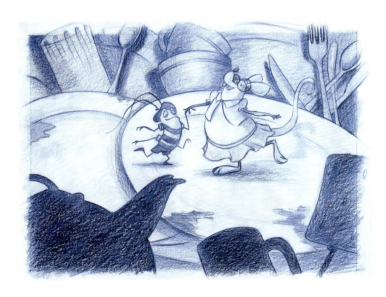

[Fig. 7-5] Props and backgrounds literally put the characters into perspective. Reproduced by permission of William Robinson.

[Fig. 7-6] A 'giant' may have large hands and a small head in proportion to the rest of its body. A very fat character might have hands and feet that are smaller than normal. Contrasting shapes within the design scale a character against itself.

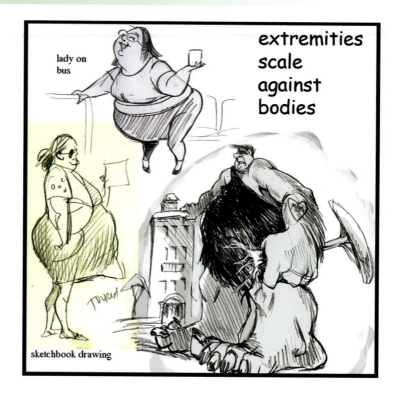

Contrasting shapes are used to create visual interest and scale portions of the character *against itself*. Impressions of gigantism can be created by distorting the scale of the head and hands relative to the body as shown in Figure 7-6. A prop building and tree aids in establishing the giant's size. A very fat character's body size may be exaggerated by diminutive feet and hands.

Varied proportions create interesting character designs that read well at a distance. In Figure 7-7, character (a) is evenly proportioned with a smooth surface and no strongly defined forms. The design was drawn as an outline with no variation in the scale of the body parts. The exterior of the character was modeled first and the skeleton added later. Figure (b) was designed *from the inside out*, beginning with its skeleton. The limbs and body were carefully designed to display an interesting variety of scales and textures. Although the character was very small, its silhouette read well even in long shots.

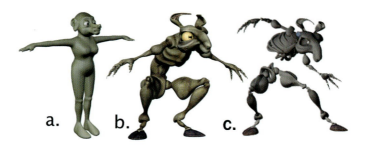

[Fig. 7-7] A symmetrical character and a second design that scales various portions of the character against itself. Reproduced by permission of Nathaniel Hubbell.

# Stereotypes of Scale

Villains are sometimes larger and heavier than the heroes. This makes the villain a more menacing presence and we automatically feel sympathy for the "little guy." Burly actors playing villains in early comedies were actually known as "heavies" and this tradition continued in some animated cartoons. There were comedians who turned this stereotype on its head. Laurel and Hardy, who were both tall men, often cast very small actors as their villains. These nasty little men and women made their lives miserable in countless films. The villainy was projected by their actions and attitudes, not by their physical presence, and their silhouette contrasted amusingly with that of the two comedians. It is easy to ignore the fact that Stan and Ollie are taller than these menaces since their characters' mental stature is so small.

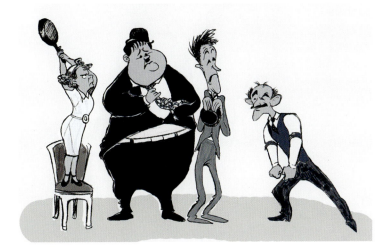

**[Fig. 7-8] Caricature of Laurel and Hardy with James Finlayson and Daphne Pollard, two of their small villains.**

Tex Avery took particular delight in having small, 'cute' characters react ferociously to large intruders, suddenly displaying outsized fangs or claws when annoyed. The scale of a mouth, the eyes, or the entire body would change dramatically in the famous *"Tex Avery 'Take'"* and return to normal when it was over.

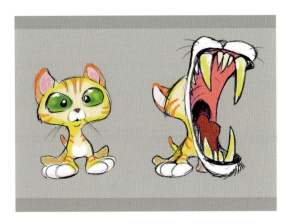

**[Fig. 7-9] A cute character doing a Tex Avery "take." Different parts of the cat's body can change scale depending on its mood.**

You may use or avoid stereotypes of scale as you use or avoid stereotypes of design. All's fair in love and animation. But what if your hero and your villain are exactly the same size?

# Triple Trouble: Working with Similar Character Silhouettes

When designing multiple characters it is common to work with contrasting silhouettes; for example, tall and thin versus short and fat.

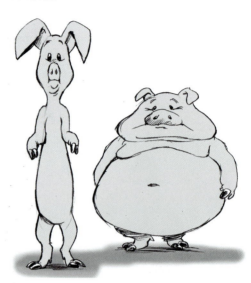

**[Fig. 7-10] Two recognizably different pigs.**

What happens when your story decrees that all characters must be the same size and shape? They could be identical in action as well as in silhouette. This was common practice in early animated films. An example appears in Figure 7-11.

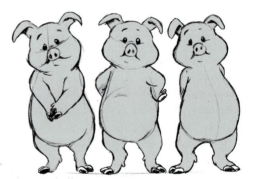

**[Fig. 7-11] Three pigs or one pig repeated three times?**

Color can differentiate between identical designs. This was also a standard way of working in the early years of animation. Figure 7-12's pigs show distinct color variations but they're still just the same pig design repeated three times.

**[Fig. 7-12] Three pigs, with color variations.**

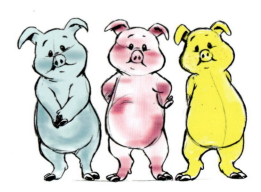

A more sophisticated method of differentiating the characters varies their body language. Identically designed characters can use distinctive poses, silhouettes, and attitudes to show differing personalities. Each will move differently from the others when they are animated since their attitudes will affect everything they do. An example of varied body language on the 'standard pig' is shown in Figure 7-13.

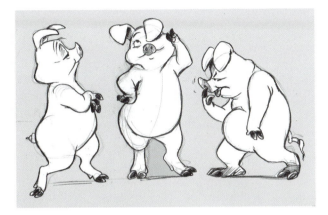

[Fig. 7-13] Prissy Pig, Pulchritudinous Pig, and Piggy Pig. Different body attitudes can create different characters. The middle pig now appears to be female.

You can associate certain props or costumes with each character. In Figure 7-14, props and costumes vary the pigs' silhouettes so that identical body construction can be used for different personalities. Costumes can also suggest specific locations and time periods.

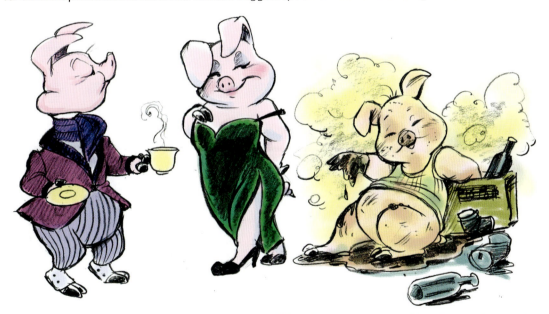

[Fig. 7-14] Piggy Props. Prissy, Pulchritudinous, and Piggy become stronger characters and suggest their settings with the addition of props and costumes.

Show your audience what you want them to see. Avoid *telling* them about it. The environment and the props associated with a character enable the audience to "*read*" the story and characters without your having to resort overmuch to filmic devices like voice-overs or explanatory dialogue.

Creative character and props designs will contribute enormously to the audience's understanding of the story. Characters and props should have readable silhouettes that reinforce the staging and help frame the action.

It is not necessary to use light backgrounds to make your characters read well in the shot. Treat prop and character as part of the same composition and work for good silhouette value on both. It is a good idea to use simple perspective in your staging so that your character and the prop do not appear to be in two different dimensions as we saw in Figure 7-1. But don't overdo it. Perspective and tonal values can be a double-edged sword.  Figure 7-15 shows a deliberately chaotic and confusing etching by

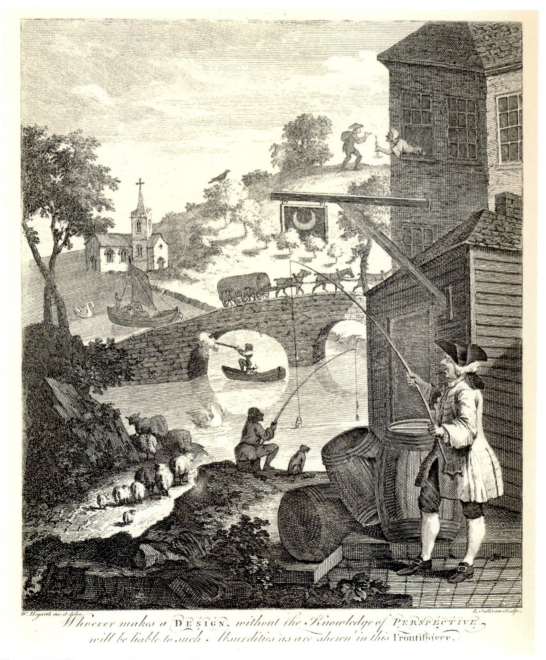

**[Fig. 7-15]** William Hogarth's parody illustration has at least 43 perspective errors. The eye is drawn into the picture by the man in the foreground but all other pictorial elements are emphasized equally. As a result, none stands out. The scene's composition is deliberately chaotic and confusing. (Nancy Beiman collection)

William Hogarth. The perspective is ridiculous and all pictorial elements are emphasized equally so no one element stands out. Compose your designs and compositions with forethought. Use contrast and staging to emphasize the important elements and gray down less important ones so that they do not cancel each other out.

The popular children's book series *Where's Waldo?* deliberately had the characters and the backgrounds drawn and rendered in precisely the same style. Each illustration featured flat lighting with no shadows, hundreds of near-identical characters with flat color, and no center of interest. *Where's Waldo?* books were designed to keep small children occupied for hours poring over incredibly complex drawings in search of the central character. You literally don't know where to look first.

A painting or a book can be looked at for hours at a time. A shot in an animated film will go by in seconds.  It is crucial to direct the viewer's eye precisely where you want it to go, whether you are working on a character design or a storyboard sequence. Test character silhouettes along with relevant props. Place the character on a simple background and shade their silhouettes with the side of a pencil or crayon. Is the character reading well in relation to the other scenic elements? Can you suggest a foreground, a middle ground, and a background with different tones?

Always consider how the character's silhouette relates to other elements in the shot.

At the beginning of this chapter I discussed how to scale a character to a chair by adding items in the shot to put them into context. An object will scale a character, but they both must work with a background that frames the action and contains good composition. Figure 7-16's pastoral scene contains strong tonal values and good silhouette value. The three trees in the background scale the pigs adequately but they are all the same size and standing in a row like ducks in a shooting gallery. The two identical pigs and the trees share a common picture plane. The staging is flat and uninteresting.

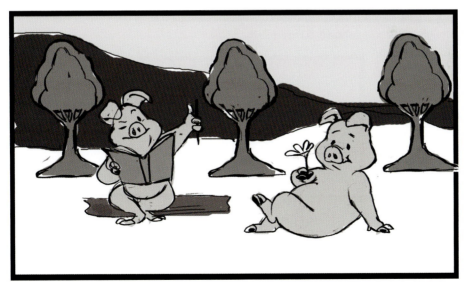

[Fig. 7-16] **Everything in the frame is drawn to the same scale on the same picture plane.**

The composition is improved when the trees and pigs are rescaled so that some of them are closer to the camera and some farther away. Figure 7-17 reads better than Figure 7-16 even though the tonal values are less dramatic. There is a feeling of depth to the scene. Tonal values are discussed in Chapter 10.

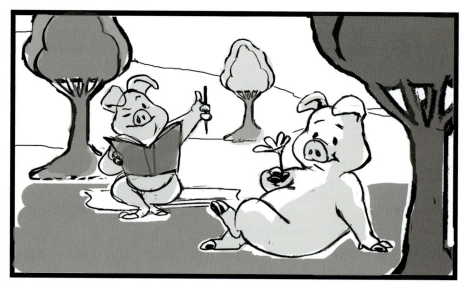

[Fig. 7-17] **Varying the scale of the characters creates a feeling of depth and interest in the scene.**

# Getting Pushy

Animation grew out of illustration, cartooning, and caricature. Character designs that are *pushed*, or exaggerated slightly from the norm, are often more successful than those that attempt to reproduce reality. This principle also applies to backgrounds and props. A caricatured Victorian chair conveys the peculiarities of the style better than a 'straight' version, as shown in Figure 7-18.

[Fig. 7-18] **Caricatured props work best with caricatured characters.**

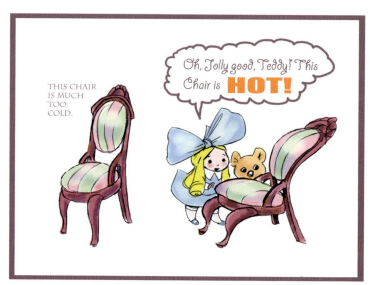

Animated camera moves may also be 'pushed' and caricatured along with the back-grounds and the characters. For example, exaggerated perspective introduces a whim-sical note into the action in Figure 7-19 (B), which is  more broadly staged than (a). Cari-catured backgrounds can work with exaggerated camera angles to spice up, or "*plus*" the staging. Animated camera angles are usually stronger than their live-action equiva-lents since everything about an animation project is a little larger than life.

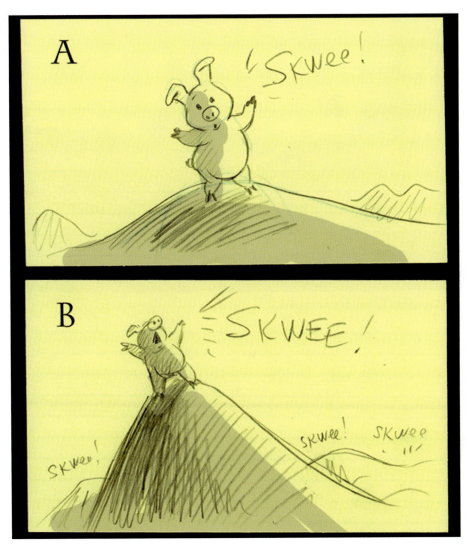

[Fig. 7-19] "Plus-ing" or exaggerating the design of the characters, backgrounds, and camera angles helps establish a whimsical mood.

Make sure that *everything*—character, setting, and story point—reads clearly *at all times* during preproduction and production. When the final project is screened your audience will not be able or willing to rewind to see what they missed, and you will not be standing by in their home or in the theater to explain what they should have seen.

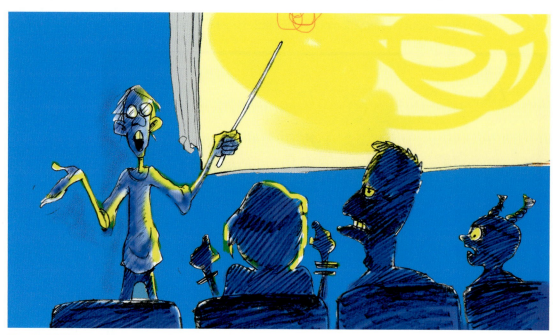

[Fig. 7-20] "What was supposed to happen here was…"

# 8

# Beauties and Beasts: Creating Character Contrasts in Design

The most important consideration when designing characters is *creating different body language and movement*. This consideration is not unique to animation.

## The Great Dictator: Charlie Chaplin's Character Acting

Charlie Chaplin made THE GREAT DICTATOR as a rebuke to Adolf Hitler. In this film, Chaplin plays two parts. His Barber character bears an amazing physical resemblance to the Dictator. They never meet. The lives of the Barber and the Dictator intersect only in the last ten minutes of the picture when the Barber replaces the Dictator after appropriating the latter's uniform. Yet all through the film the denizens of the Ghetto and the "Tomanian" bullies who oppress them do not notice that the barber resembles the Dictator. The Barber does not see this resemblance himself. Are all the characters, friends and enemies, equally ignorant? The situation, though fantastic, is believable to us and we never notice that the comparison is never made. This is because Chaplin, as the Barber, *moves in a completely different fashion* from the Dictator. The characters'

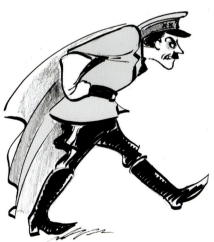

stance, silhouette, actions, and facial expressions are as opposed as their politics. The Barber smiles often. His short, graceful movements resemble those of a small mouse or bird. The Dictator tilts his head up and back in an arrogant pose or raises his shoulders in an almost feline fashion. He usually has a scowl on his face. His movements are forceful and reminiscent of a predatory animal.

[Fig. 8-1] Charlie Chaplin as the Dictator.

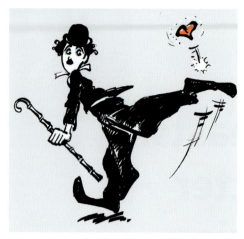

[Fig. 8-2] **Charlie Chaplin and the Chaplin Kick.**

Chaplin's performance is so skilled that it appears that a second actor plays the Dictator. When the Dictator dances with a globe we see the only occurrence of a famous gesture of Chaplin's 'Little Tramp' character—a backward kick. The Tramp uses it to dispose of cigarette butts but the Dictator disposes of the world. The kick is the one gesture that the two characters have in common, but different contexts change its meaning.

At the end of the film when the Barber dresses as the Dictator, his gestures still differ from the aggressive, arrogant movements of the tyrant. We believe that one of Chaplin's characters has truly replaced the other. THE GREAT DICTATOR is a film that all animators should study.

# I Feel Pretty! Changing Standards of Beauty

"Beauty is only skin deep. Ugly goes clean to the bone."

—Dorothy Parker

It is difficult to design attractive human characters. They can easily become dull and flat. Beauty is a variable concept that is affected by time and place. What is beautiful in one era or culture appears grotesque in another.

[Fig. 8-3] **A literal interpretation of a 19th-century poem produces monsters. (Nancy Beiman collection)**

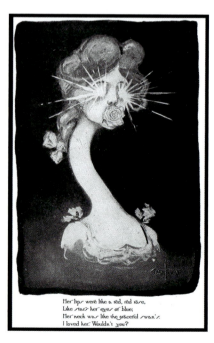

In the late 19th and early 20th century a woman was considered attractive if she wore a corset.

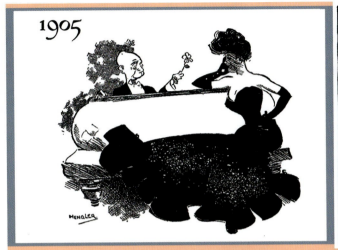
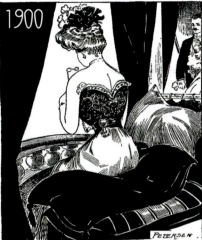

**[Fig. 8-4] A tightly corseted waist was once the gold standard of female beauty. (Nancy Beiman collection)**

Men once wore clothing that showed their legs—and much more—to be considered masculine, as the Regency gentleman (circa 1822) demonstrates in figure 8-5.

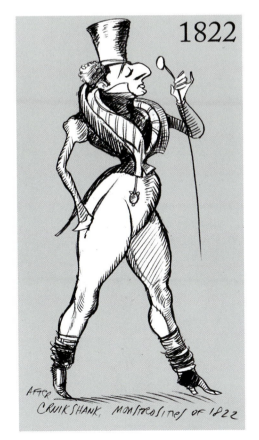

**[Fig. 8-5] A tightly corseted waist was also once considered macho!**

Certain design constants may be applied when designing 'beautiful' characters.

Beautiful people in Western culture often have asymmetrical faces. Take a full-face picture of a popular actor or actress; duplicate one half of it and flip it using a mirror or computer graphics program. Then try this exercise with a picture of your own face. The two resultant composites will show significant differences and may suggest two different people. Most of us have asymmetrical faces. Perfect faces are rare but not unheard of. T. Hee claimed that a 1930's actress with flawless features was the most difficult caricature assignment of his career. A small imperfection can enhance the beauty of a face. The great actresses of the 1930s—the Hepburns and Garbos and Crawfords and Dietrichs—all had slightly asymmetrical features that made their faces more interesting to T. Hee (and millions of viewers) and gave him something to caricature. A perfect face inspired a less interesting drawing.

**[Fig. 8-6] Caricature of actors and actresses with asymmetrical faces by T. Hee. (Nancy Beiman collection)**

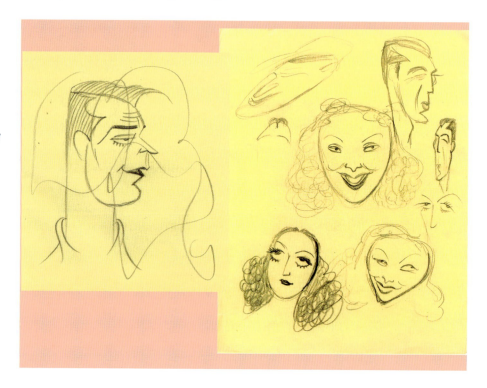

Human beings seem to respond to features that are symmetrical but not perfect. Perfect features can sometimes seem 'plastic'. Figure 8-7 shows a drawing of an attractive girl with asymmetrical features. She illustrates a major design principle—the *line of beauty*.

**[Fig. 8-7] A pretty girl that is constructed along an S-curve, or "Line of Beauty." Reproduced from Scribblings 2 by permission of Dean Yeagle.**

The Line of Beauty was described by William Hogarth but it appears in the art of many cultures. The Line, a modified S-curve, is used to construct living objects. Straight lines are used for 'dead' or inorganic ones. The girl in Figure 8-7 and the cats in Figure 8-8 illustrate the line of beauty very well. Their bodies are a pleasing combination of contrasting curves and straight shapes constructed along an S-curve.

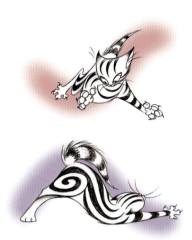

**[Fig. 8-8] Cat and kitten constructed along the Line of Beauty. Reproduced by permission of Nina L. Haley.**

A good design will use both straight lines and curved shapes to create "fast" and "slow" areas as shown in Figure 8-9. The eye travels at slower speed and lingers longest in the more detailed areas. Faces, and particularly eyes, are viewed first.

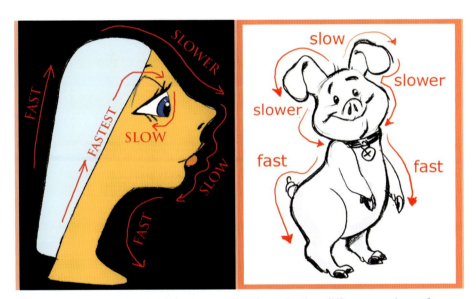

**[Fig. 8-9] The eye travels at different speeds when viewing different sections of a design, lingering longest on detailed areas. Our attention should remain longest on the important parts of the design. "Fast" and "Slow" areas are indicated in red.**

It is possible to create movement in a still drawing since different areas are viewed at (fractionally) different times. A busy design that contains complex patterns and textures in all areas such as the one in Figure 8-10 can be difficult to animate and watch.

**[Fig. 8-10] A busy design can be distracting to watch. (Nancy Beiman collection)**

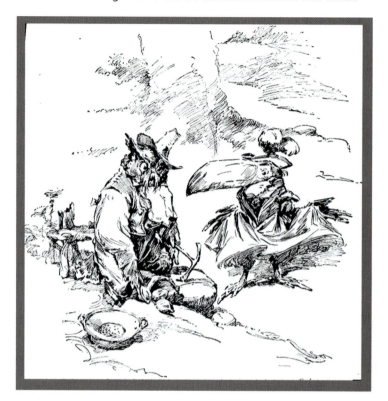

# A Face That Only a Mother Could Love?

CUTE AND NON-CUTE: Other species attract us if their body and facial proportions resemble those of human infants. Puppies and kittens are "cute" because of their rounded, regular features—a design that appeals to mammalian mothers. Babyish features typically are small and delicate, occupying a smaller area of the skull than an adult's. The human baby's head and torso are huge when compared to the hands, feet, and limbs. The puppy or kitten's body is small and the paws and head are very large. In Figure 8-11, the baby, cat, and puppy's eye levels are approximately one-third from the bottom of the skull. (An adult's would be situated at the halfway mark.) The eyes are large while other facial features are very small.

The Roswell Alien in Figure 8-11 shares the babyish proportions of the kitten, puppy, and human but the scale is now dramatic to the point of caricature: its eyes are huge, with no whites showing; the nose is eliminated and the mouth is a lipless slit. We see this as creepy instead of cute. Human beings are also unlikely to find a young insect 'cute' since their proportions are completely unlike the mammalian pattern. The caterpillar's eyes take up nearly all of its head shape and there is no clear differentiation between the head and the body. So, insect babies will seem cute only to insect mothers. Animated insect characters have all been humanized to a greater or lesser degree so that we will find them appealing rather than alien.

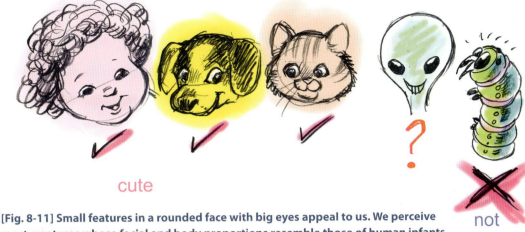

[Fig. 8-11] Small features in a rounded face with big eyes appeal to us. We perceive most creatures whose facial and body proportions resemble those of human infants as "cute."

# Gods And Monsters: Contrasting Appearance and Personality

The features of a human face are centered in an inverted triangle. Eyes are always on either side of the nose and the mouth appears underneath (unless you are Pablo Picasso). We are conditioned to find this design beautiful. Breaking this triangle can break our sense of connection to the humanity and beauty of a face's design. Some of Picasso's deconstructions of the human face are disturbing to view. People with deformed faces (for example, the Elephant Man or Quasimodo the Hunchback) can cause a great feeling of discomfort in the viewer. Designs that do not relate the facial features to each other will usually be considered 'unappealing'.

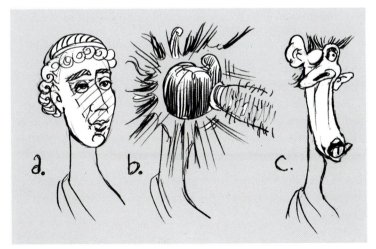

[Fig. 8-12] Breaking the pattern of a human face makes us feel very uncomfortable.

Characters with highly deformed or asymmetrical facial proportions are called MONSTERS. Humans are attracted or repelled by facial proportions and expressions. Highly irregular faces can excite fear in the viewer. Some famous monsters have partly destroyed faces or faces that lack an eye or an ear, or have too many eyes and ears. Leonardo da Vinci wrote that the "eye is the window of the soul." Shakespeare was more accurate when he had King Duncan in *Macbeth* state, "There's no art to find the mind's construction in the face."

A handsome man may 'smile, and smile, and be a villain' and an ugly duckling may have a heart of gold. The Phantom of the Opera and the Hunchback of Notre Dame are examples of two misunderstood monsters. Erik's facial burns mirror his damaged soul; Quasimodo's spirit is noble despite his deformed face and body, since his actions are kind, brave, loving, and generous. Not that he fares any better than Erik in the end.

A character's design may announce its personality or work in contrast to it.

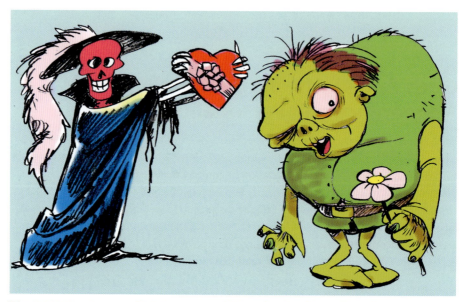

[Fig. 8-13] **Monsters can frighten us even if they do nice things. There is a contrast between the horrifying exterior and the noble interior.**

Both the Phantom and Quasimodo reveal human depths under the deformed face. Their actions reveal their spiritual beauty but these characters are never considered physically beautiful. The contrast between interior and exterior makes them more appealing than the 'beautiful' characters in their stories. Ugliness is easier to portray than beauty since we are more able to agree on what is ugly than on what is beautiful. While beauty may be in the eye of the beholder, the artist is able to create it.

So what makes a Princess beautiful? Her appearance will ultimately depend on the time and setting of the story. A noblewoman in Renaissance Italy will not look like a noblewoman in medieval Japan.

Though your audience is not going to be composed of historians, period character designs should contain elements that suggest the era with a touch of the modern to enable audiences to appreciate them. They should be individuals, not mannequins with period costumes. Here are some suggestions on how to get started. Look at basic clothing shapes and use the ones that best set the period and the character. Don't be literal. You can use silhouette for the look of the period without reproducing every flounce and ribbon on a dress.

➤ 1. *Research styles.* Learn something about the fashion silhouette of the period. For example, the silhouette of a man in 1860 differed radically from that of a woman. The man's and woman's silhouette are nearly the same in 1926. Use clothing and props of the period to develop the character. (Figure 8-14)

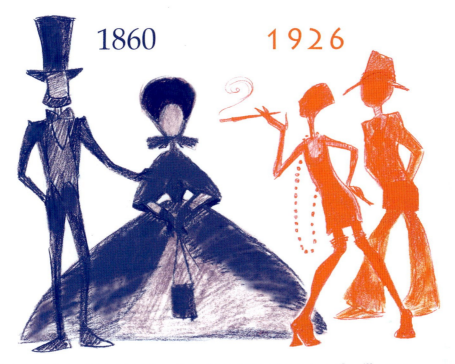

[Fig. 8-14] **Male and female silhouettes have changed over time. The silhouette of 1860 shows the greatest contrast between male and female shapes in costume history. The silhouette of 1926 shows very little difference between the two genders.**

➤ 2. *Use more than one source for reference.* Source materials do not have to be from the period in which the film was set. You may use an object's silhouette to suggest a character type. For example, an inflexible character might be based on a rock. A flighty human character might have some birdlike qualities. Illustrators' work is a useful source for period reference. Avoid recycling designs from other animated films since audiences are more likely to have seen them before.

➤ 3. *Draw a variety of character designs* and then combine the best features of each in the final design. Some inexperienced designers tend to draw one character and stay with it. Experiment with different proportions and character types and see what appeals to you. Never stick with the very first sketch unless, of course, it is the best one (as occasionally happens).

➤ 4.   *Use the features of an actual person for inspiration.* This need not be a caricature and it does not apply merely to human characters. Combining the features or body type of a human with those of an animal will make the animal (or human) unique. The facial expressions of a living person can bring an historical character to life.

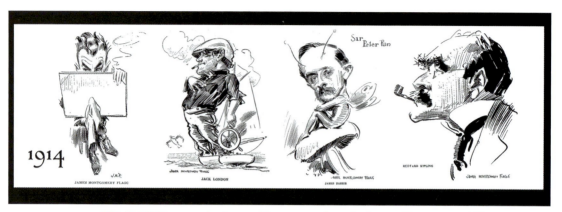

[Fig. 8-15] These caricatures of famous authors by James Montgomery Flagg were drawn from life. Incorporating the features of actual people into character designs gives them a touch of life and sparkle. What animal characteristics do some of these drawings suggest? (Nancy Beiman collection)

➤ 5.   *Draw from memory as well as from life.* Since no two people have precisely the same life experience, this technique will make a design *yours.* This is why it is vitally important to keep a sketchbook and a clip file; the clip file will give you ideas for color and designs, the sketchbook will show you people who make an impression on you by their appearance or actions. Keep your old sketchbooks for future reference.

➤ 6.   *Avoid literalism in design.* We do not see dragons, whales, giant monsters, or lions every day or even view dogs and cats in the same way we do other humans. An animator or designer may take artistic liberties with an animal's appearance and movements—all may be forgiven if the story is working! Only when you strive for the super-realistic human design does the stiff, lifeless appearance known as the *'cryogenic effect'* set in. If you design 'realistic' humans, the character must move like one—hiccups, blinks, and all—so as not to appear doll-like and lifeless. Stylized design and animation of human characters will make them appear more alive than will slavish copying of real life.

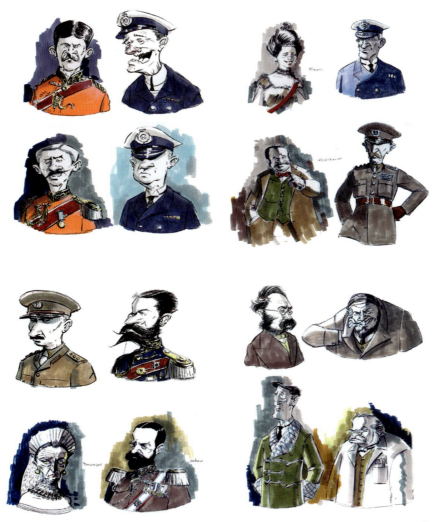

[Fig. 8-16] These character designs for a video game set during World War I caught the martial flavor of the era without being absolutely authentic. The facial features were based on antique photographs. Reproduced by permission of John McCartney.

Animation design changes over time. Some design styles become clichés because of the tributes paid to them in other films. If you work some of your own experience into the design and get inspirational material from a variety of sources, the resulting characters will become your original creations instead of a retread of someone else's work.

*Remember:* Animation is not Reality. *It's much better!*

# Location, Location, Location: Art Direction and Storytelling

# 9

The art director sets the film's period, location, prop and character design, and color style. Production design develops at the same time as the characters and storyboards.

The setting is an important storytelling element. Setting and props can influence a character's actions or support a story point.

A film's style should aid and support the story. Design styles should not be used because they are popular or because some other artist worked that way. Over-designed characters with a lot of *pencil mileage* take a long time to draw and are difficult to animate. Well-designed characters suggest complex shapes instead of illustrating them literally. You don't need to draw every hair on a character's head. An animated character must be able to express a variety of emotions, have a design that moves easily and well, and contain strong silhouette value. Characters with these features, in any design style or medium, are called *good actors*.

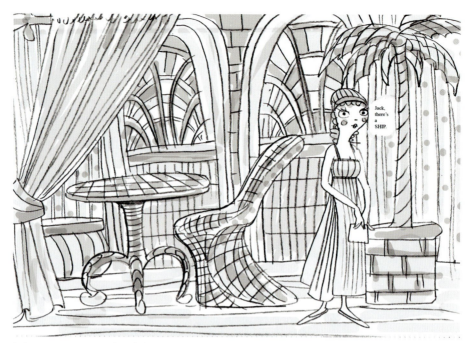

[**Fig. 9-1**] **An example of design overkill in a background. What are we supposed to notice first? The tonals and design are confusing and there are many tangents.**

Objects that are important to the story and to the scene should be visually prominent on your storyboards and backgrounds. Less important objects can be played down and merge into shadows with very close values so that they do not compete with the center of interest. Detail should not overpower the characters. Period styles and props are there to help set the scene, not upstage it. (Figure 9-1)

Atmospheric sketches can be created before storyboarding begins to explore the setting's design, color, and lighting. A floor plan is useful if your project takes place in a specific location, since it enables you to place the characters accurately in the scene. Background details and props will be drawn on the storyboard if the character interacts with them. Master backgrounds may be drawn up at the beginning of pre-production to help the storyboard artist. The Master background might not be used in the finished film. It places doors, houses, and other important objects in specific locations so that the board artist may stage the shots better. The characters are frequently included to indicate scale. Figure 9-2 is an original master background from a student film. A man sits in a house playing the piano. He plays piano with one finger. He looks tired. There is a Christmas tree and some presents in the corner of the room and a dog lying on a carpet.

The background is bare. It seems as if the man has just moved into the house or that he is too poor to own anything but the piano, tree, and dog. We know nothing about him or about where this film takes place. The Christmas tree gives the only hint of a timeframe.

A house is never 'just' a house. Objects inside a real house tell us about the inhabitants. A room is never completely empty unless the occupant is a monk who has taken a vow

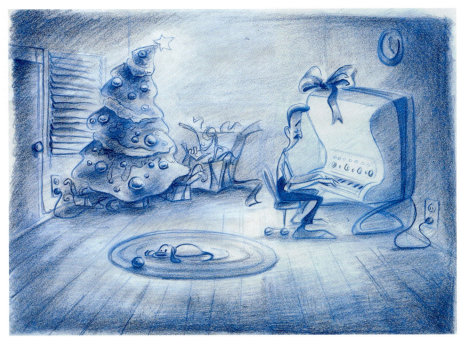

**[Fig. 9-2] Master background, House interior, first pass. Reproduced by permission of Brittney Lee.**

of poverty. People collect objects that reflect, and sometimes define, their personalities. A golfer might leave clubs in a corner. 'Horsey' people have pictures of horses on the walls. Parents have pictures of their children on the dresser. Pet owners will have pet photos and pet toys everywhere. A child might have toys all over his or her bedroom. A poor character could have pictures cut from a newspaper tacked on the wall. Set-dressing is an important element in live-action film, but it is crucial in animation since every object in an animated film's setting and background should help tell the story and provide background information about the characters. Best of all, it does not require dialogue. The general rule in animation is: *Show, don't tell*. A pictorial introduction is far superior to voice-over narration or explanatory titles.

Animated characters depend on the audiences' suspension of disbelief to be accepted as real. A good setting can go a long way toward eliminating that disbelief and make the viewer accept animated drawings as living beings with a past.

Your opening shots are like the opening sentences of a short story. They introduce your characters and setting and establish the viewer's interest in their situation.

Both characters and backgrounds can depict emotions and feelings in visual shorthand.

It is possible to tell *too* much in a shot. Backgrounds can be crammed so full of detail that nothing registers with the viewer (Figure 9-1). Design the placement of objects in the shot in the same way you would read a sentence aloud. Emphasize some words more than others. Don't shout every word and do not mumble. Get to the point quickly, use varied inflection and pacing to keep the audience interested, and don't let irrelevant anecdotal material interrupt the story.

Let's return to the piano player. We know that it is Christmas time since there is a tree in the corner. What else can be added to the background to set the stage for the story? If there is a red ribbon tied on the piano and a fireplace hung with stockings is added to the blank wall and the tree is surrounded with unwrapped presents, we get an idea of what has taken place in the room and what time of year it is. The piano is a Christmas present. Perhaps the man is still learning how to play the instrument. If the fire is lit, the time (night) and location (a cool climate) are set. Clutter in the foreground adds depth to the scene and provides a frame for the character action. The final background translates the gray tonal values into color and provides us with even more information. Warm browns and golds predominate and the cheery fire provides the main light source. The colors suggest a cold winter climate at night. We suddenly know this fellow a lot better; he's no longer just 'a man'. He's a wannabee piano player and dog owner who is manfully trying to master his unfamiliar Christmas present. The film's setting and characters are neatly introduced without using a single word of dialogue. (Fig. 9-3)

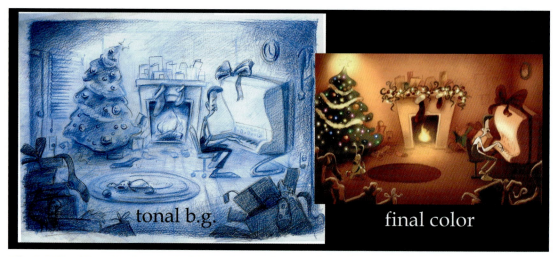

[Fig. 9-3] **Final tonal background with overlays and a color frame from the finished film. The setting now tells us a lot about our characters' lives. Reproduced by permission of Brittney Lee.**

In the last shot of the film we get a surprise. As we cut from the interior to the exterior of the house the colors shift dramatically. Warm pinks and greens and golds now dominate the scene. It seems that the Christmas story does not take place in the cool northern climate that was suggested by the design and lighting of the previous shots, but in the Southwestern United States. It isn't even nighttime! There is a radical disconnect between the style and color of the interior and exterior backgrounds. But it's still Christmas time. Snowmen (presumably made of plastic) stand on a vibrant green lawn and there are plenty of Christmas lights scattered amidst the flowers, palm trees, and sunshine. These details added an additional comic touch to the final scenes of the movie (Fig. 9-4).

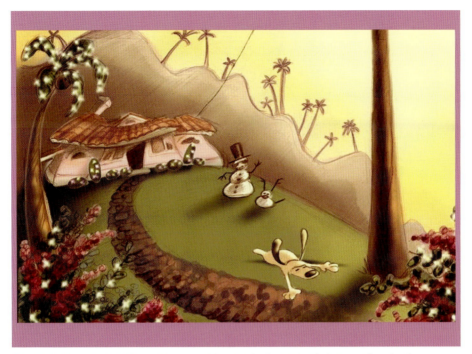

[Fig. 9-4] It's not nighttime, it's not cold outside, but it is Christmas time in the American Southwest! The art direction, color, and even the time of day in the last shot are completely different from the rest of the film. The season of the year and the characters remain consistent. Reproduced by permission of Brittney Lee.

Note how the color and lighting changes instantly transport us to a sunny desert in the late afternoon. Color and light are powerful tools that can create emotional resonance and add additional dimension to your storytelling.

Here is another example of how background design can tell part of the story. An ordinary five-year-old girl is having a tea party with stuffed toys in her ordinary bedroom. The extraordinary element in this story is the odd bird that literally crashes her tea party and tries to eat one of the toys.

The original atmospheric drawing had two or three toys in the room and nothing at all on the walls. Additional objects were added to create scale. We are now absolutely certain that we are in a child's bedroom, and that the child is very fond of stuffed toys (Fig. 9-5). Pools of light with slight shadows isolate the figures in the tonal sketch and direct our attention precisely where the filmmaker wants it. Pastel-candy colors on the characters and the final backgrounds accentuated the childlike and vaguely laughable quality of the intrusive bird. A soft spotlight effect highlighted the area where the action took place.

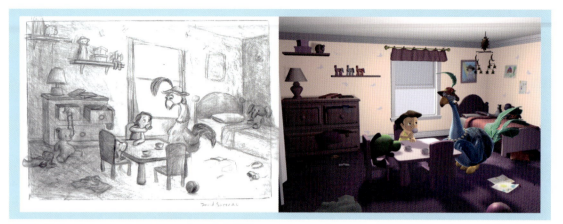

**[Fig. 9-5] A child's tea party, with a guest. The final CGI staging is very close to that of the original design. Reproduced by permission of David Suroviec.**

When considering a setting for your film, ask yourself the following questions:

➤  1.  Is this time period appropriate for the story? What year is it? What season? What time of day? Could this story take place in an unusual geographical location?

➤  2.  Is this a visually interesting time period or style? Some periods have better design elements to work with than others. (There is a reason why very few films are set in the 1970s.)

➤  3.  What shapes and colors suggest the period? Faded earth tones suggest different time periods than bright, plastic colors. Perpendicular architecture with strong verticals suggests the Gothic Middle Ages. Strong horizontal lines are reminiscent of late 20th-century architecture. These details can be used as visual patterns throughout the film.

➤  4.  What materials are everyday objects made of? Are they handmade or mass-produced? Are they made of wood or metal or plastic? Textures and colors taken from everyday objects can be used on the characters to help maintain visual continuity.

➤  5.  If the setting is a natural one, is it a jungle or a forest, outback or desert? What colors dominate each of these locations? (Colors can, of course, be changed for artistic reasons but you should know where you are starting from.)

➤  6.  Does the story take place on this planet or in this dimension?

➤  7.  If not, establish the rules of the fantasy world at the start of the story. What design elements can suggest that we are not in the real world?

➤  8.  What is the tone of the story? Is it whimsical, crazy, or serious? This will affect the treatment of the backgrounds.

➤  9.  Will your colors be sunny or dark? Are pastel colors more suitable for the story than saturated colors? Would the story still work if it was set in a different period?

➤  10.  Do the characters fit into this setting or does the story make use of *anachronisms* to create conflict or interest in the story?

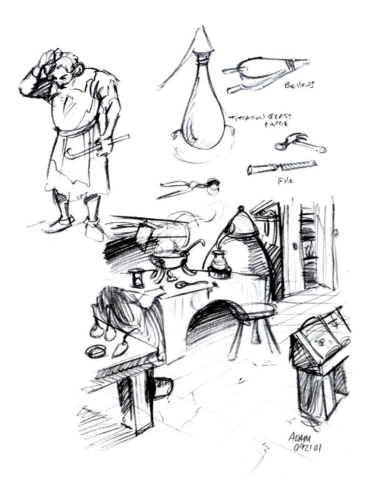

[Fig. 9-6] These conceptual sketches were drawn for a film set in the medieval period. The artist researched props that might be found in an alchemist's lair. Reproduced by permission of Adam Fox.

An *anachronism* is a style or device that appears out of period. They are usually unintentional mistakes (such as Roman legionnaires wearing wristwatches). Anachronisms can also be used intentionally as shown in Figure 9-7. In SITA SINGS THE BLUES, 1920s pop tune lyrics provide humorous commentary on a story from ancient India. The art direction combines Indian and Art Deco designs. It is perfectly logical to show Hanuman the Monkey King playing jazz trumpet in this film's *universe*.

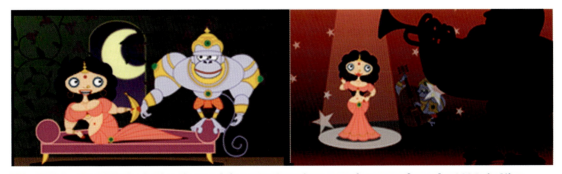

[Fig. 9-7] Ancient Hindu deities sing and dance to American popular songs from the 1920s in Nina Paley's SITA SINGS THE BLUES. The series design incorporated stylistic elements from both eras. Reproduced by permission of Nina Paley.

Remember that reality in animation is whatever you want it to be. It's not necessary to remain slavishly faithful to one design or historic period in your art direction as long as the mixture of styles is believable and the story point is conveyed clearly.

If the story takes place in "a typical house in modern times," can the backgrounds contain details that suggest the personalities and tastes of the characters? Do they have hobbies or interests that might tell us something about them? For example, if your character is a teenage girl, would she have posters on her wall? What sort of books might she have in her room? Does she play a musical instrument? Does she collect anything? Would these books, instruments, and collections look different if the girl was a Goth? And how do you define "typical"? A "typical house" will not look the same in Lesotho or Lapland. Typical houses also vary between Maine and California, Paris and Marseilles, London and Blackpool.

What sort of detail suggests a fantasy setting? If your story is set in Cookie Land or the King of the Cats' court, would the characters own human-style chairs and tables? What would they be made of? It's very unlikely that the King of the Cats would sit on a hard wooden chair, so *think like the character* when you design furnishings for his palace. Cushions or beds might be more appropriate for a cat. Cookie people might use meringues or cotton candy for pillows.

What is the scale of the characters to the background? Are they overwhelmed by their surroundings or do they fit comfortably into the world that you are creating? If your characters are very large, you might make their home furnishings small in comparison so that the contrast in size is intensified. A very small character will look smaller when it works with a large-scaled object that the audience is familiar with.

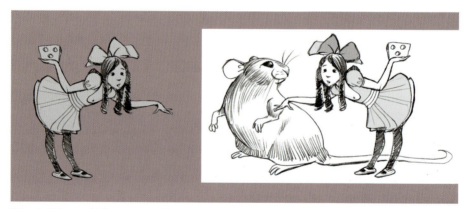

[Fig. 9-8] A small character only appears to be small when it is compared with another object. If Thumbelina is seen in isolation, we have no idea of her scale.

Be creative with your art direction. Investigate color and see how it sets the mood for your story. Assemble reference materials for color and design from magazines, photographs, paintings, Internet sites, and books. Research different periods and locations and keep the reference materials in front of you as you construct your setting. Use gray or blue tonal values on master backgrounds to establish the lighting. Be sure to set the characters into the shot for scale. Work on animation paper at full size.

Animator Milt Kahl once said, "There ain't nothin' harder to do than *nothin'*!" A house is never just a house! Don't leave rooms bare. Find items, textures, and colors that help set the period and tell us something about the occupants. Good storytelling and characters will carry the picture long after "timely'"references fade into the past.

ONE HUNDRED AND ONE DALMATIANS is a *tour de force* of retro modernism. When the film was released in 1961, its look was contemporary—the characters lived in a London that contained cars and trucks and television. The new Xerox technology gave the characters a sharp graphic look. Ken Anderson's art direction used an interesting mixture of 19th- and 20th-century styles. The human heroes wore everyday 1950s clothing, played jazz music, and lived in a Georgian terrace house (circa 1840). The dogs and crooks watched television shows that parody 1950s quiz shows and serials. The villainess, Cruella De Vil, drove a 1920s-era automobile, lived in a garish Victorian mansion (circa 1885), and wore a caricature of 1950s *haute couture*. The mixture of historic locations and contemporary references gave the film a more interesting design quality than it would have had if all its props and settings dated from the 1950s, although its strong story guaranteed its success.

ONE HUNDRED AND ONE DALMATIANS has aged gracefully into a period piece yet nothing in it looks dated. This is because the story and characters remain appealing and the art direction fresh and original. The film now has the same period charm as a story set in a fantasy kingdom

**Exercise:** Draw a master background in gray tonal values full size on a sheet of animation paper. We are in a country town near the seashore on a late summer day in the historical period of your choice. There are two houses on the background. One has a barbecue out back, a surfboard on the front lawn, and flowers in the windows. The next-door house is made of gingerbread and has odd growths in the front yard. Creatures fly in and out of the attic. The front yard features a deep hole with a chain leading into it and a sign marked "Beware." The surrounding fence is made of lollipops and candy canes. Now do some rough thumbnails for the characters that live in these houses. What is the scale of the scene? Are the characters human? Work for contrasts between the houses and their occupants. Even conventional-looking characters will seem less normal if they live in the second house. Add the characters to the master background with appropriate props. Lastly, add color to set the mood and time of day.

Do this house exercise a second time with different settings and colors. If you boarded the same story twice using the different locations, you'd end up with radically different results even if you never changed another thing.

Now that you have done this assignment, create a similar background using your own characters and settings.

Chuck Jones said "I don't want realism. I want *believability*." Animated film creates its own reality in animation and design. Place your characters into the setting and develop both in the context of the story. The audience will accept your alternative reality. In animation, normality is whatever you want it to be. Like Alice, you might find Wonderland down a rabbit hole.

Once you have established your location and characters you are ready to begin storyboarding your production.

# Part Two

# Technique

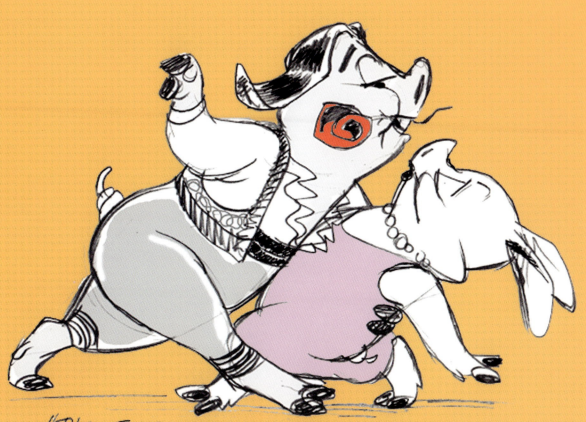

"THE FOUR HORSEMEN OF THE APIGCALYPSE."

# Starting Story Sketch: Compose Yourself

# 10

## Tonal Sketches

At this point you have a rough story idea and rough character designs to act it out.

The verbal blueprint for your project must now be translated into visuals. A rough character *lineup* (such as the one in Figure 7-4) or an atmospheric sketch sets the characters' scale to each other, to the background, and to important props. *Placeholder*s such as the ones in Figure 10-1 are used to stage the action and acting on the boards if character designs have not yet been finalized.

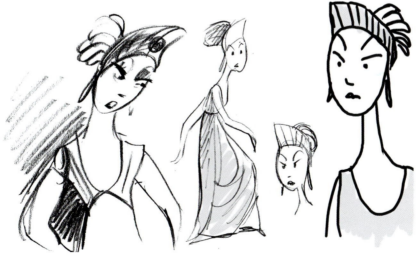

[Fig. 10-1] **Very rough drawings will read as the same character if the silhouette values are good. This woman's headdress and oval face make her easy to recognize when different artists draw her.**

Scale must be determined at this stage to prevent problems later on. A storyboard us- ing two adult-sized placeholder characters will need to be completely redrawn if one of them is later redesigned as a child, since eye-lines and horizon lines will change. Rough drawings will read as the same character even if different artists draw them, as long as the character silhouette remains consistent. This system saves time since storyboards may be produced quickly using non-standardized placeholders. Some- times boards are redrawn when final character models are set.

The characters' appearance and personality will develop as they act and react on the storyboards. Storyboard drawings are frequently pasted up into "*action only*" model sheets to assist the character designers since the rough drawings show actions and ex- pressions that the character needs to be able to perform in the film. This mutual feed- back works equally well in feature, student, or independent films.

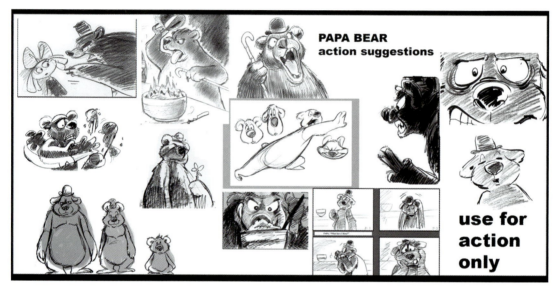

[Fig. 10-2] This action model sheet of Papa Bear is composed of rough storyboard drawings that capture his personality and typical actions. It is used by the animator for acting tips and by the designer as reference for the character's final appearance.

The most important considerations in story sketch and character design are *selection*, *simplification*, and *emphasis*. You *select* what you want the viewer to see, *simplify* the staging so that there is a defined center of interest, and *emphasize* important elements in the scene.

The following elements are used to create a story sketch:

Line, value (light and shadow)

Silhouettes and shapes (consider both positive and negative space)

Texture

Color (occasionally)

■ *Each board drawing should read from a minimum distance of 15 feet.* Storyboards must read from a distance since they are commonly pitched to a large audience in a large story room. Tonal modeling enables the drawing to read from a far greater distance than boards done only in line. The two boards in Figure 10-3 demonstrate greater and lesser degrees of readability. Try viewing this illustration from the other side of the room. If you wear glasses, view the boards without them.

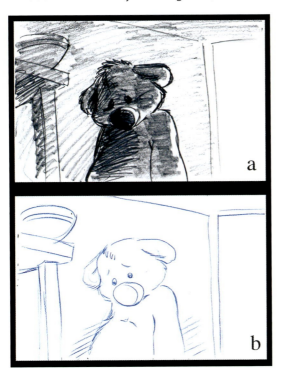

**[Fig. 10-3] Storyboard (a) will be visible from the other side of the room. Storyboard (b) will not read unless the viewer is very close to the boards.**

■ *The optical center of the screen is higher than the actual geometric center of the screen.* The optical center is where the viewer's vision goes first. It is located slightly above the actual center of the screen. Objects placed at the optical center will automatically draw the viewer's attention. Staging and design can be utilized to counter the natural tendency to look at the optical center. Optical and actual screen centers are depicted in Figure 10-4.

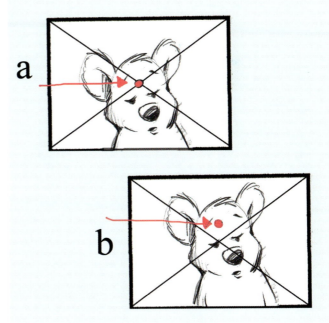

**[Fig. 10-4] The Optical center of the screen (a) is higher than the actual center (b). It is a frame's focal point that is recognized first by the human eye.**

**Exercise:** Create a simple palette of basic tonal ranges by dividing a rectangle into four sections as shown in Figure 10-5. The rectangle need not be very large.

a. Use a soft pencil to put your darkest value in the top panel. Label this "a."

b. The lightest value is determined next. It will be at the bottom of your chart. If your lightest value is white, leave the bottom panel blank. If you are boarding a shadowy or foggy scene, the lightest value could be gray and not pure white. Whichever way you go, put your lightest tone at the bottom of the diagram and label it "b."

c. Next, take a value that is roughly halfway between the darkest and lightest. Put that tone on the second panel from the top and label it "c."

d. Take a tone halfway between your middle value "c" and lightest value "b," put it in the third panel, and label it "d."

Refer to these values when completing the storyboard exercises.

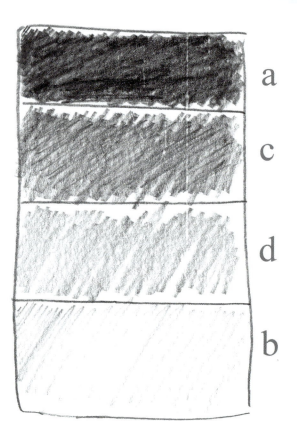

**[Fig. 10-5] A progression of tonal values. Four should give you enough range to emphasize areas of the frame that you want the viewer to see first. You must be able to create the tones quickly on hundreds of boards. Contrast between these values can create a wide variety of moods and lighting effects.**

Why use only four values? Why not use a dozen? Storyboards are revised so frequently that it would be a shame to spend hours creating full *presentation boards* only to see most of them "go by the boards" when the story changes (as it assuredly will). Simple tonal values add depth and readability to the boards with a minimum of tears. The number 'four' is merely the smallest number of values I recommend that you use. It is permissible to use five. You should not spend all your time working on fussy tonal details in the drawings at this stage. Your object should be to work quickly, concentrate on depicting important story points, and make the boards read well using simple line and a few distinct tonal values.

Tonal values set the mood of the sequence and direct the eye to the most important areas of the frame. Use tonal values to maximize readability. Line drawings are the least effective communicators. Figure 10-6 is a busy composition with no real emphasis on any particular area.

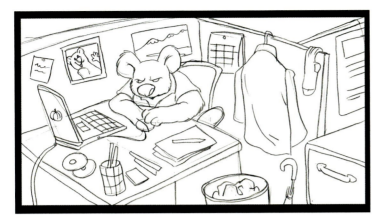

**[Fig. 10-6]** This linear composition is confusing and we don't know where we are supposed to look.

The strongest tonal contrast should appear on the areas of greatest importance. Poorly applied tonal values can read as badly as the pure lines used in Figure 10-6. In Figure 10-7, the coat on the wall appears to be the center of interest since it contains stronger tonal contrasts than the main character.

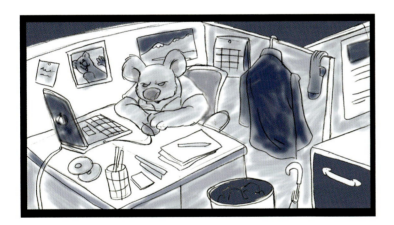

**[Fig. 10-7]** Our office guy is at his desk. His coat appears to be the center of interest since tonal values have been poorly applied.

Good tonal values will create a feeling of depth in the scene, enable a drawing to read for the requisite 10-15 feet, and direct the eye to the center of interest. In Figure 10-8, the background has been "knocked down" (had its contrast reduced) by making it a single value. Different values indicate depth of field in the scene. The character is isolated by a pool of light that helps set the mood and improve the drawing's readability.

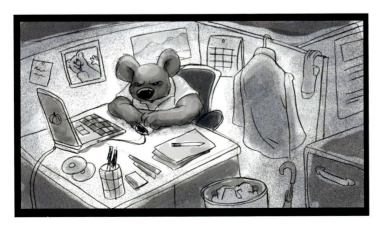

**[Fig 10-8]** In this version tone places different elements at varying distances from the camera. Foreground silhouettes frame the shot and direct the eye toward the character. Background elements can be simple suggestions since they are not as important.

Exercise: Draw a storyboard panel in line similar to the one shown in Figure 10-6. Pin it on the wall and view it from the other side of the room. Does the image read clearly? Next, shade the central figure with your darkest tonal value (A). Use the lightest value (B) on the background and the two medium values (C, D) for prop or background detail. Pin the second drawing on the wall and view it from the other side of the room. The second drawing should read more clearly.

## Graphic Images Ahead!

Silhouettes read best, but tone can work just as effectively to highlight important areas of the storyboard frame. Some common techniques used in graphic illustration are shown in Figure 10-9.

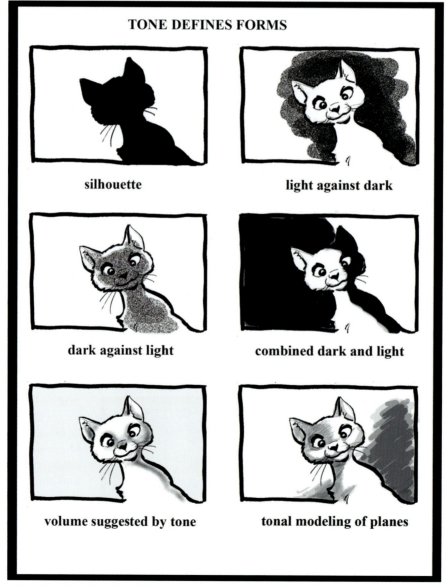

TONE DEFINES FORMS

silhouette

light against dark

dark against light

combined dark and light

volume suggested by tone

tonal modeling of planes

[Fig. 10-9] There is more than one way to skin a cat, or draw one!

Layout man Ken O'Connor always stressed that you "should not paint the Sistine Chapel ceiling for a three-second shot." In other words, it is a waste of time and effort to put extensive detail onto your backgrounds if the scene is too short and the action too fast for the audience to see it. Background patterns can interfere with the character action. Figure 10-10 shows some problem backgrounds and their solutions. Elaborate backgrounds are better suited for long and medium shots. Simple tonal backgrounds work best for closer shots.

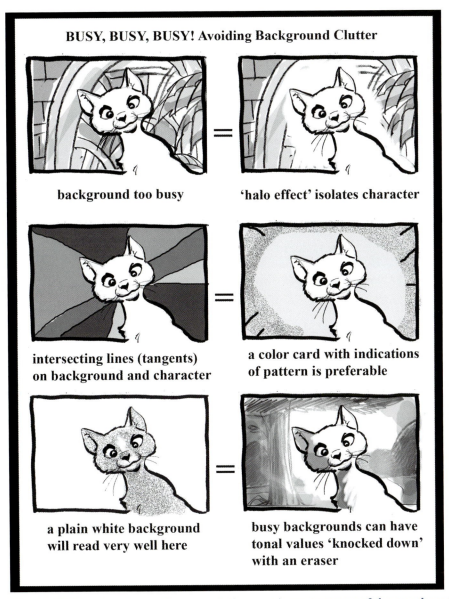

[Fig. 10-10] **The character performance is the most important part of the storyboard in an animated film. Background detail should support it, not interfere with it.**

Backgrounds can consist of a solid color (known as a *'limbo'* or *color-card* background) that fits in with the rest of the sequence. If you have established your location and color scheme in earlier shots, scenes on color cards will seem to take place in the same location as boards with detailed backgrounds. Cutting, color, and consistent screen direction will create the illusion of action in a continuous space. Chuck Jones' DUCK AMUCK uses many 'limbo backgrounds' with Daffy Duck emoting full-figure on the blank white movie screen for a large part of the picture.

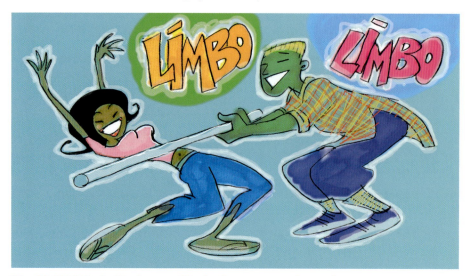

[Fig. 10-11] A 'limbo' background is also known as a color card.

# The Drama in the Drawings:
# Using Contrast to Direct the Eye

The human eye is drawn to the area of greatest contrast just as it is naturally drawn to the optical center of the frame. The most dramatic contrast is between black and white as shown in Figure 10-12, but this principle applies even if your tonal values are relatively close, as Figure 10-13 demonstrates.

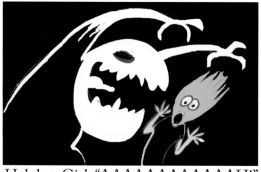

Helpless Girl: "AAAAAAAAAAAAH!"

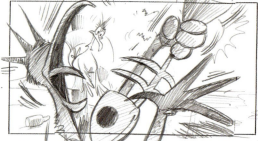

Punk Gull: "AAAAAAH!"

[Fig. 10-12, Fig. 10-13] A screaming gal in a monster movie and a screaming gull in a beach picture. The eye immediately goes to the areas of greatest tonal contrast even when the values are close, as shown in Figure 10-13.

I recommend that you use pencil, graphite, or charcoal to apply tones. It's relatively easy to take an eraser to a board that is done in graphite or charcoal and "carve out" lighter values and highlights.

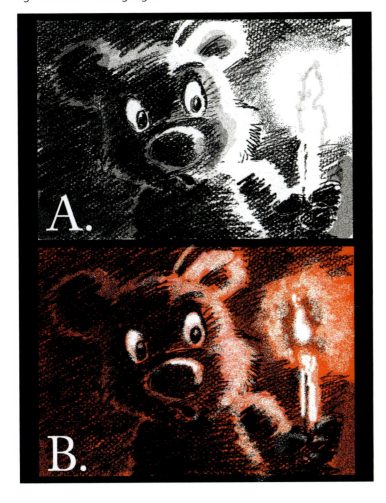

[Fig. 10-14] Boards may be drawn on black or colored paper with white and colored pastels and pencils. Highlights may be "carved out" with an eraser. The red panel is more dramatic than the black-and-white version.

It's very hard to change a tonal value on a board that's been done in marker. This is not an issue if you are comfortable with this medium and don't mind doing your boards over again when changes are made. A marker board appears in Figure 10-15.

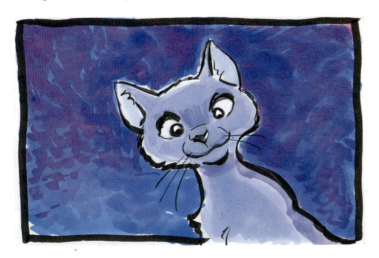

[Fig 10-15] An example of a storyboard with tonal values done in marker.

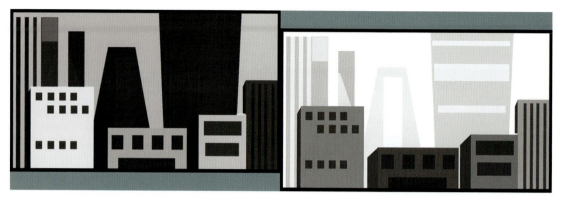

[Fig. 10-16] Computer graphics make it easy to vary tonal values on the same background.

You may wish to do your storyboards on computer but this has its drawbacks. The computer screen's small size (when compared to that of a storyboard) makes it difficult to view more than two or three panels at a time—which can lead to serious problems since entire storyboards must often be reworked and reviewed on a daily basis. A computer screen may only be seen clearly by three or four people. Drawn panels pinned to the wall are the easiest way for a group of people to view all of the artwork in a sequence at once during a pitch or *turnover* session. Paper storyboards can be easily and inexpensively changed by adding, rearranging, or deleting panels. The story *crew* is not dependent on the availability or functionality of software, hardware, codecs, or operating systems. Computer graphics programs can easily resize, *flop*, change tones, and re-composite existing artwork when you create the *story reel* or *animatic*. They are invaluable aids to animation production—after the boards have been drawn.

## The Best Laid Floor Plans

For the sake of argument let us assume that your story and characters work with props and visual landmarks in a recognizable location. Drawing a simple floor plan will help you stage major scenic elements, such as doors and windows, along with furniture and other inanimate objects. If your picture is set outdoors, you can place landmarks such as rocks, paths, streams, and trees into the floor plan. 'Wild' forests are always meticulously planned in animation!

Floor plans are usually shown from a three-quarter angle or a top-down view. I prefer the top-down view since it shows all portions of the location equally well and lets you block your character's action with little effort. The three-quarter view is useful for establishing character scale to props or other elements in the shot. A three-quarter floor plan is necessary for CGI projects that literally create the background in the third dimension, as shown in Figure 10-17.

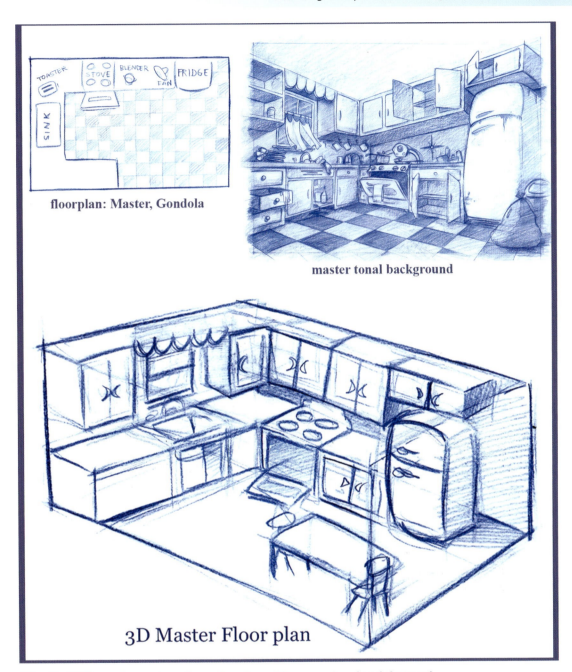

floorplan: Master, Gondola

master tonal background

3D Master Floor plan

[Fig. 10-17] The artist creates a floor plan viewed from overhead and the tonal background based on it. A three-quarter view floor plan is a more accurate indication of scale. Reproduced by permission of William Robinson.

At this stage you may work up a tonal Master Background based on your floor plan, but this is not always necessary. I have worked on productions that were handled both ways. In some instances the art director provided a master background with tonals for the board artists to work with. This was a useful tool since the action involved multiple characters in a busy kitchen with several work tables on the floor, a huge fireplace along one wall, prop-laden shelves, and doors at opposite ends of the room. An example of a master background and an elaborate floor plan of this type are shown in Figure 10-18. Master backgrounds typically include the characters to indicate relative sizes and scales.

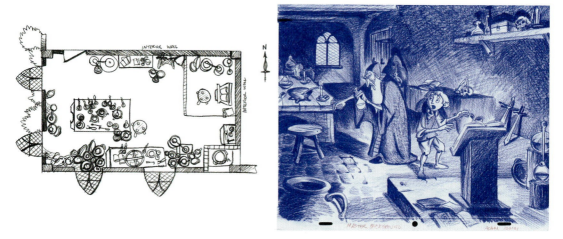

[Fig. 10-18] This floor plan locates the windows and every dish on the table. The master background includes the characters for scale. Reproduced by permission of Adam Fox.

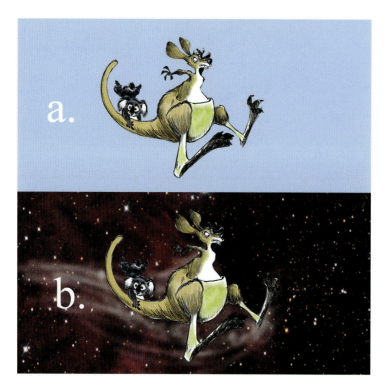

[Fig. 10-19] Characters (a) pose on a color card or (b) move through outer space.

Not every location needs a floor plan. Figure 10-19 shows characters on a color card (a) and (b) on a background in deep space. The kangaroo and koala appear to be stationary when placed on a color card. The starfield background suggests that they are flying. It is not necessary to plot the location of each planet or nebula in the background since the characters do not interact with them.

# Structure: The Mind's Eye

Whose viewpoint is the action seen from? Do we see it from a God's-eye-view or from the perspective of one of the characters? Staging will affect the mood of the scene. Figure 10-20 shows two panels illustrating a very old joke. The flat staging in (a) reads well enough, but it does not indicate the atmosphere or the characters' mood. Figure (b) uses an upshot to literally put the kangaroo's head in the air as he delivers the corny punch line with obvious distaste. Several versions of the second panel are thumbnailed below the storyboards. Thumbnail 1 uses the same flat staging as storyboard (a), but the camera has pulled back to add depth to the shot as the kangaroo walks away from the bar. Characters may advance or retreat from the picture plane to create the illusion of the third dimension.

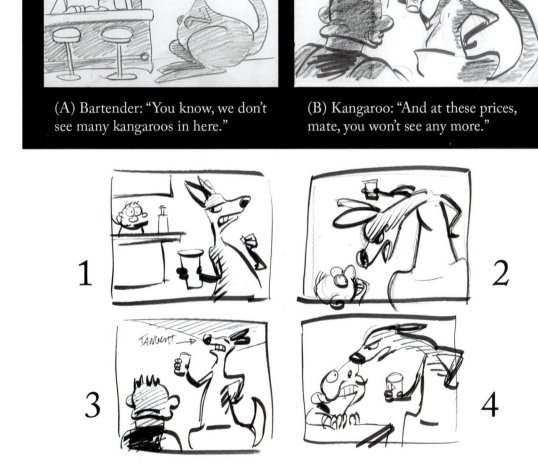

(A) Bartender: "You know, we don't see many kangaroos in here."

(B) Kangaroo: "And at these prices, mate, you won't see any more."

[Fig. 10-20] "This kangaroo walks into a bar...." A dramatic upshot in the second panel shows the relationship of the characters in the shot. Thumbnails show how the scene would read with different camera angles and character attitudes.

*Work for an interesting variety of shots*. Each shot must contribute to the story. Don't use extreme cuts because you *can*; use them when they are the best way to stage the action. Medium shots and long shots distance us from the characters; close-ups can show us their reactions and inner thoughts. Successful animation has been created in one single shot, but it tends to be very short. Use film grammar correctly. Thumbnail a scene from different angles to see which one works best for your story. An example of this technique is shown in Figure 10-21.

**[Fig. 10-21] Thumbnail drawings by T. Hee showing three possible angles for the same storyboard panel. (Nancy Beiman collection)**

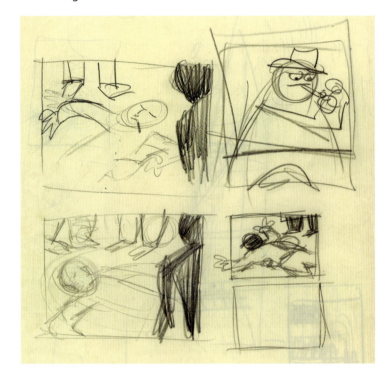

The mood of the scene changes along with the staging. Low-angle or high-angle shots can indicate tension or show one character dominating another in the scene. The viewpoint can be ours, or that of one of the characters. Ken O'Connor recommended drawing a floor plan with cameras blocked in at different angles, as shown in Figure 10-22.

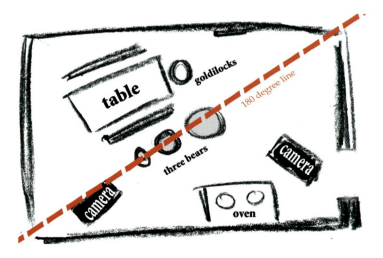

**[Fig. 10-22] Ken O'Connor suggested adding camera indications to a simple floor plan. This helps the artist choose the best angle for the shot.**

Here are some guidelines to follow when creating storyboards:

- Work for clarity of staging.
- Simple staging is always the best.
- Make sure that your shots work into one another.
- Use good film grammar.

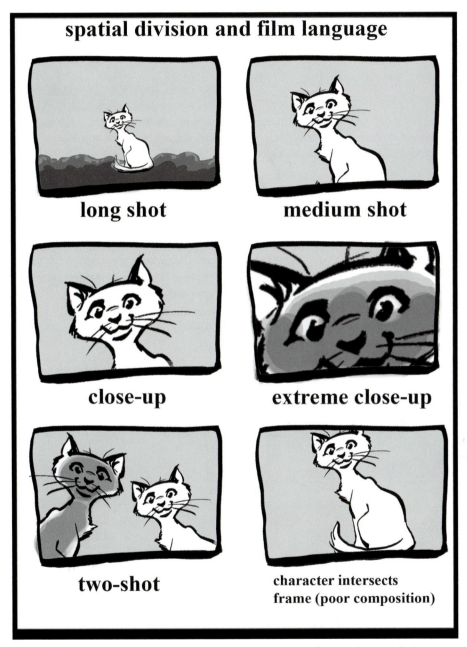

**spatial division and film language**

long shot

medium shot

close-up

extreme close-up

two-shot

character intersects
frame (poor composition)

[Fig. 10-23] Use the language of film to tell your story. A close-up is more intimate than a long shot. Don't jam characters against the frame line.

"Matching horizons on a cut" is a common error. Characters will appear to pop on and off the screen if the background perspective remains the same in every cut. Maintain eye-lines when characters are speaking to one another. Figure 10-24 shows an example of poor eye-line continuity and matching horizons. Who are Goldilocks and Papa Bear talking to and where are they standing?

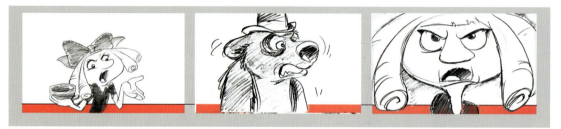

[Fig. 10-24] Poor film grammar will distract from your story. Characters' eye-lines should make us believe that they are looking at one another. Matching horizon lines on a cut give the impression that the characters are popping on and off the same background.

*Do not animate the camera*. Work out action thoroughly for story points before determining cuts and camera moves. Concentrate on the best staging of the action. Use the moving camera to help tell the story, not distract from it.

*Design your frames*. Use props and the design of the character to create good silhouette value within the frame. Certain objects can serve as directional elements or "pointers" to direct the viewer's attention to a specific part of the frame. All elements in the frame should have a purpose and help tell the story. The wolves in Figure 10-25 are giant "pointers" leading our eyes to the center of interest.

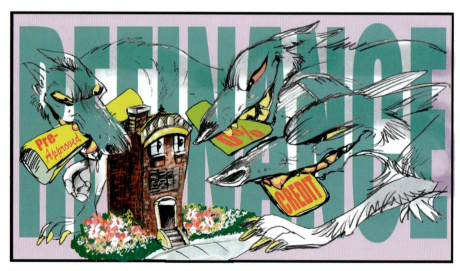

[Fig. 10-25] Directional elements in the background and foreground act as "pointers" directing your attention to the center of interest. Illustration by Nancy Beiman from the film IN DEBT WE TRUST, reproduced by permission of Globalvision Inc.

*Tangents* are intersecting lines that direct the viewer's attention to a specific point. This tangential action can be involuntary. It is commonly used in design and graphics, but is generally avoided in animation since it flattens the composition and destroys the illusion of depth in the frame. Figure 10-26 shows two frames with numerous tangential absurdities such as a tree that appears to grow from a little girl's head. The tangents are corrected in Figure 10-27.

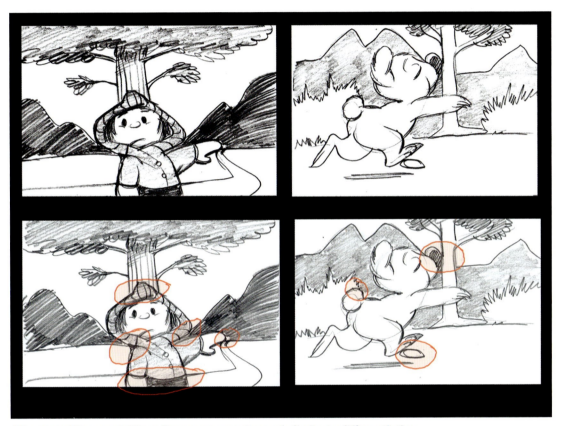

[Fig. 10-26] Tangential lines flatten perspective and eliminate differentiation between the characters and the backgrounds. They can also direct the eye to an important part of the composition, but too often the tangent distracts from the center of interest. Tangential areas are highlighted in red.

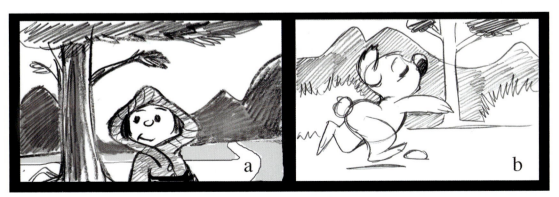

[Fig. 10-27] Panel (a) moves the background, (b) moves the character. Tangents disappear and the illusion of the third dimension is restored.

*Use tonal values, not pure line.* Storyboards work best in tone. Linear ones do not read as well from a distance and they won't show moods or time of day. There is also a danger of losing the characters against a busy background. Tonal values can be applied and modified to direct the eye precisely where you want it to go. (Figure 10-28)

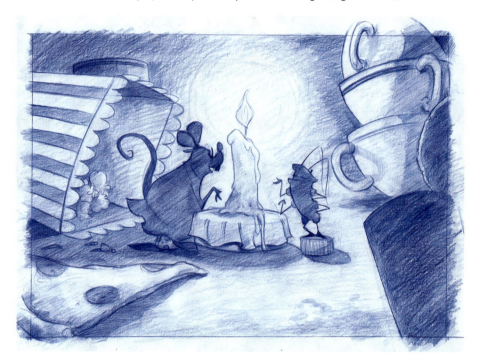

**[Fig. 10-28] Close tonal values helps knock the patterns in the background down and focus our attention on the characters. A section of the tonal background can be rubbed out with a kneaded eraser for a 'halo effect' around the center of interest. Reproduced by permission of William Robinson.**

Color should not be used unless it is absolutely necessary. Sometimes color will help put over a story point—for example, when red is used for Little Red Riding Hood's cloak as shown in Figure 10-29b.  A blushing or intoxicated character might have its nose or face colored red to convey the story point.

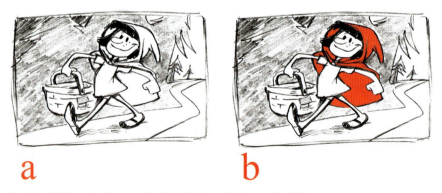

a                                        b

**[Fig. 10-29] Rendering result: Red Riding Hood reads right.**

Figure 10-30 shows panels from a storyboard that used the characters' color as an important part of the story. Color, especially the color of the symbols on their heads, signified life. Gray values symbolized death and sadness. Color gave individuality to characters with nearly identical silhouettes. The boards could have been done in grayscale but were far more effective in color.

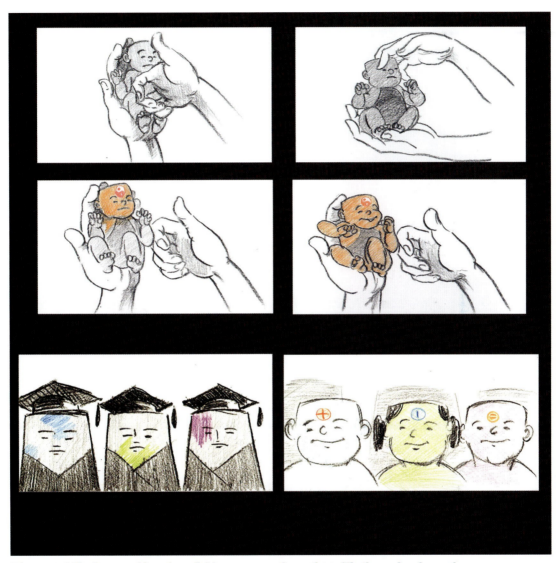

[Fig. 10-30] The hero and heroine of this story were brought to life through color and bore brightly colored life-symbols on their foreheads. Gray tonal values were used for the backgrounds and a symbolic death-figure. A character died when its color faded to gray. Reproduced by permission of Rui Jin.

Lastly, avoid placing the character directly against the frame line. This creates a tangent, and it is also weak staging. A portion of the aperture is lost when the film is projected (depending on the medium, the "safety" area can be up to 15% of the picture area). Portions of your character may be cut off by the frame. All lettering must be created inside this 'safety zone' or else it may be cut off when the film is projected, as shown in Figure 10-31. Figure 10-32 corrects the problem. Note that the man's arm is no longer parallel to the frame line.

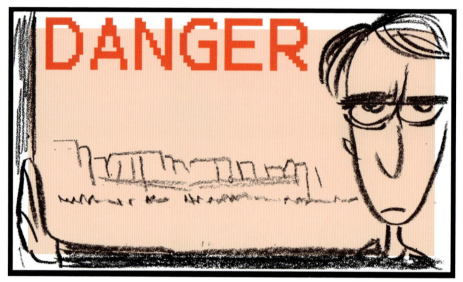

[Fig. 10-31] Characters and lettering must fall within the letter-safe area. Modern monitors have larger safety areas than older ones, but a portion of the frame is invariably lost. Characters' heads and bodies should not intersect the frame. The portion of the image that is in the white area will be cut off when the film is screened. Red tones indicate the lettering safety area.

[Fig. 10-32] The action and text now appear well within the letter-safe area. The man's arm is staged at a diagonal to eliminate parallels with the frame.

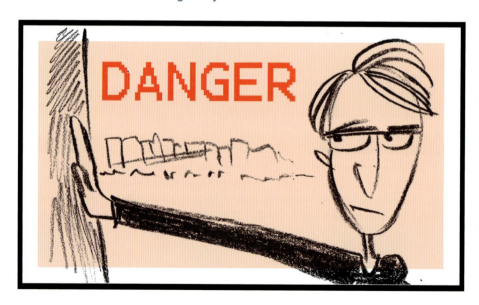

All the world's a stage and the people merely players. But animators design the stage and the players and then stage the action. Chapter 11 examines this paradox.

# 11

# Roughing It: Basic Staging

The visual elements and spatial relationships of the animated picture are constantly changing in fourth-dimensional space. Each scene must read instantly whether their time onscreen is long or short. Here are some tips that will help your boards read clearly and well.

Indications of light and shadow should be kept simple. Four values are commonly used: light, dark, and two medium values, as described in Chapter 10.

Line defines *contour*. The contour is the *shape*, or silhouette, of the object or character.

**[Fig. 11-1] Line defines the contours of an object. Size relationships can create an illusion of depth but the third dimension is easier to indicate with tone than with mere line.**

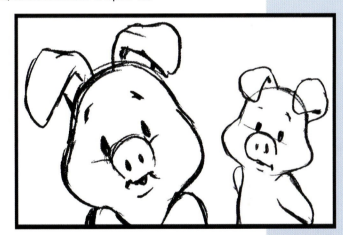

Tone defines the *volume* of the objects and characters. Volume indicates the third dimension. Tone also serves to define the depth of field in the shot. Certain objects will seem closer or farther away with the aid of tone.

**[Fig. 11-2] Tone creates the dimension in backgrounds and characters.**

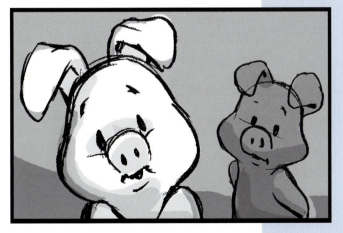

The darkest part of a shadow appears nearest the light. Reflected light will create a lighter value on the side of the object that opposes the light source.

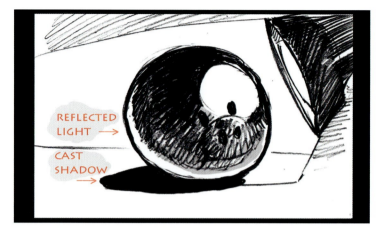

**[Fig. 11-3]** Direct lighting creates strong shadows. The farther away the light is from the subject, the more diffuse the shadow. Cast shadows are strongest of all.

Objects at the optical center of the frame will normally be noticed first but strong tonal contrast and directional elements can direct the eye elsewhere, as shown in Figure 11-4. Remember that the optical center of the frame is higher than the actual center (See Figure 10-1 for a simple example).

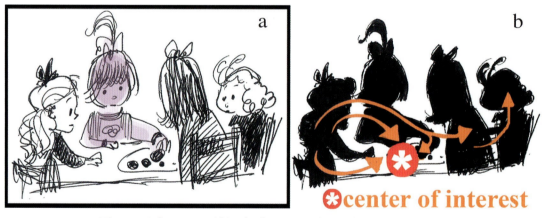

**[Fig. 11-4] Elements within the frame can direct the eye away from the optical center. The pink girl's arm provides the strongest pointer leading to the plate of cookies. Figure (b) shows the visual pattern of the composition.**

Different eye levels or horizon lines indicate that we are viewing the scene through the eyes of particular characters. Figure 11-5 shows two different subjective views of the same background. The perspective and camera angle are more caricatured in the dog's-eye view.

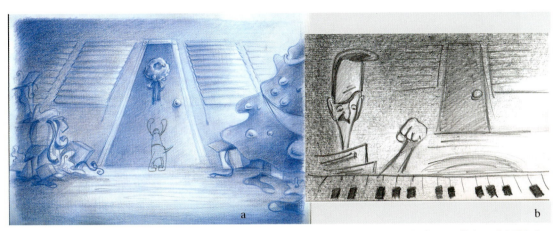

[Fig. 11-5] (a) This dramatic upshot shows the door viewed from the eye level of a small dog. (b) This is the same door viewed from the eye level of his owner. Reproduced by permission of Brittney Lee.

In Western culture we read text from left to right. We read film frames the same way. A character will *read* 'first' when it is on the left side of the frame as shown in Figure 11-6. The eye goes to the figure at screen left and moves to the group at screen right a millisecond later.

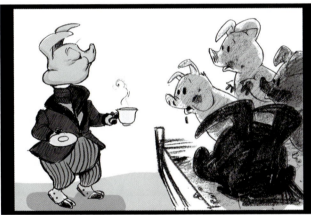

[Fig. 11-6] One figure appears to dominate the crowd as well as the scene because it is standing at screen left, where our eye naturally enters the frame. The character is also isolated by tone and by the positive and negative space in the frame. The other pigs read as a group rather than as individuals.

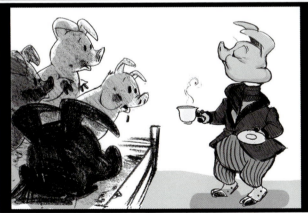

[Fig. 11-7] The crowd is now the center of interest. Nothing has changed except for the orientation of the storyboard panel. It has been "flopped," or reversed.

If this figure's composition is reversed the group at the left is seen before the isolated figure. *Flopping* the panel dramatically changes the meaning of the scene. In Figure 11-6, our point of view is that of the elegant pig. In Figure 11-7, we have a pig's eye view of elegance—direct from the pen.

These two shots would not work if they appeared consecutively on an actual storyboard, since the artist has *crossed the line.*

Care must be taken to avoid *crossing the line*, or breaking the compositional 180-degree arc when staging scenes. The picture plane is divided in half to establish the viewer's perspective. The "Line" also bisects the characters, which must always have the same left-right directional relationship to one another. Consecutive shots staged from opposite sides of the 180-degree axis as shown in Figures 11-6 and 11-7 would be disorienting to the viewer if they were in an actual film since the characters appear to have suddenly changed places. A simple diagram of the 180-degree line appears in Figure 11-8. The closer the camera is to the central axis, the more dramatic the staging of the shot. The Line runs through the center of interacting characters in a scene. The storyboards for scenes following a '*flopped*' panel must usually also be flopped to maintain the continuity.

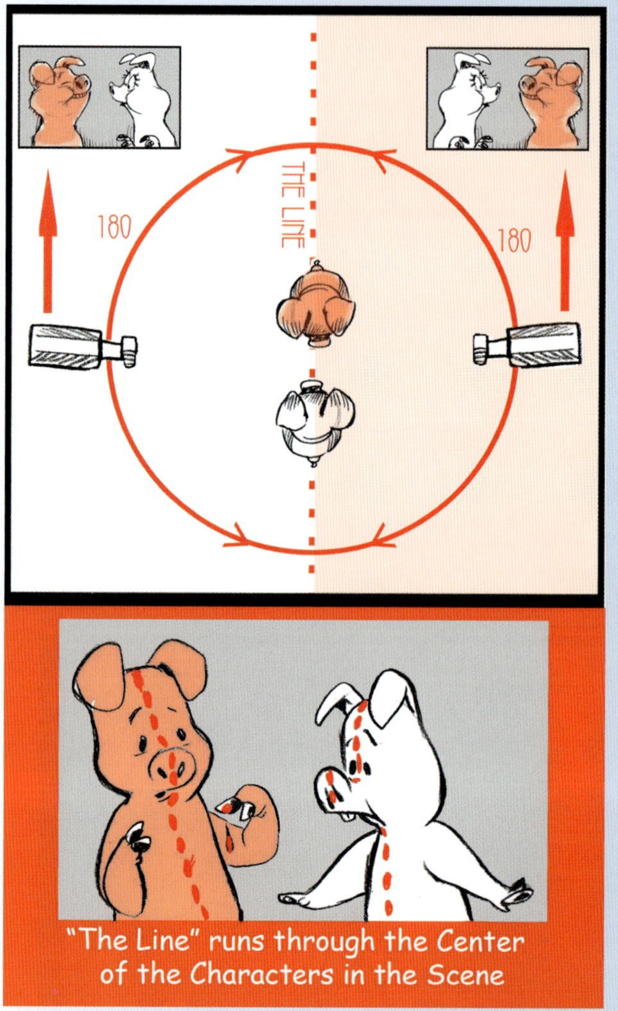

**[Fig. 11-8] The camera will usually remain on one side of a 180-degree axis to prevent confusing reversals of directional elements. The dramatic content of a scene is enhanced when the camera is staged very close to 'the line'.**

"The Line" runs through the Center of the Characters in the Scene

A *neutral shot* has a character heading either toward or away from the camera. It may be intercut with shots that contain strong directional elements without fear of breaking the 180-degree staging rule. You may cut to shots staged on the other side of the Line.

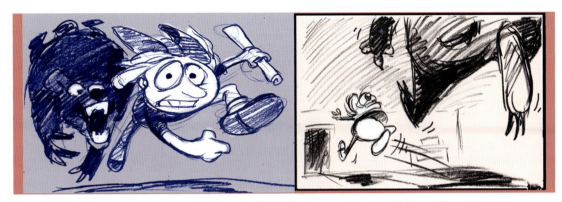

[Fig. 11-9] **Characters moving toward or away from the camera are staged neutrally. You may cut from a neutral shot to any other angle and maintain directional continuity. Overhead views can also function as neutral shots.**

Negative and positive space must both be considered when designing storyboards.

A figure may be isolated while in the midst of a crowd. Figure 11-10A shows a crowd scene with one pig at the optical center of the panel. The frame has been carefully designed to draw the eye toward the central character. (1) The central pig contains the greatest value contrast. (2) Dark negative space on the background forms a letter 'V' creating a pointer that isolates and leads to the center of interest. (3) The foreground pigs are rendered with close tonal values so they do not distract from the center of interest. Their animation will be underplayed. (4) Background characters are handled as one unit that isolates the main characters and frames the action.

Tonal values can be used to direct our attention to different areas of the scene at different times. In Figure 11-10B, a pig at screen left now contains the greatest tonal contrast. The eye views this pig first but the central pig is still differentiated from the crowd (though to a lesser extent) by the same design elements described in Figure A. The eye travels from the character with greatest contrast to the character isolated by directional elements in the frame. This example is only a still frame. Tonal values, positive and negative shapes, directional elements and spatial relationships between characters are constantly changing in an animated motion picture. These elements must read well at all times. The viewer's attention must be directed to the center of interest even when it is in rapid motion.

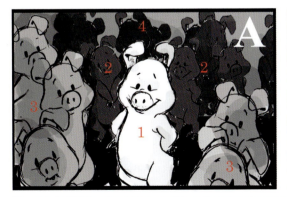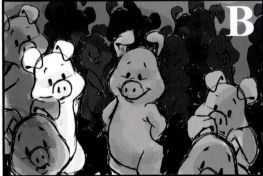

[Fig. 11-10] **Negative space and tonal contrast can vary in one scene over time. Tonal values are used to direct our attention to (A) one figure in the middle of a crowd; (B) a secondary figure interacting with the main character.**

*Arrows* can be used to establish the direction of the incoming motion when characters enter the frame from off-screen. The arrow determines the direction of action *outside* the frame. Speed lines (borrowed from the comics) are used to indicate the direction of action *inside* a frame. Figure 11-11 shows Papa Bear entering from off-screen as Goldilocks 'speedily' exits.

**[Fig. 11-11] Papa Bear enters from offscreen with the help of a directional arrow. Goldilocks makes a break for the door, trailing speed lines.**

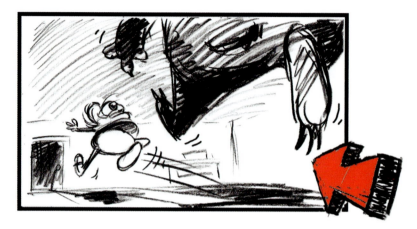

Do not use arrows to point out the center of interest within the frame. Your staging should read well without them. Add another panel if action continues within a scene.

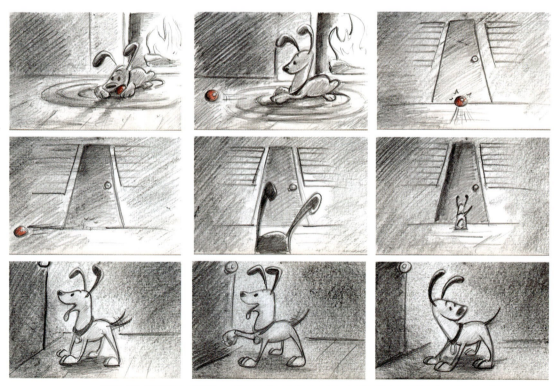

**[Fig. 11-12] Use additional panels, not arrows, to depict continuing action in a scene. Reproduced by permission of Brittney Lee.**

The storyboard blocks out and 'rehearses' animated characters' performances. Animators use these visual guidelines to tailor their acting to the needs of the story. A skimpily-boarded sequence will not convey the character's thoughts or motivation to anyone but yourself.

Since anything is possible in an animated world, characters and objects may appear in several places at the same time. Multiple drawings in a panel represent *separate phases of one action occurring in a short period of time.* Arrows or (preferably) speed lines show us the progression of the movement. Two panels are used to show the action in Figure 11-13 to prevent confusing overlaps in the bouncing ball's flight paths.

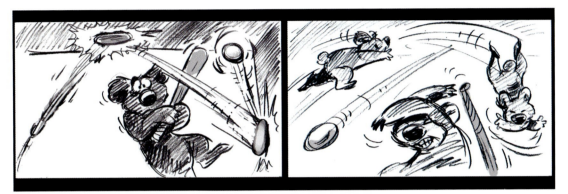

**[Fig. 11-13] An animated object may appear simultaneously in several locations. Multiple drawings on the same panel indicate rapid movement taking place in a short time period. Additional panels are used for longer actions.**

One panel is not sufficient illustration for a scene unless the scene is very short. Figure 11-14 is an example of a poorly-conceived storyboard panel. Arrows and multiple limbs substitute for acting. Each panel should contain one idea; this panel has three. Which one should we notice first?

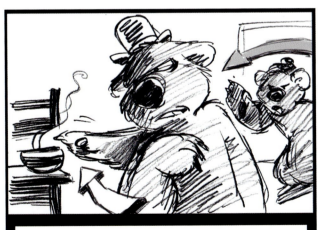

**[Fig. 11-14] One panel is not sufficient to illustrate complex actions taking place over time. This type of action is best illustrated on multiple storyboards.**

PAPA: "If only I could just ONCE have porridge that was *just right!* So who's to know if I..."
MAMA: "What are you DOING!"

Each storyboard should contain one idea. The number of boards per scene varies with the complexity of the idea. Papa Bear's moral dilemma is displayed in two scenes, the first of which is illustrated on one panel. In the second scene, we pull back (truck out) from a close-up of Papa Bear to reveal Mama's horrified reaction to his dastardly villainy.

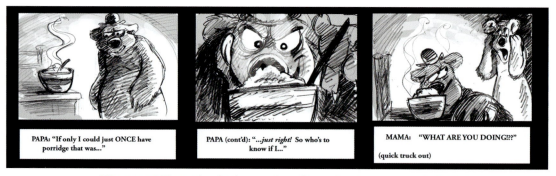

PAPA: "If only I could just ONCE have porridge that was..."

PAPA (cont'd): "...*just right!* So who's to know if I..."

MAMA:   "WHAT ARE YOU DOING!??"

(quick truck out)

**[Fig. 11-15] The action in the previous figure has been expanded into two scenes on three storyboards. The acting is emphasized and the staging helps pace the action.**

Use a new storyboard panel to convey each new action. Otherwise, the boards will become hopelessly confusing to read and you will find it extremely difficult to time action well when shooting your *story reel*.

# I'm Ready for My Closeup: Storyboard Cinematography

Characters have the best silhouette value when seen in straight profile, although action staged exclusively in profile can create confusing cuts. A profile shot of a character heading from screen left to screen right (Fig.11-16a) followed by one of another character heading from screen right to screen left (b) leads us to assume that they meet (c) since both characters are traveling (in profile) on the same plane. A cutaway shot can be inserted between them to correct the misapprehension. A better solution would be to use different camera angles and perspective to show that the characters are moving in three dimensional spaces. (Figure 11-17)

**[Fig. 11-16] The two birds collide since they are traveling in opposite directions on the same plane.**

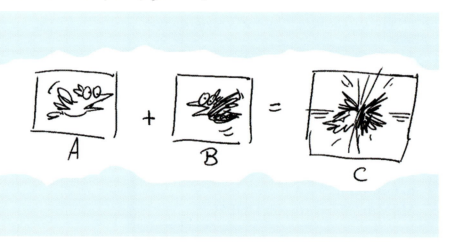

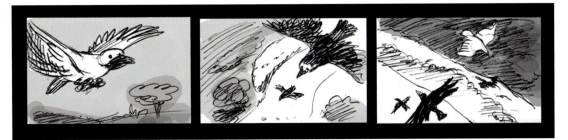

[Fig. 11-17] **Varying the angles creates a feeling of three-dimensional spaces and eliminates the collision course.**

A three-quarter view of a character is usually more interesting than a frontal or profile shot since it creates a feeling of depth and the third dimension. Both pigs in Figure 11-18 read well, but the three-quarter view allows for more depth in the staging and acting than the profile shot.

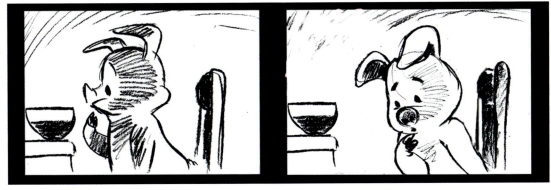

[Fig. 11-18] **A three-quarter view is more interesting than a straight profile since it adds the illusion of depth and dimension to the character.**

Characters staged in the center of the frame should be in dynamic poses so that the negative space isn't divided evenly. Avoid the 'gingerbread man' look by putting some torque on the body so that the pose is not completely symmetrical. Examples of the 'gingerbread man' and more dimensional staging of the same pose are shown in Figure 11-19.

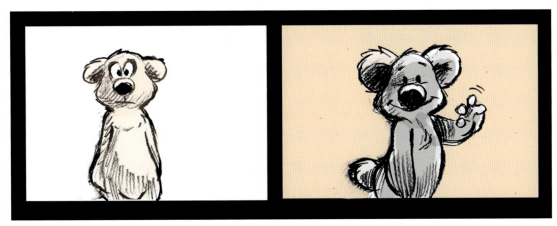

[Fig. 11-19] **"Frontal views" read better if the character is placed slightly off center in the frame and turned slightly into three-quarter view. Most animated characters look best from a three-quarter angle. A straight frontal view often falls flat.**

Overlapping shapes will create the illusion of depth. Tangents will flatten the composition and destroy the illusion of depth. (Examples of tangents and their cure are shown in Figures 10-18 and 10-19 in Chapter 10.) Large shapes in the foreground will appear to be closer to the picture plane. The illusion may be assisted by the use of tone, as shown in figures 11-20 and 11-21. Distant objects can sometimes have much lighter values than items in the foreground.

**[Fig. 11-20] The foreground buildings appear to be in the shadow of the sun-dappled skyscrapers since they contain the darkest tonal values.**

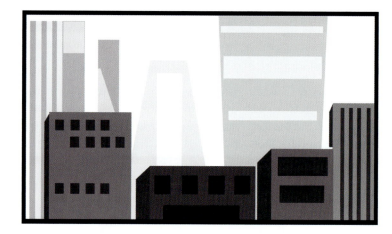

**[Fig. 11-21] The panel's atmosphere undergoes total change when the lightest values appear on the foreground buildings.**

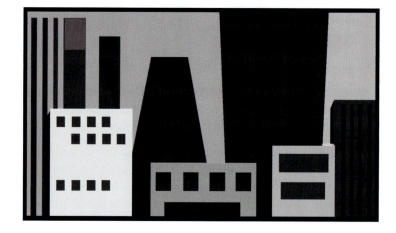

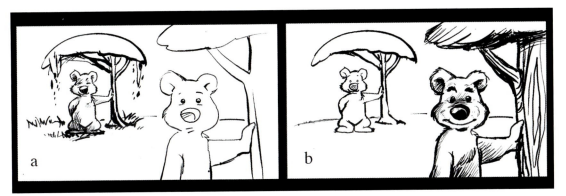

[Fig. 11-22] A close object that contains no interior detail will appear more remote than an elaborately rendered background area, and vice versa.

The eye may be led around the frame by contrasting tonal values or colors, variations in positive and negative space, directional elements in character and background designs, and the amount of detail that appears in specific areas of the frame.

Detail varies with scale. Important scenic elements should contain more detail than secondary items and distant objects should be rendered with fewer details as they recede from the picture plane. The Close-up Bear in Figure 11-22(a) is rendered in a sketchy style commonly used for more distant objects and so appears more remote than Far-away Bear, who is the center of interest in (a) but recedes into the background when the detailed areas are reversed in (b).

Tonal values determine the scale of objects in smoky or foggy scenes. Values grow closer and outlines become fainter as elements of a foggy scene recede from the picture plane. There will be very little depth of field and characters may only read as silhouettes.

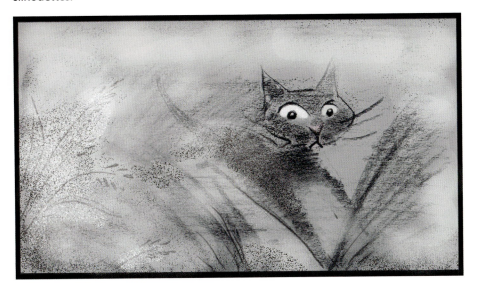

[Fig. 11-23] A smoky or foggy scene uses tonal values to set the scale of objects in the frame. There is little depth of field and values are very close.

Good design principles will create contrasting visual patterns on the boards. Each individual project will use different solutions but visual patterns are only half the battle: storyboards also pace the action so as to create *patterns in time.*

Exercise: Analyze one sequence of a classic live-action film by stopping the DVD or video during each scene and drawing simple thumbnails of each shot's composition. Observe how the camera is used and when and why cuts are made. Next, repeat the exercise with one sequence from a classic animated cartoon of your choice. What are the similarities and differences between the two media?

It's now time to get with the beat … a *story beat.*

# 12

# Boarding Time: Getting with the Story Beat

A sculptor was once asked how he carved an elephant from a block of wood. He replied, "I take this knife and carve away anything that does not look like an elephant."

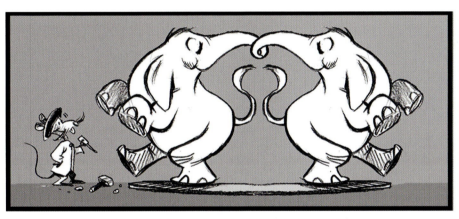

**[Fig. 12-1] The Elephant in the Room, or removing the inessentials.**

Like sculpture, animation develops complex forms from simple beginnings. Unlike sculpture, finished animation does not simply appear as extraneous material is removed. Animation is like patchwork. A series of small parts is assembled according to a pattern, resulting in a whole "quilt." Refinement of story, production design, and animation can sometimes continue right up until the completion of the project. A sculpture can be viewed from many different angles. A motion picture's viewpoint is locked. The director 'directs' your attention to specific areas of the frame and the editor sets the viewing time for each shot, exercising total control over the production. Storyboard artists function as a combination of director and editor. They create the blueprint for the remainder of the film.

Storyboard drawings describe an idea. They are not a series of individual drawings. They may be lovely works of art in their own right, but if a story point does not *communicate instantly* the boards are not working.

Split screens are occasionally used when depicting simultaneous action in animation, but not for long periods of time. The simultaneous motion of several animated characters can prove extremely distracting. Methods that work in still drawings or graphic novels may not work as well when competing with sound effects, animation, and camera movement.

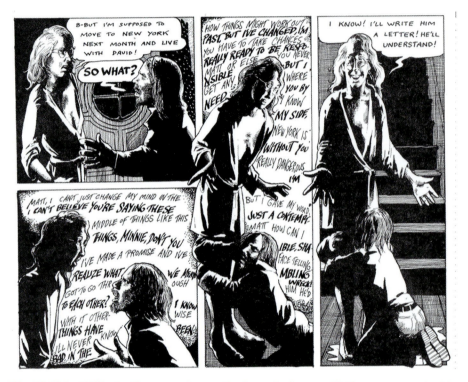

[Fig. 12-2] A still illustration may change the frame's shape, split the screen, and add lettering to the design without creating visual overload. Excerpt from *David Chelsea in Love* reproduced by permission of David Chelsea.

The reader of a graphic novel may take as long as they like to view the artwork. It is possible to put an immense amount of information into one panel without creating confusion. The animation viewer's comprehension of a scene's content is dictated by its length. Visual overload can easily ensue if too much action is crammed into a frame.

If major story points and character relationships are not planned well at the beginning of the project, they will have to be reworked later on. Weaknesses tend to become more obvious as the production advances, and changes become more expensive in proportion. This is why animation is edited first, in storyboard form, before the animation begins. Beat Boards are the next step in this process.

# Working to the Beat: Story Beats and Boards

An animation story, like live action, is broken down into sequences that are determined by story beats. A story beat is a major turning point in the story. Animation storyboards will use *beat boards* (also known as *outline boards*) to illustrate the major story points before the rest of the storyboard is completed.  Figure 12-3 shows a simple example.

Beat (1) Little Red Riding Hood starts out for Grandma's house.

Beat (2) She meets the Wolf.

Beat (3)) The Wolf goes to Grandma's house and puts on Grandma's clothes.

Beat (4) Little Red Riding Hood meets the Wolf in the house.

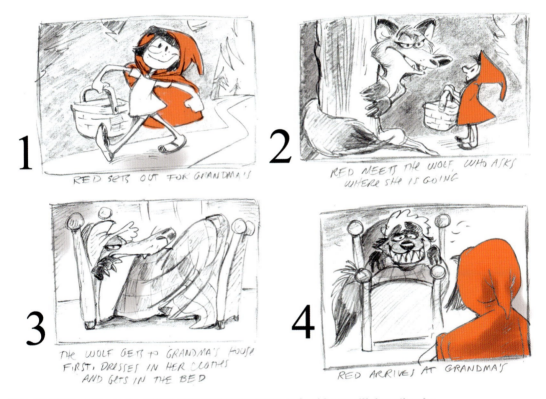

[Fig. 12-3] **Story Beats for LITTLE RED RIDING HOOD. A final beat will describe the resolution of the story. Color helps Red Riding Hood read better. Written captions clarify the action. Draw a final beat board describing how you might end this story.**

It is customary on longer productions to assemble a board in which beat boards describe the major action in every sequence. The beats for an entire feature will fit on one or two storyboards. Each sequence will then have its own set of story beats developed as the boarding progresses. It is crucial to work on a large scale at this early stage, refining the story and adding complexity, subplots, and acting only after the main story points are set. Beat boards are also useful on short projects, particularly if you are depicting changing moods and emotions. One or two story panels are used per beat. They are accompanied by separate panels containing a brief description of the action. Figure 12-4 shows Beat Boards for one sequence of a simple story.

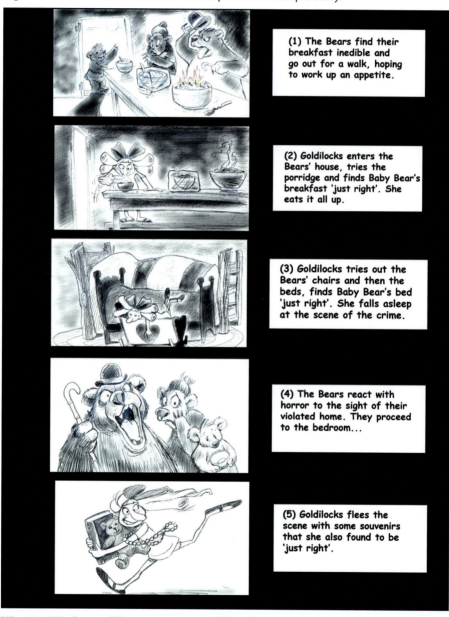

(1) The Bears find their breakfast inedible and go out for a walk, hoping to work up an appetite.

(2) Goldilocks enters the Bears' house, tries the porridge and finds Baby Bear's breakfast 'just right'. She eats it all up.

(3) Goldilocks tries out the Bears' chairs and then the beds, finds Baby Bear's bed 'just right'. She falls asleep at the scene of the crime.

(4) The Bears react with horror to the sight of their violated home. They proceed to the bedroom...

(5) Goldilocks flees the scene with some souvenirs that she also found to be 'just right'.

[Fig. 12-4] Each panel illustrates one story beat for GOLDILOCKS AND THE THREE BEARS. (1) The Bears find their breakfast inedible and go out for a walk. (2) Goldilocks breaks and enters, eats Baby Bear's porridge. (3) She remains at the scene of the crime in Baby Bear's bed. (4) The bears return and discover the intruder. (5) Goldilocks makes her getaway.

The Story Beats are visual 'sentences' illustrating the major developments in the story. They are used as a guide for the remainder of the production. Embellishments of personality animation, art direction, and timing are developed later.

Why use Beat Boards at all? Why not start at Scene One, Panel One and continue straight ahead to the end of the story? If you start with Panel One and keep going to the end, you may never reach it. There is a danger, when working in this straight-ahead manner, of losing sight of the main theme. This is a particular problem on longer films where each story artist will work on a different story beat. The story crew must see how their section of the project fits into the bigger picture so that they do not go off on a tangent. Entire sequences may be edited out of the film if communication is not established between the directors and the crew. A short film may be boarded at such length that it is not possible to complete the project in the allotted time period. Story beats are like signposts on the production roadmap. Beat boards are a visual representation of the story's beginning, major plot twists, and --most importantly-- ending. They divide your film into clearly-defined sequences and simplify production. Beat boards tell you where you are going and make sure you stay on the road.

# Do You Want to Talk About It?

 If you gave a short speech containing a synopsis of your film, each major development could be represented by one sentence (see Figures 12-3 and 12-4 for examples). Each beat board should represent one sentence of your synopsis. You may find it helpful to say the story point out loud before drawing it on paper, or write it down in the margins of the drawing.

Nursery rhymes provide excellent examples of story beats since they are the bare bones of story with no extraneous material. Generally, each line of a rhyme will describe one story beat. Here is an example of a couplet with three distinct story beats:

*Yesterday upon the stair, I met a man who wasn't there.* (Beat 1)

*He wasn't there again today.* (Beat 2)

*I wish, I wish he'd go away!* (Beat 3)

We receive the following information about the characters and settings:

- The action takes place in one location over a period of two days.
- The 'man who wasn't there' disturbs the narrator in some way.
- One character is a man.

No other information is given. We do not know the time period, who or what the narrator is, or what type of building the 'stair' appears in. Staging the action upon an exterior stair rather than an interior one would completely change the story.

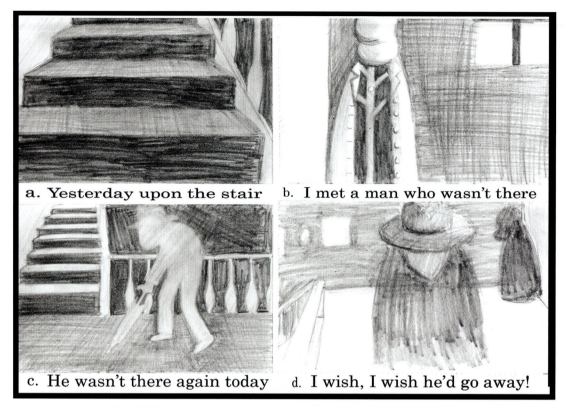

a. Yesterday upon the stair    b. I met a man who wasn't there

c. He wasn't there again today    d. I wish, I wish he'd go away!

**[Fig. 12-5] These beat boards have one line of the rhyme printed under each panel on a separate slip of paper. Modular construction enables you to reposition the slips to indicate changed timing of visuals or dialogue. Reproduced by permission of Sarah Kropiewnicki.**

The beats for this story are already worked out for you. The next step is creating thumbnails of the location—interior stair, exterior stair, how lighting can indicate the passage of the two days, do we see the narrator or is a subjective camera used? Go with the most interesting results. The simplest staging is usually the best. Figure 12-5 shows sample thumbnails for the "Man Who Wasn't There" beat boards.

Once the thumbnails have been worked out, more elaborate beat boards are drawn up. Blank 4 × 6 inch index cards make excellent storyboard panels. You can get them in colors to help depict emotions and lighting.

It is extremely important that the action be readable. Work with the four values of gray tones and make sure that the boards read from the requisite distance of 10-15 feet.

Test your tonal values to be sure that they are reading well. If the values are too close, they may run together and make it difficult to see the action; if they are too far apart, you may have a variety of centers of interest on the same board that makes it difficult to establish where the eye is supposed to look first.

View the boards upside down, in reverse, and through narrowed eyes. (This last trick lowers the contrast and enables you to see if the values are reading separately or running together.)

You should now be able to find the major developments in your own stories and create beat boards to illustrate them. Your *first beat* will introduce the setting and characters. Your *second beat* can introduce a problem or obstacle that the characters must deal with. Your *third beat* might show a twist that develops when they try to deal with the problem. The *final beat* will be the resolution of the problem, or the end of the story. In a short film, you may not have more than three or four beats. Longer productions will have more beats. Remember, any little details of acting and characterization are worked out at a later period. Beat boards are a visual synopsis of the story, not the finished storyboard.

> More than one set of beat boards can be created to tell the story from different characters' perspectives. Now is the time to experiment with story interpretation. This book stages THE THREE BEARS from Papa Bear's viewpoint. How would the story change if Baby Bear's, Mama Bear's, or Goldilocks' viewpoint was used instead? The Eye lines, camera angles, and action would differ greatly.

Not every film will end on a high note. Examples of films with downbeat or bittersweet endings include THE TRIPLETS OF BELLEVILLE by Sylvain Chomet, ANNA AND BELLA by Borge Ring, ONE FROGGY EVENING by Chuck Jones, and THE GUARD DOG by Bill Plympton. Your story and characters will dictate your ending. Just be sure that you *have* an ending. Design the finale in beat board stage so that you do not wind up having the picture simply come to a stop. It is okay to use more than one board for each beat if the story point reads better as a result.

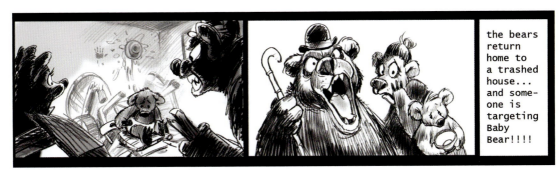

**[Fig. 12-6] Two panels may be used to illustrate a story beat. It is not good to use too many at this stage since the beat board describes the basic outline of the story. Details of acting and timing will be determined later.**

Once you have created beat boards for your story, you are ready for your first *pitch,* or presentation before an audience. A beat board enables you to show, and tell, the basic story *(pitch it)* to an audience in a compact form and receive immediate feedback on whether your storytelling is working.

A great way to test the readability of your beat board is to have *someone else* pitch it for you. If they cannot understand what is going on, the boards are not working. A good beat board should read instantly to everyone.

Storyboard panels can be mounted on sheets of foam core or pinned on bulletin boards. Make sure that the panels are reading from 10-15 feet away, and write a short description of the story point on a separate card. They are generally pinned to the right of the panel so that the artwork 'reads' before the description.

Use a pointer to indicate each board as you *pitch* it to friends and colleagues. (A ruler or wooden dowel works well. Laser pointers can be distracting and are not recommended.) Describe the actions in the scene and act out the character parts as you point to each panel. You may read from the descriptive cards or embellish the printed descriptions if you feel that this will help your presentation. Acting is important! "Perform" the different parts and vary your vocal intonation to bring the characters to life. (Storyboard pitches are discussed in more detail in Chapter 18.)

Note the reactions of your auditors during and after the pitch. Did they understand everything in the story? Were they able to follow your pitch? You may find that everything is reading well, in which case I congratulate you. More typically, you will have to redraw some panels to improve or clarify the story. Don't worry if some drawings need to be changed at this point. It is better to nip potential story problems in the bud so that you won't have to rework the boards later on after hundreds of drawings have been done.

Beat boards are your first story checkpoint. The story beats build the framework of your film and create the story's setting and conflicts. They tell us who the characters are, what they want, and what happens to them. Story beats are like the foundation of a house. You can't build a lasting structure on a bad foundation. Get a strong story now so as to prevent collapse later on.

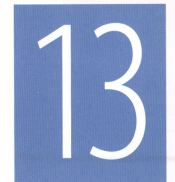

# The Big Picture: Creating Story Sequences

It's now time to start refining your story by breaking it down into sequences. Beat boards give you the *plot* of the story. Sequences add *subplots* and give a film structure. They enable filmmakers to vary the pace of the storytelling, develop the characters' personalities, and create realistic production timetables. Feature directors sometimes work as a team handling alternating sequences to help simplify the film's production.

Feature animation stories are commonly divided into three *acts* defined by the beat boards:

➤ Act I. Introduction of the characters and their conflict.

➤ Act II. Complication of the situation and a setback for the hero.

➤ Act III. Resolution of the conflict.

Each act is broken down into sequences by the *Story Head* and the director(s). Character development and story are fleshed out. More than one sequence may be used to illustrate the same story point. Storyboards will be redrawn and sequential order may be changed. Existing scripts will be rewritten to incorporate revisions made on the boards as a verbal story is transformed into a visual one.

A sequence is *a series of related scenes illustrating a story beat*. A beat board is like a storybook. The important story points are conveyed in one or two illustrations. Several story points may be conveyed in one illustration. In animated film, several sequences may illustrate one story beat. Figure 13-1 would illustrate two different sequences if the story was produced as an animated film.

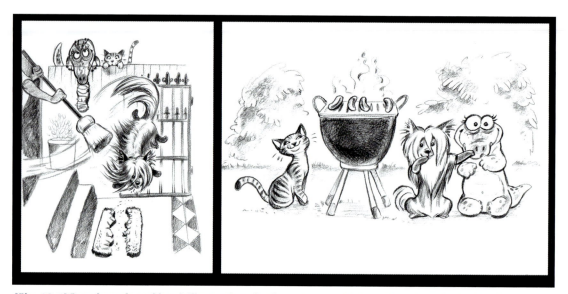

**[Fig. 13-1] Beat boards and book illustrations both portray multiple actions in a single drawing. Illustration from *Duffy and the Invisible Crocodile* by Nancy Beiman, reproduced by permission of Patricia Bernard.**

A sequence can take place in a single location (for example, in Grandma's house).

A sequence can also be a *series of scenes in different locations that illustrate the same story point* (as in a dream sequence or action sequence). Animated sequences may go into production while other sections of the film are still being storyboarded. This is why it is desirable to solidly map out your main plot and character arcs in the beat board phase, so that your sequence details and subplots will fit within the larger structure. A short film may consist of only one sequence or be divided into one or two sequences depending on the story. Animation is produced like a patchwork quilt: small pieces make up the whole. It would be difficult if not impossible to complete a feature on time and on budget were it not divided into sequences.

# Panels and Papers:
# A Word About Story Board Materials

Television storyboards illustrate the script. There is no time in the schedule to allow the board artist to experiment with different approaches to the material. Everything has to be right the first time. Television and commercial boards are drawn comic-strip style with more than one panel on a page and camera moves indicated as shown in Figure 13-2, since the story and setting do not change much from script to final film.

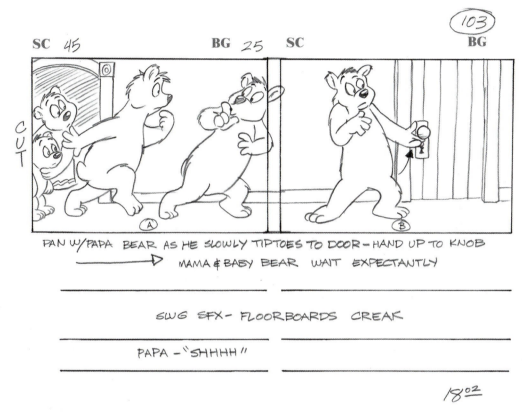

[Fig. 13-2] A television animation storyboard has special panels for the picture, the action description, and the soundtrack. Several panels usually appear on one page. Reproduced by permission of Nelson Rhodes.

The storyboard *is the 'script'* of the feature film. Feature boards are drawn on separate panels since they may be re-pinned in different order during a turnover session. This cannot be done if more than one drawing appears on a page. Blank index cards work very well, but any blank pad may be used for storyboards in a pinch.

Feature board artists are allowed to rewrite or add new dialogue if it helps the scene. Dialogue is written on separate cards and pinned beneath the story panels. The dialogue can be shifted to a different character or cut if the action reads well without it. The modular approach works equally well with short personal films. Work with individual boards and sticky notes and plan for change. (There will always be changes!)

# Acting Out: Structuring Your Sequences

A feature film is divided into acts that are divided into sequences. Some animated features are composed of sequences that are actually discrete short films based on a common theme. Examples of this type of film include Walt Disney's FANTASIA, Bruno Bozzetto's ALLEGRO NON TROPPO, and Bill Plympton's THE TUNE. The omnibus film eliminates the need for a continuing storyline.

Different moods, characters, and techniques may be used in one film. Each short film will contain its own sequential structure. Film titles will sometimes have a separate sequence number if animation begins before or plays under the main credits. Here are fictional sequences and numbers from Act I of the animated feature THE STRANGE CASE OF THE THREE BEARS.  All sequences in an animated feature film are given descriptive names as well as numbers. The names are written down in sequential order before storyboarding begins. Naming a sequence gives the director and story artist a description of its action. This enables them to see the film's structure and pace the story without having to view all of the storyboards simultaneously.

Sequence numbers will change if they are edited into the film in different order than originally planned. Decimal points are added if a new sequence is inserted between two older ones. A sequence may be renumbered (with its "OLD" number retained in parentheses) but its name will remain consistent throughout the production so as to avoid confusion. The decimal point in Sequence 1.5 indicates that it was added between Sequences 1 and 2 at a later date. The "OLD" number is retained since it is possible that Sequence 1.5 could be put back in its original order and renumbered as Sequence 4.1. Sequence 4.5 was also added after the main sequences were numbered. Note that Sequences 2 and 7 are O.O.P., or "out of picture." Sequences are not renumbered when one is edited out. The finished film will cut from Sequence 1.5 to Sequence 3 and from Sequence 6 to Sequence 8.

Do these sequence names describe the action? How many sequences illustrate each of the story beats depicted in Figures 12-4 in Chapter 12? Which sequences might be cut without harming the story?

# Production A113: "THE STRANGE CASE OF THE THREE BEARS"

## *ACT I:*

Sequence 1: The Bears' Bad Breakfast

Sequence 1.5: Bearly Remembered (Old Sequence 4.1)

Sequence 2: OOP

Sequence 3: Goldilocks Breaks into the House

Sequence 3.5: Goldilocks' Golden Memories

Sequence 4: The Chairs Are There

Sequence 4.5 Jolly Happy Bear Song

Sequence 5: Bedtime for Goldilocks

Sequence 6: The Bears Head Home (Jolly Happy Bear Song II)

Sequence 7: OOP

Sequence 8: The Creep Sleeping in My Bed

Sequence 9: Goldilocks Escapes

Figure 13-3 illustrates Sequence 1, **"The Bears' Bad Breakfast,"** which introduces the main characters and their conflicts. The action in the sequence takes place at a specific time and place with a set group of characters and illustrates one idea. It introduces our heroes and is therefore essential to the story.

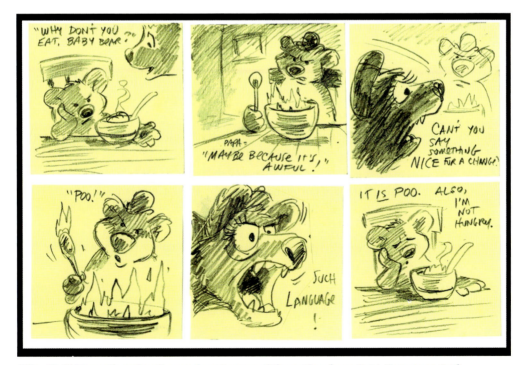

**[Fig. 13-3] These thumbnails rough out some of the action from Act I, Sequence 1 of THE STRANGE CASE OF THE THREE BEARS.**

Figure 13-4 is an excerpt from Act I, Sequence 1.5, "Bearly Remembered," where Papa Bear has a flashback to his troubled past. This is an example of a subplot that leads to character conflict—Papa Bear and Goldilocks have met before! The action takes place in a new location and introduces a new character. The decimal point indicates that the flashback sequence was added to the story after the main sequences were boarded and its old number, 4.1, tells us that it formerly appeared at a later point in the film.

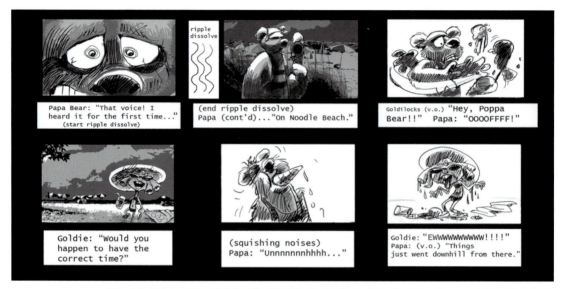

[Fig. 13-4] Sequence 1.5 is a flashback that takes place in more than one location but all drawings illustrate the same story point. Backgrounds can be drawn on the first panel of each scene and eliminated once the character relationships are established.

Sequence 2 is out of the picture (O.O.P.). Sequence 3 takes place in the same location as Sequence 1. A different sequence number and name is used since the action takes place later in the film and a new story idea is introduced.

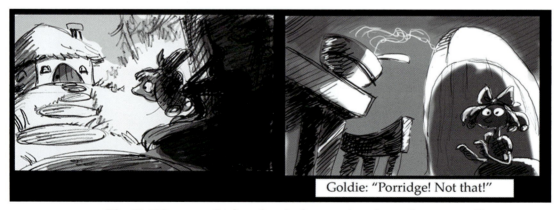

[Fig. 13-5] Sequence 3 takes place in the same location as Sequence 1. The same backgrounds and props will be used for both sequences.

Simple descriptive names indicate each sequence's content and story point. A sequence's name is usually a clever pun. This makes the name easy to remember even if the memory creates the occasional shudder.

It does not matter which type of names you choose for your sequences, since they will never appear in the finished production. The names simply indicate what the sequences are about. Identifying each sequence by name and number will be very helpful to you whether you are on a long production containing two dozen of them, or a short one with three or four. Sequences often go into production out of sequential order. The names and numbers keep artistic materials organized and keep the crew informed about the story's twists and turns. Sequences are prioritized with an A-B-C system since some might be edited out after storyboards are completed (there are two OOP sequences in the outline for the Three Bears feature).

# A-B-C-Sequences: Prioritizing the Action

Each sequence is assigned a letter "A," "B," or "C" to indicate its importance to the story. The "A" sequences *are essential to the story* and often have the most extensive and complex action. They are boarded first. The "B" sequences are still important but are less difficult to board and animate. The "B" sequences may go into production before the "A" sequences gets out of pre-production. The "C" sequences may be edited out without damaging the story. "C" sequences are put into production last so that they may be cut from the film if time or money runs out. The same prioritization is used for scenes within the sequences.

## KNOW YOUR A-B-C's

- An "A" scene/sequence is an essential story point that *must be* in the film and cannot be eliminated.

- A "B" scene/sequence is also important, but it can be shortened or restaged if time and budget require it.

- A "C" scene/sequence is one that contains material that may be amusing but not essential. It can be cut without compromising the story.

Label your sequences and scenes and work on them in order of importance. Prioritization ensures that the important story points are finished. Inessential sequences may be cut so that the film can be completed on time.

Character relationships are set up in Act 1 of the feature-length story. Act 2 (conflict), which opens with Sequence 10, provides an opposing figure (or villainess) as Goldilocks and her crony Little Red Riding Hood team up to blackmail Papa Bear, who has been eating Baby Bear's just-right porridge for years and blaming the theft on Goldilocks. Act 3 (climax and resolution) shows the Bears' climactic struggle to defeat the Goldilocks gang. Papa admits to his faults so that Justice may triumph. When it does, they all go out for a pizza. Please note: *There is no formula for animated film stories*. Use this structure as a guideline only!

# Arcs and Triumphs

A 'big picture' view of the film will help you develop the hero's *character arc*.

A character arc is created when the story's action changes the hero in some way by the end of the film. Character arcs can be described in the original *outline* for the film. In this book's version of THE THREE BEARS, Papa Bear blames Goldilocks for the theft of Baby Bear's porridge when he is the one who's been secretly eating it. At the end of the picture, Papa Bear admits his character weakness and overcomes his fears to defeat the menacing Goldilocks. (Mama Bear probably learns to be a better cook!)

Characters that do not grow and change as the story progresses tend to be flat, one-note creations with little depth, as depicted in Figure 13-6.

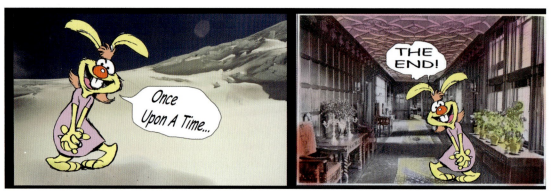

[Fig. 13-6] A hero without a character arc remains unchanged from start to finish. This may not keep the viewer interested in his story.

Breaking your story down into sequences helps you analyze the rhythm of your film and develop the characters' personalities over time. Storyboards for large portions of a feature film (and all of a short film) may be viewed simultaneously. Changes can be made on the spot. The original story structure may need revision if several action sequences and song sequences appear consecutively or too many sequences are set in the same location. The modular storyboards make this relatively simple to do.

Each storyboard artist must be familiar with the story outline and know how the characters develop. On longer film projects the story staff periodically views work-in-progress on boards or on reels, so that story points and gags are not inadvertently repeated. If the artist does not know what happens before and after his/her sequence, the character's performance may be inconsistent throughout the picture. A rather exaggerated example appears in the next figure.

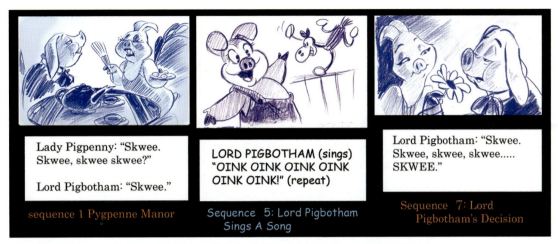

Lady Pigpenny: "Skwee. Skwee, skwee skwee?"

Lord Pigbotham: "Skwee."

LORD PIGBOTHAM (sings) "OINK OINK OINK OINK OINK OINK!" (repeat)

Lord Pigbotham: "Skwee. Skwee, skwee, skwee..... SKWEE."

sequence 1 Pygpenne Manor

Sequence 5: Lord Pigbotham Sings A Song

Sequence 7: Lord Pigbotham's Decision

**[Fig. 13-7] Story artists sometimes work in isolation. It's very important to know what happens before and after their sequence so that it fits into the context of the picture.**

Feature animators often thumbnail character actions and staging for all the scenes in a sequence at once so that the acting remains consistent throughout even if the scenes are animated out of order. If the animator has an understanding of the story and the character, it is possible to come back to a sequence put on hold months earlier without making it obvious that portions of it were animated at different times. My animation of the Fates in HERCULES was put on hold after a few scenes were completed while another part of the sequence underwent storyboard revisions. I was able to keep the 'actresses' in character when I returned to the Fates sequence seven months later because I had first thumbnailed the action for every scene after viewing the story reel and the storyboards for the sequences preceding and following the Fates. I was able to tailor my animation so that it fit into the film's context.

The script or outline will be rewritten to incorporate modifications made on the storyboard as sequences are developed. Walt Disney Studio story man Floyd Norman describes how THE JUNGLE BOOK changed between outline and storyboard:

"The guys [in the story department] would just kick around a lot of ideas. Larry Clemmons was our official writer. What Larry would do was put together an outline of the way a sequence might "play." Then this rough script outline was handed out to the story artists who would take it and embellish it. Everything was wide open. We would try anything. It wasn't structured and no one was saying "You can't do this or that." [Vance Gerry and I] were given Mowgli and the snake [sequence] and so we started working out some gag ideas. The first version of THE JUNGLE BOOK as envisioned by Bill Peet was a much darker film. This was not to Walt Disney's taste. We really just took the story and redid it. When we showed it to Walt he liked it and said, "Do more with this." He had the Sherman brothers write a song ("*Trust in Me*"). People still talk about it. We had no idea the film was that good! You never know. I guess the audience tells you."

(Interview with Nancy Beiman, August 29, 2000)

## Naming Names

Characters in animated film, including incidentals, receive names for precisely the same reason that sequences do. If a scene contains multiple characters it is far easier to direct action on "Julie and Steve" than "the pink fish with the blue eyes" and "the octopus with the bowtie and moustache" since there may be more than one moustached, bowtie-wearing octopus in a scene, as shown in Figure 13-8.

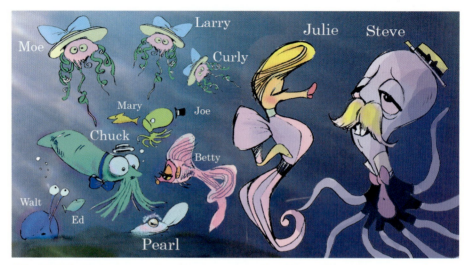

[Fig. 13-8] Animated characters have names so that it is easier to direct the action in scenes involving more than one character. "Julie and Steve" may never have their names mentioned in the film. The incidental characters in the scene are also named.

An animated film will usually have story development and story revisions occurring simultaneously. Breaking the picture into sequences helps keep the characters, the story, and the filmmaker's head pointed in the right direction.

Now that you have named and numbered your sequences and characters and determined your characters' arcs you are ready to stick in your thumbs—thumbnail drawings, that is—to stage the action and acting for each sequence. But things are going to get *rough!*

# 14

# Patterns in Time: Pacing Action on Rough Boards

"Time is an illusion. Lunchtime doubly so."
—Douglas Adams, *The Hitchhiker's Guide to the Galaxy*

Time seems to slow to a crawl and stop when you are listening to a dull speaker. A short lecture given in a monotone can appear to last for hours rather than a few minutes.

Conversely, a good speaker who varies his or her inflection and pacing can make a long speech fly by and leave the audience wanting more. I once auditioned an actress for a narrator's role in a film I was directing. Since I wanted the character to have a sexy voice but didn't want the actress' choice of material to influence my decision, I requested that she read distinctly 'un-sexy' material for the audition. The actress found an ex-

tremely dull exterminator's treatise on the life cycle of the bedbug and declaimed it in a breathy, Marilyn-Monroe style voice that reduced the crew to hysterics. She got the part.

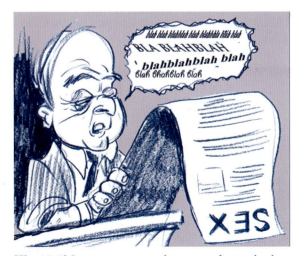

There is an old saying that it's not what you do, but how you do it. Good timing and good delivery can make a scientific analysis of insect pests interesting, while monotonous droning speech can make a fascinating subject seem dull to the listener.

**[Fig. 14-1] A monotonous voice can make a gripping topic seem dull.**

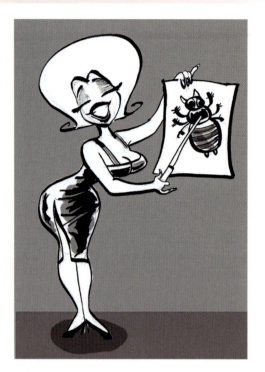

**[Fig. 14-2] Varied and well-paced verbal and visual delivery can generate audience interest in a plebian subject.**

Film has a language, a vocabulary, and structure. A film's editing and pacing can correspond to natural pauses and punctuation in human speech. Evenly-paced visual rhythms can be just as monotonous as speech that lacks inflection.

Animation storyboards cannot simply set up the shot the way live-action boards do. Animation boards will block in every aspect of the character's performance. Consider them rehearsals for the animated action. A new storyboard is added when any of the elements listed in Figures 14-3, 14-4, 14-5, or 14-6 change.

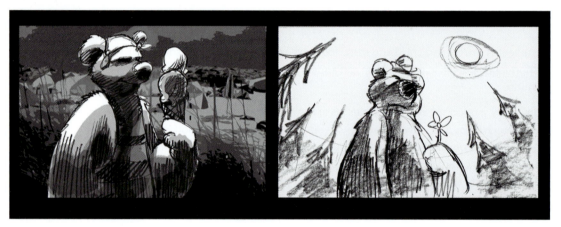

**[Fig. 14-3] Change of Scene.**

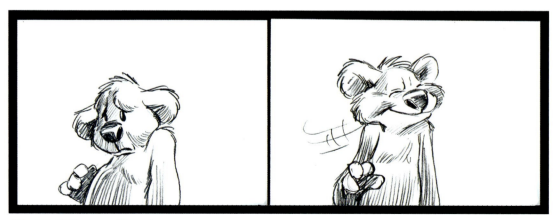

**[Fig. 14-4] Change of Emotion.**

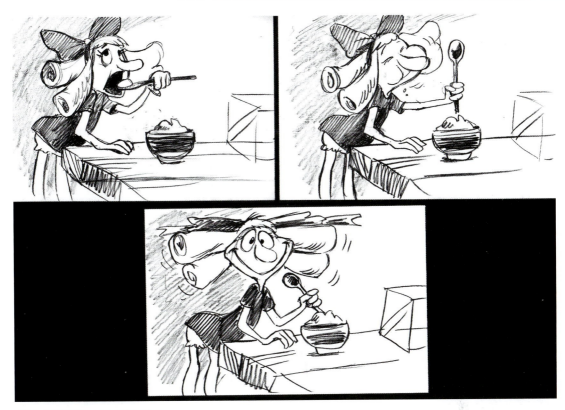

[Fig. 14-5] **Change of Action.**

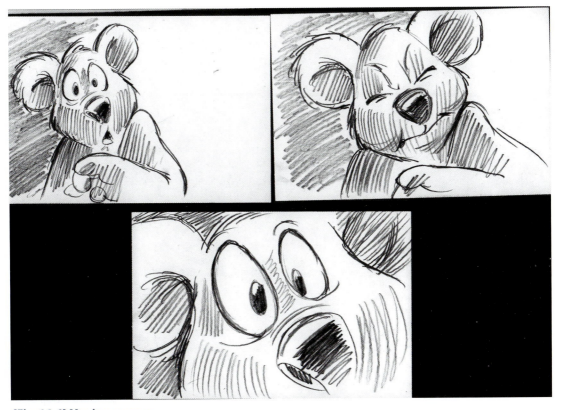

[Fig. 14-6] **Moving camera.**

Action sequences will use many storyboard drawings to choreograph progressive character and camera moves in minute detail. Spontaneous-looking actions and 'quick cuts' must be planned well in advance. A flashback or montage sequence may include scenes set in a variety of locations featuring many different characters. The scenes work in combination to illustrate one theme.

Acting is also blocked in storyboard. Important changes of attitude and expression are storyboarded to help guide the animator in his or her performance. There is no serendipity in animation preproduction. Figure 14-7 shows thumbnail drawings for fast action.

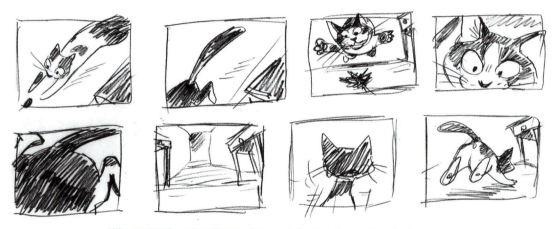

[Fig. 14-7] Thumbnails may be used for staging action before going to full-sized boards. Action sequences will need more storyboards than most other sequences.

While the animated film's final timing and pacing is created when the boards are *up on reels* (assembled into story reels with soundtrack), it does not begin there. These pictures not only tell the story, they make the movie. Timing and pacing are created on the storyboards by varying camera angles and cuts. Scenes may 'play' short or long depending on the story point that is being made and staging that is used to convey it.

Figure 14-8A shows three boards with identical staging. They give the impression that the pacing of the action is just as dull. Perhaps the characters could have moved around more—but even a simple conversation can convey deeper meaning if a variety of shots are used as shown in the second example. The camera angle and perspective in Figure 14-8B are caricatured along with the characters.

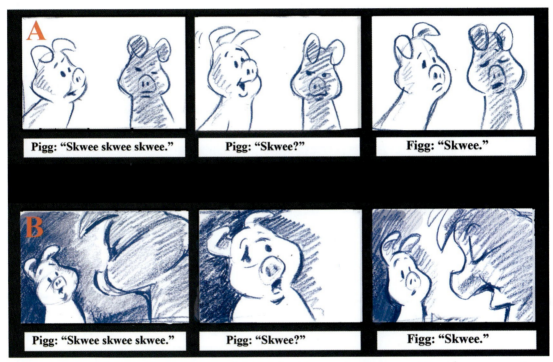

| Pigg: "Skwee skwee skwee." | Pigg: "Skwee?" | Figg: "Skwee." |
| Pigg: "Skwee skwee skwee." | Pigg: "Skwee?" | Figg: "Skwee." |

[Fig. 14-8] **Unvarying visuals can cause a viewer to lose interest in the story. Different camera angles help the storyboard artist create dramatic tension within a scene. Animated perspective is 'forced' and deliberately exaggerated to create an emotional effect.**

Vance Gerry, the great story artist, wrote that the storyboard artist was only concerned with telling the story. Gerry was of the opinion that the story artist should only present ideas and not concern himself or herself with a cinematic approach to the story, since cinematography was the provenance of the director. In modern productions this rule no longer applies. The industry has changed greatly since Gerry's time, and so the modern storyboard artist should be fully conversant with the language of film. The pigs' acting becomes more compelling when they are given props to work with and staging that helps establish the mood and the setting, as shown in Figure 14-9. A story is being told visually and the dialogue is distinctly secondary to the action!

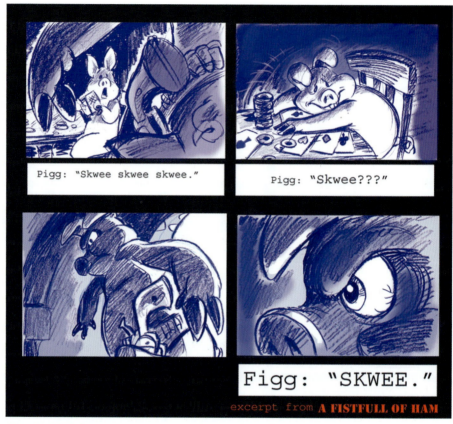

[Fig. 14-9] Dialogue scenes are more interesting when characters have something to do. Props and camera angles help set the scene's atmosphere. Animated camera angles are more caricatured than the angles used for live action boards.

*Workbook,* an intermediary stage between boards and layout, was created in the mid-1980s when live-action producers first came into the animation studios. They found traditional rough-and-ready storyboards too hard to read. In workbook, layout artists redraw the storyboards to *tie down* camera and character moves and make the boards more cinematic. Workbook contains a rougher version of the camera *fielding* seen in television storyboards.  Figure 14-10 shows two workbook sketches for a camera move.

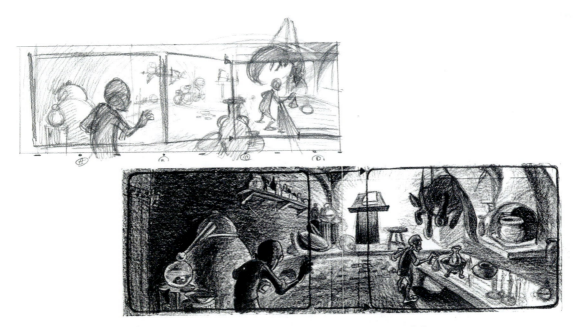

[Fig. 14-10] A workbook sketch from MAGIC by Adam Fox. A camera truck is indicated along with (a) and (b) (starting and ending) fields. Background and foreground elements are carefully composed to frame the character's actions. The workbook is designed shot-by-shot after boards are finalized. Reproduced by permission of Adam Fox.

Workbook resembles television boarding since it contains recognizable backgrounds and detailed camera moves. It is a form of layout and hence falls outside the scope of this book, but keep in mind that while some projects might accept quick, rough 'acting' boards and leave the final background and staging to the layout department, the story man or woman is usually required to indicate camera angles and cuts. If you are making your own short film, you may *be* the layout and story departments. Composing the camera, characters, and background objects in the panel makes it easier to follow the continuity, particularly in action scenes. It will also add dimension to your characters' acting and make it easier to convey important elements in the story.

Stage your action in *thumbnail* sketches before proceeding to final storyboard. Thumbnails can be done on one sheet of paper. The story artist roughs out many small sketches to find the most effective staging for the action in a scene or sequence. The action sequence may use more *pencil mileage*, but you will find that the sequences with emotional depth and acting will be most difficult to do. Sometimes less is more in these instances. Final boards are drawn after the thumbnails establish the staging.

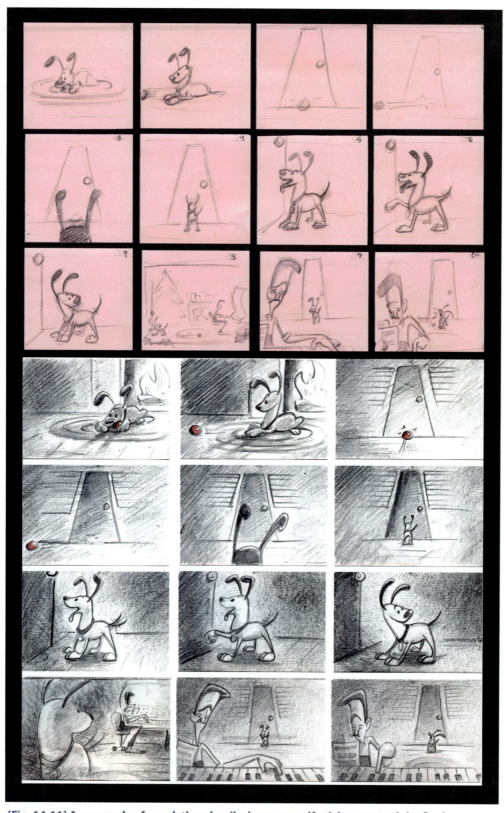

[Fig. 14-11] An example of rough thumbnails drawn on self-stick notes and the final storyboards for the same shots. Reproduced by permission of Brittney Lee.

A recent and very effective tool for the story man or woman is the simple self-stick notepad. These pads come in a variety of sizes and colors and enable the artist to create modular 'mini-boards' without the need for pins or large display spaces. Different colored notes can suggest light and mood changes. It is possible to display the thumbnails for an entire sequence in a very small area. The sticky pages are easily replaced or removed and can be arranged in different order with little effort. There is no need to scratch out or cut up thumbnails that were created on the same page. After the rough staging is finalized, full-sized storyboard drawings are worked up from the thumbnails as shown in Figure 14-11.

A background may be drawn only on the first panel of a scene and left blank on subsequent panels. If the shot is static the viewer will understand that the remaining panels of the scene take place in the same location. Details are added to later panels if the character moves to another location in the scene or interacts with background or foreground elements. A pan shot needs some indication of the background on every panel so that the camera move reads well.

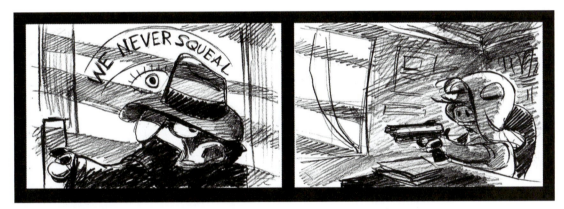

[Fig. 14-12] **Background indications are drawn in each panel of a pan shot to indicate that the camera is in motion.**

Storyboard panels should contain only one idea per panel. If a scene is complex and involves a good deal of acting or action, panels are added as needed. Here is an example of how the same action can be boarded to appear short or long. The thumbnails in figure 14-13 are a brief indication of the action in the scene.

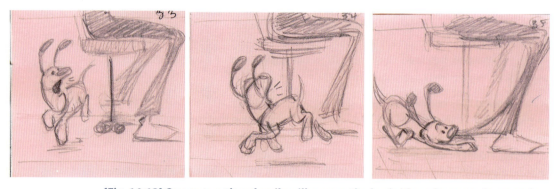

[Fig. 14-13] One or two thumbnails will convey the basic idea of a scene, but not the characters' acting. Reproduced by permission of Brittney Lee.

The next figure depicts the same situation as Figure 14-13 with additional panels added so that the characters' acting reads clearly. As a result this scene appears longer even though the timing for the film may not have changed a bit. Note how even a simple action assumes more importance when illustrated on a series of storyboards.

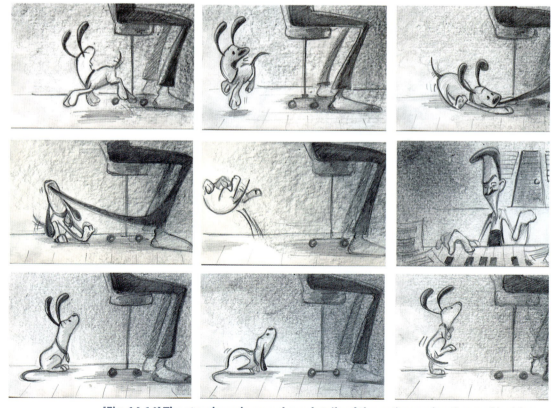

[Fig. 14-14] The storyboards now show details of the action and acting and incidentally slow the pacing of the scene before any animation or filming has been completed. Reproduced by permission of Brittney Lee.

A simple action may be simply staged, as shown in Figure 14-15. There is some hint of Papa Bear's desperation but the action comes before the acting. Four drawings convey the impression of rapid action in a short scene.

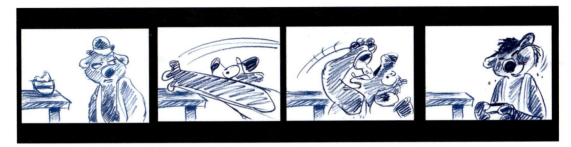

[Fig. 14-15] **Papa Bear's basic action is blocked. The scene is short and direct.**

A larger number of storyboards retimes the action in Figure 14-15 and expands Papa Bear's emotional performance. Papa Bear's desperation builds as he grows bolder and finally breaks down and quickly eats the porridge. The elaborate visuals in Figure 14-16 give the impression of a lengthy scene but the drawings may represent the same amount of time depicted in Figure 14-15's four boards. Final timing is established by the director when the *story reel* or *animatic* is created.

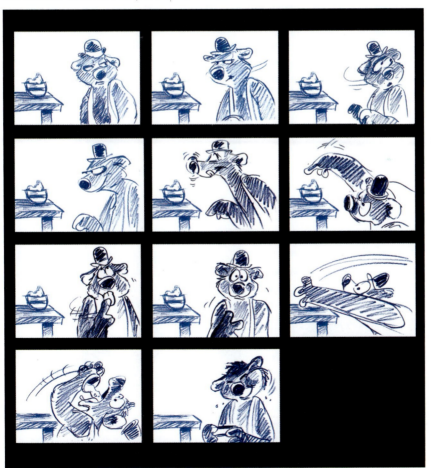

[Fig. 14-16] **Additional storyboards can change the acting even if the timing remains consistent. Papa Bear's acting is now the main focus of the scene.**

Both of these interpretations are acceptable depending on whether the director wants to emphasize the acting or the action in the scene.

*"One must have a heart of stone to read the death of Little Nell without laughing."*

—Oscar Wilde

A dramatic scene can become comic if the timing and pacing are right.

DRIPALONG DAFFY, directed by Chuck Jones, contains a hilarious parody of HIGH NOON. Two gunslingers advance along a Western street. We hear only footsteps and jingling spurs. Jones cuts to one 'artistic' view after another, alternating shots of the endlessly approaching duelists. Each shot is more elaborately framed than the previous one and the camera moves farther and farther away from the actors. Midway through the sequence the audience begins to laugh at the artificially drawn-out timing of the duel and the self-reverential staging. The too-numerous scenes become comic since the 'artistic' angles upstage the action and emphasize the fact that nothing much is going on.

The lengthy buildup to the shoot-out (which never actually takes place) turns drama into comedy. A dramatic acting scene will become comic if the emoting goes on just a little too long. There is a fine line between pathos and bathos that should not be crossed unless the 'emoting' is comic, as shown in Figure 14-17. Hold a dramatic pose too long and it becomes funny. Underplay strong emotional scenes. Provide hints that let the audience understand what is happening. Do not drive an emotional point home with a sledgehammer. Less is more.

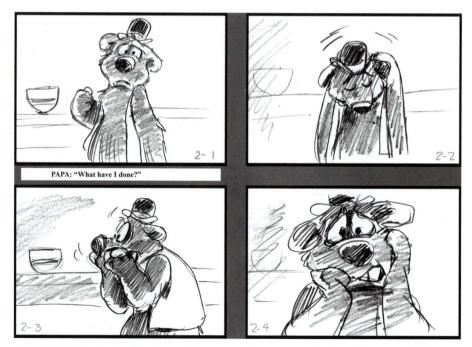

[Fig. 14-17] **Underplaying drama lets the audience participate in the story. If the emoting goes on too obviously for too long, drama can turn into comedy.**

One or two panels may suffice to depict a scene's action if the character's attitude does not change. Figure 14-18 shows thumbnails for a scene that is visually weak. Dialogue is placed on separate cards underneath the panels. Two boards are enough for this scene since the character's attitude or body language does not change during the delivery of the line. The characters are only "talking heads."

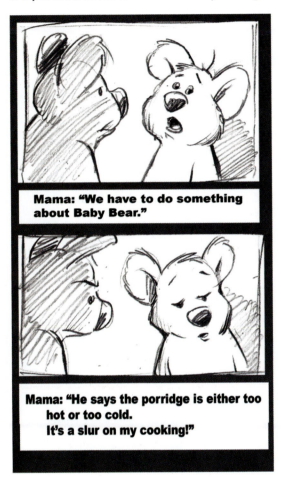

Mama: "We have to do something about Baby Bear."

Mama: "He says the porridge is either too hot or too cold.
It's a slur on my cooking!"

**[Fig. 14-18] A long speech may be depicted on one or two storyboard panels if the character's attitude does not change from the beginning to the end of the scene. This staging is adequate but not very interesting. "Talking heads" should be avoided in long dialogue scenes.**

A new board is used for each attitude change. Figure 14-19 illustrates the same line used in Figure 14-18, but in this interpretation we cut away from the close-up of Mama Bear to Baby Bear and some props. Mama Bear's lengthy dialogue is now indicated as a voice-over in two panels. "Talking heads" quickly become tiresome in animation. These boards give us more insight into the characters' performances and depict more interesting action than the earlier example. Animators will draw out the conflict even more when the characters begin to move.

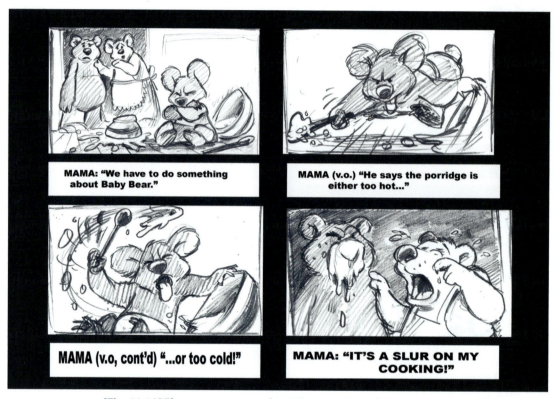

[Fig. 14-19] **The scene now cuts from the complaining parents to the more interesting Baby Bear. The dialogue is spread over several scenes. Two panels are lip synched and two are marked 'V.O.' for 'voice-over'.**

Boards that attempt to depict every key pose in the scene can appear precious and mannered. Figure 14-20 is an example of storyboard overkill or "animating on the storyboards." This board artist is spending a lot of time doing something that is properly the provenance of the animator.

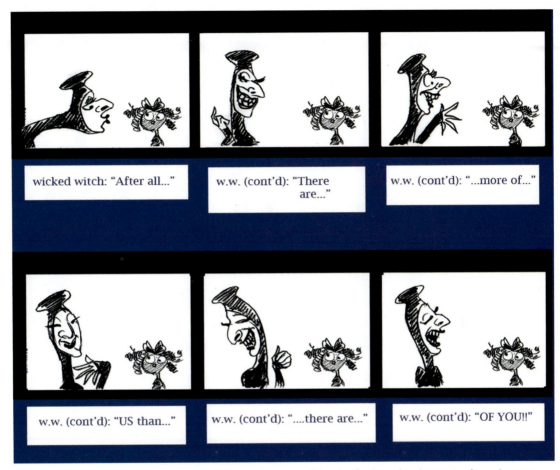

[Fig. 14-20] Six boards for one line of dialogue leave nothing to the imagination or to the animator. When in doubt, it is better to have too many boards than too few, but most will probably be tossed out or turned over during a storyboard review.

Figure 14-16 also uses a series of boards to illustrate action in one scene. There is an important difference between the two examples. Papa Bear's attitude changes during his scene. He is also acting and interacting with a prop. The Wicked Witch's attitude in Figure 14-20 remains consistent throughout the scene. She is not given anything to do except talk. There is no need for the lengthy series of storyboards. The scene works more effectively when the action appears on one panel, as shown in Figure 14-21.

**[Fig. 14-21] Use the minimum number of boards that best convey the action and acting in a scene. The Witch's attitude does not change, so her dialogue can be illustrated on one storyboard panel.**

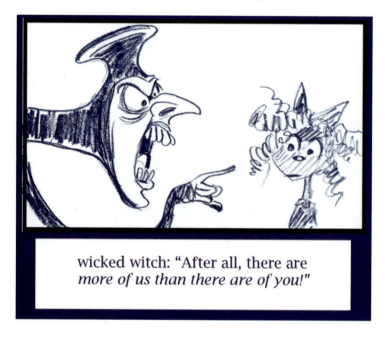

wicked witch: "After all, there are *more of us than there are of you!*"

Remember that dialogue and acting will be modified during the course of the production. If you spent time drawing twenty panels for one line of dialogue when you could have conveyed the action and acting adequately with three or four, you will have much more work to toss out should the scene change. Do not waste time on self-indulgent exercises like the one shown in Figure 14-20.

Storyboard artists use graphic symbols to represent cinematic transitions such as fade-outs and fade-ins, swish pans, and cross dissolves. These symbols are indicated in Figure 14-22. A 'fade-out-fade-in' or a cross-dissolve imply a short passage of time. A fade-to-black will generally indicate a longer interval between sequences. A fade-up from black at the beginning of a sequence helps to gradually introduce your audience to your animated universe. Camera rotations, camera moves, and quick cuts serve as punctuation marks. Do not use them simply for their own sake.

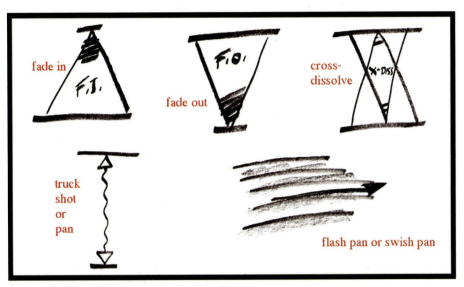

[Fig. 14-22] Cross dissolves, fade-ins, fade-outs, and swish or flash pans are always drawn on separate storyboard panels. This makes it possible to shift or remove them if the storyboard is changed. Use these devices as punctuation marks to pace your action and sequences.

I worked on a film that contained an upbeat song and dance sequence. The story reel was assembled in the style of a live-action music video, with extremely short cuts averaging 12 frames or one-half second in length. The scenes were each illustrated with one storyboard panel. The sequence worked well when the boards were assembled into story reels but proved extremely confusing to watch when it was fully animated. The artists were mystified at first but finally understood that we were victims of visual overload. We viewed one storyboard drawing *per scene* in the story reel, so we were able to absorb the information it contained in very little time. The action became difficult to follow when a dozen animated drawings played in the 12 frames formerly occupied by a single panel. Each shot featured a new background and characters. The song provided story continuity but the quick cuts competed with the rapid-fire lyrics. It officially takes *four frames for the audience to visually register a cut*. This sequence's rapid pacing, constantly changing settings, and complex visuals meant that each shot needed more than four frames to register with the viewer. All of the short scenes were lengthened by an average of 12 frames each so that the sequence would read, and since the song's length remained constant, some scenes had to be cut to accommodate the new edit.

A live-action music video *can* use very short shots. A live-action film's audience does not need time to suspend disbelief and accept the characters as 'real' beings. Music videos are not part of a longer film and do not need to worry about story continuity.

Pace your scenes by using a variety of short and long scenes where required. Use filmic punctuation, such as fades and cross-dissolves, to avoid visual overload. The story must be told in a clear and understandable fashion. There is no set blueprint for a film's construction and interpretations of story materials will vary by filmmaker and culture. Variable pacing will maintain an audience's interest in the story.

# Climactic Events

A feature will build from small climaxes in Act One to stronger ones that illustrate the complications developing in Act Two. The strongest climax will usually occur in Act Three. Think of the story line as a roller-coaster where the twists and turns gradually build toward the biggest thrill just before the recovery at the end of the ride. Figure 14-23 shows a sample chart from the story of *The Three Bears*. A series of small climaxes leads up to the major conflict. The Bears' emotional roller coaster is on a higher level at the end of the sequence than it was at the beginning.

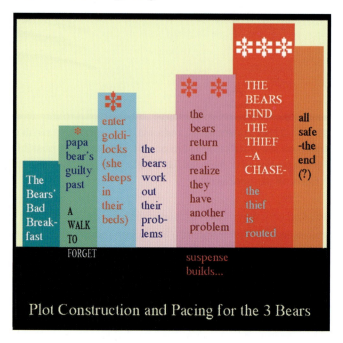

[Fig. 14-23] The story climaxes of THE THREE BEARS gradually become stronger with the strongest climax occurring near the end of the story. The denouement, or summing up of the story, comes after the climax.

Climactic charts are not commonly used in storyboard, but you may find it helpful to sketch one out when plotting an original story. The strongest climax should come just before the story's denouement. If the major conflict occurs in Act Two, the film's third act can literally be anticlimactic. (Some films are constructed in this fashion. Circumstances alter cases.)

A script, if it exists, is a framework on which the story is built. A good story man or woman will *"plus"* written material with visuals that translate verbal descriptions into images. Good boards develop the characters' personalities and the plot in equal measure. Avoid literally illustrating a script. Your visuals may lead you in another direction as they develop. A script suggests dialogue, story outline, and some character traits, but the boards bring these materials to visual fruition.

Storyboard takes a tremendous amount of work but your technique should never show onscreen. Everything in a film should develop from the characters' conflicts and seem to *happen by chance*. If you hit your audience over the head with a story point, it, and they, will ache.

We now come to the climax of the storyboarding process: the creation of the animated performance.

# 15

# Present Tense: Creating a Performance on Storyboards

*"Have a very good reason for everything you do."*

—Sir Laurence Olivier

*"Writing is 1 percent inspiration, and 99 percent elimination."*

—Louise Brooks

You are now ready to begin creating in-depth storyboards that flesh out the acting and actions of the characters. If you are working on your own film, you will have your outline, beat boards, rough character models, and atmosphere sketches completed by this stage and your sequences should be clearly defined.

If you are on a professional production you will most likely be working in a totally different system. A television storyboard artist will be handed a model pack, or *"Bible,"* with all characters, props, and backgrounds already designed. Each artist will be assigned a script for a sequence or for the entire show, and given a deadline to finish boarding it. All characters must be drawn accurately or *on model* and camera moves and background detail must be clearly indicated on the boards.

Feature storyboard artists work as a team or *crew* under a *story head* with each artist handling one sequence of a film or working with a few pages of a script or outline that was written in advance. The story head works out the sequences and beats with the film's directors, creates the beat boards, and decides which artists will board which sequences. Atmospheric sketches and rough character designs may not yet exist. Each artist will work separately from the others but will have some idea of what the rest of the picture is about so that their sequence fits into the story. The story head reviews and approves the thumbnails for each sequence and the artists then draw rough boards that are presented to the directors in a *first pass.* If this goes well, the rough boards may be reworked and detail added, turning them into *presentation boards.* It is far more likely that they will go through many rough revisions before they are finalized. Feature films spend an average of two years in development. Some have taken longer.

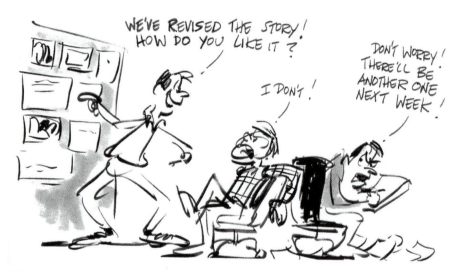

[Fig. 15-1] **Feature films can take a long time to complete if their story problems are not worked out at the beginning of production. Reproduced from *Son of Faster Cheaper* by permission of Floyd Norman.**

Commercial animated films were not always produced this way. In the early days, the story men and women were the writers of the picture. They drew thumbnails of the characters and the staging, wrote story outlines, and then worked their thumbnails up into finished boards. The writers and directors at the Warner Brothers cartoon studio often worked in groups and bounced ideas off one another. Writers such as Mike Maltese and Tedd Pierce would eventually put the witty dialogue for Bugs Bunny and Daffy Duck directly on the storyboards. The final script was written out for the voice artists to read during recording sessions. Walt Disney Studio story man and art director Ken Anderson stated that he would write his own outlines for feature films, sketching the character designs at the same time, and that the storyboard always took precedence over the script. In the instances where a feature began with a writer's treatment, it was not uncommon to have the story change 180 degrees by the time the storyboards were completed. (A transcript of my interview with Ken Anderson is included in Appendix 3.)

The *Story Head* on a modern feature film will act as a "third director," in the words of story head and director Brenda Chapman. The story head has specific responsibilities: he or she will focus entirely on the story, while the directors are responsible for every aspect of the film. The story ideally is a collaborative process, with the writers working directly with the artists and the directors having final approval.

A story head will pick their *crew* of artists, give them their assignments or *handouts*, and ensure that the artists function as a unit. He or she keeps track of each sequence and notifies the crew of developments and changes, sometimes on a daily basis. At times the story head will provide rough thumbnails for the storyboard artist to use, along with a description of the characters' attitudes and acting. Most of the time the artists are given free rein to interpret the material in their own way. Individual artists will be assigned to sequences that play to their particular strength. Some will excel at action scenes while others might be better 'cast' on comedy scenes. Story artists will write or replace dialogue and add "business" that helps flesh out the written material. They may revise the script and create or delete characters if the story seems to require it. Freedom to do this will depend on the production, but the better films I've worked on welcomed constructive change, or *plus-ing,* at this stage of development. Scripts that are set in stone tend to produce weaker films.

When a story man or woman receives an assignment from the Story Head, he or she will first rough out thumbnails to experiment with staging. In Figure 15-2, two different sets of thumbnails have been drawn up for a short sequence. One version is staged in medium shot and the other is staged entirely in close-up. The dialogue is written under each frame. The two interpretations might be combined in the final film.

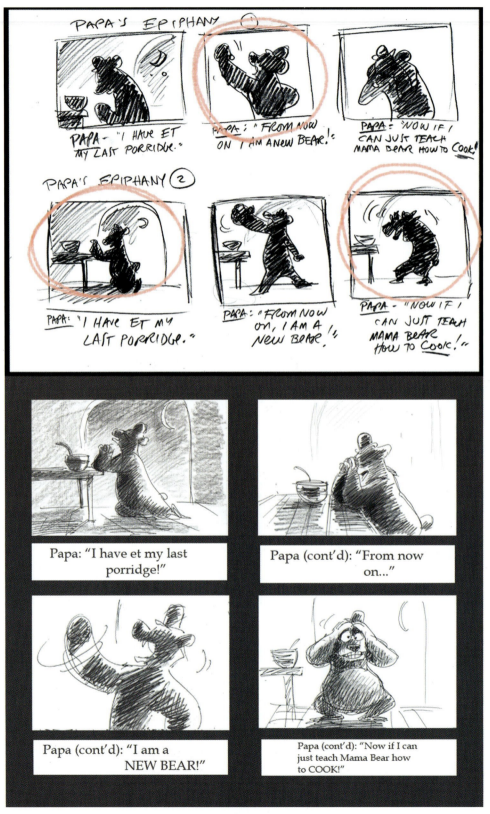

[Fig. 15-2] The sequence is thumbnailed in two alternate views. The final may use elements from both versions.

The story head will review the thumbnails with the storyboard artist. If the story head approves the roughs, a rough storyboard will be created for the director(s). This board will be *pitched* in a *first pass* and changes will be suggested in a *turnover session*. The process will be repeated until the story is acceptable to the directors, at which time the boards may be left *rough* or highly-rendered *presentation boards* may be drawn to replace them, depending on the production and the people involved. Some directors will use extremely rough storyboards and others might require more polished examples for the *story reel*. Storyboard pitches are discussed in detail in Chapter 18 and the story reel is described in Chapter 19.

If the characters have not yet been designed, rough *placeholder* characters as shown in Chapter 10, Figure 10-1, are used on the boards. The storyboard artist will have a major influence on the final appearance of the characters since they are drawing the acting that will be required in the film. Storyboard drawings that best convey the characters' personality and typical actions are frequently copied and pasted up into model suggestion or *action-model-only* sheets. Character designers and animators receive copies of these suggestions as a reference guide. The drawings and designs will be refined and standardized as the rough model sheets are created but the action sheets can be used for acting reference by the animators all through the picture.

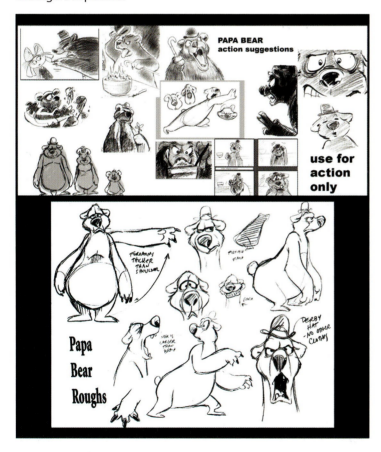

**[Fig. 15-3] Storyboard sketches are selected for expressiveness and pasted up into an action-model-only sheet. This may be used as reference by the animator all through the picture since it conveys Papa Bear's acting range very well. The model sheets will try to retain the spirit of the storyboard drawings even if the character's final design bears little resemblance to the storyboard sketches.**

Portions of the script will be rewritten if the material is not working successfully on the storyboards. If there is a major story change, the art direction and character design may also have to be reworked.

A good story artist is open to change, since this is the one thing that is guaranteed to happen on all productions. The story man or woman has to know what to change so that the story baby is not thrown out with the bathwater. Sequences will be deleted if they no longer work, and will be replaced by new ones that may be replaced in turn. It is essential that the storyboard artist not take the reworking or deletion of his or her art personally. Storyboard is about change. There is nothing wrong with changing your drawings. It's highly unlikely that any storyboard will get it right the first time and it's not uncommon to have to redo entire boards if the story artist's vision does not coincide with that of the directors.

An original story is hardest to storyboard. Fairy tales have a basic story that is already worked out; original stories must find their own way. When the story is not yet set, some sequences will be experimental. Storyboard artists will thumbnail many rough sequences and much of this material will go unused in the final film. But, as with all animated work, it is best to change the story while the film is still in development rather than try to make repairs later on. Changes to animated films become more expensive the later they occur in production. Some films have had their entire stories changed when they were well into animation. Years of work and a good portion of the budget were wasted. If the story is well conceived and develops in a believable fashion, much heartache and waste may be avoided. But it is essential for the directors, producers, and story head to agree on what they are trying to say.

It is a common practice to hire "name" actors to do the character voices, caricature them in the character designs, and assume that the audience's recognition of the voices will carry the film. This can be a "crutch" in the opinion of story man Ken Anderson. Or, it can add genuine depth to the character. Jiminy Cricket, Cruella de Vil, and Shere Khan's final designs were based on caricatures of the actors who did their voices.

 "It's a dangerous situation to get into, basing a whole conception of character around a voice talent," says director John Musker. "We did write [the Genie in ALADDIN] for Robin Williams, not knowing whether he would do the voice or not" (interview by Nancy Beiman in *CARTOONIST PROfiles*, no. 97, March 1993). Had Robin Williams not been available, the part would have been rewritten, although the basic story of ALADDIN would not have been affected. Voice acting is 50 percent of the animated performance, but the visuals and the story construction should be supplemented by the soundtrack, not the other way around. A strong animated story and good characters will carry the picture so that its success does not depend on audience recognition of celebrity voice talents.

# Working with Music

Animation and music go together like peanut butter and jelly. The popular cliché of the animator is that of the frustrated actor. I maintain that we are frustrated *dancers*—we work out story in motion, like ballerinas, though in most cases without the tutus. A good *scratch track* will help you time your action when you are assembling your *story reels* or *animatics*. This is discussed in Chapter 19.

Animated musicals have been with us since the beginning of sound film. What makes the good ones work? The secret is this: the songs don't just "happen." You will find that the songs in successful animated musical films fall on major *story beats* or turning points in the story and help to advance it. Songs can describe the characters' dreams and motivations or comment on the action. Poorly-timed songs can stop a story dead in its tracks. Remember to never lose sight of your story. Never have someone burst into song just 'because they can' unless you are doing a parody of a movie musical.

Use a few boards to illustrate one or two lines of a song in the sequence just as you do when creating beat boards from story outlines. Songs, like poems, have recognizable beats that can be translated into visuals. If you are working with instrumental music, synchronize the action to the musical beats.

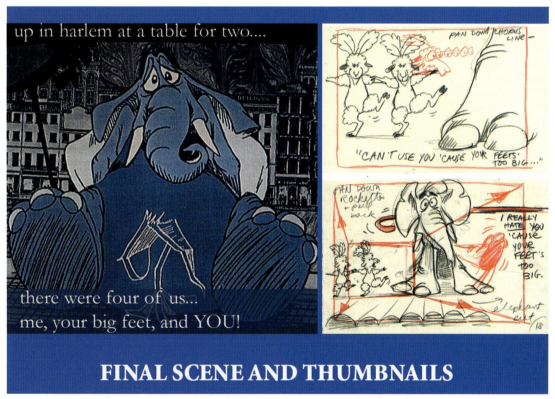

**[Fig. 15-4] My film YOUR FEET'S TOO BIG was edited to the witty song lyrics by "Fats" Waller and to the rhythm of the music.**

# Visualizing the Script

So what does a story artist do when they are handed a couple of pages of a script? A feature film *may* have a script at an early stage, though it will be subject to change depending on what develops on the boards. Let us use a familiar story to illustrate one way of adapting a written script to a storyboard. Here is a short excerpt from a hypothetical script based on the Sherlock Holmes story *The Adventure of the Abbey Grange* by A. Conan Doyle.

SEQ. 1.1 (HOLMES, WATSON)

DARKNESS.

FADE UP and PAN to a gaslight that illuminates the frame as a hansom cab pulls up in front of a dark building. It is 2 A.M. on a rainy London night in 1897.

SHERLOCK HOLMES:

Stop here, driver.

The cab comes to a stop and SHERLOCK HOLMES rushes rapidly out the open door.

EXT. 221B BAKER STREET—NIGHT

Lightning illuminates the house number as we hear a door slam.

INT: WATSON'S BEDROOM—A FEW MOMENTS LATER

The room is in near-total darkness. There is an indistinct figure in a bed. Rapid steps advance upon the stairs and a door bursts open. A figure with a candle stands in the doorway for a moment, contemplating the scene.

SHERLOCK HOLMES:

Watson!

Holmes' face is illuminated by the candle. He is a thin-faced, wide-awake man dressed in the traditional deerstalker and cape.

SHERLOCK HOLMES:

Sir Eustace is dead, his head knocked in with his own poker!

Holmes advances toward Watson's bed with the candle.

SHERLOCK HOLMES:

Come, Watson, come! Into your clothes and come.

Holmes pulls the blankets from the bed, revealing Watson in pajamas. Watson does not get up. Holmes rushes to the dresser to get Watson's clothing and tosses it onto the bed.

An animated script will not contain extensive descriptions of the background since that is the story artist and art director's job. Only a bare-bones description appears for now.

Adaptations of literary stories are notoriously hard to do. Some are far more visual than others. Some provide clues to the character's personality. Sherlock Holmes is a familiar character with established mannerisms. Here are the points you should consider when translating any story to storyboard:

- What is the tone of this story? Is it dramatic, comical, satirical, or tragic?
- What do the characters feel? Are they happy, apprehensive, or indifferent?
- Whose viewpoint will we see the action from? Do we identify with a particular character? Are they large or small? This will determine the camera angles.
- How does the action progress, and why does it happen?

This example is only an exercise. In an actual production your story head or your directors would tell you how they wish the story to be interpreted. You would also be able to read the entire script to see how matters progress in earlier and later scenes.

The first step is to break down the scene 'by idea.' Draw extremely rough thumbnails for each setting and determine which area of the frame will be the center of interest. Create a 'concrete poetry' sentence that describes the action in the setting, writing directly on each object in the panel as shown in Figure 15-5. Illustrate sentences, not words, and don't include dialogue. There are two main settings in the sequence: (a) the exterior of Holmes' and Watson's house, and (b) Watson's bedroom.

An animated sequence can be constructed like a sentence. Use the concrete-poetry method to clarify your thoughts and emphasize what is primary and what is of secondary importance in the sequence. Holmes is the active figure so the sentence and staging in the *Abbey Grange* excerpt focuses on him.

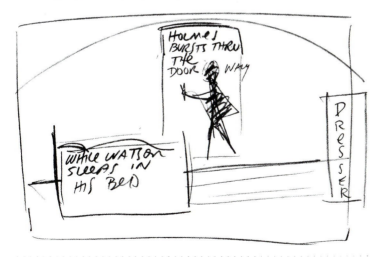

**[Fig. 15-5] A sentence describing the setting, characters, and action is written inside the thumbnail panel. "Holmes bursts through the doorway while Watson sleeps in the bed." Once the stage is set, the action can begin.**

I decide that this story will be staged as a comedy. I will contrast Sherlock Holmes' frantic action with Watson's immobility. I decide that Watson doesn't want to get out of bed because he has had too much to drink the night before. Does the script say this? No, but since this is my own production I have perfect freedom to add additional material to flesh the action out. The same material could just as easily be staged dramatically. The director or story head will guide you on a professional production.

I next draw thumbnails in silhouette to examine possible staging and then rough out the action with the pictures and dialogue on separate panels as shown in Figure 15-6. I decide to keep the final action in silhouette for artistic reasons. Instead of following the script directions literally, I add some material with Watson going back to sleep and get Holmes over to the dresser before his last line so that he doesn't see Watson's reaction to his wake-up call. The last shot offers an explanation for Watson's behavior.

You should always work for clarity in your drawings. The staging and acting should never be open to misinterpretation. Add another storyboard drawing to clarify the action or acting if the meaning of a scene is in doubt. It is preferable to have too many boards than too few to convey the story. The boards must direct the viewer's eye where you want it to go and not have distracting elements in the frame.

Since the characters in this story appear in silhouette on many of the boards, I use a spotlight effect from the doorway to frame Holmes, who remains in silhouette throughout. He is the center of interest since he is the greatest contrast in the frame and appears in the optical center. Light from the candle directs your attention toward Watson's bed, where I'd like you to look next. When the action becomes more frenetic I draw the characters on the white panels without rendering the backgrounds at all. We accept that the action continues in the same dimly lit room. I was able to build on this ludicrous start by having things go from bad to worse. Holmes eventually wakes Watson with a hotfoot, causing his friend to leap onto the chandelier, which falls, hitting Holmes on the head. The ending showed Watson solving the crime and getting "the girl" while Holmes is recovering (and still wearing the chandelier).

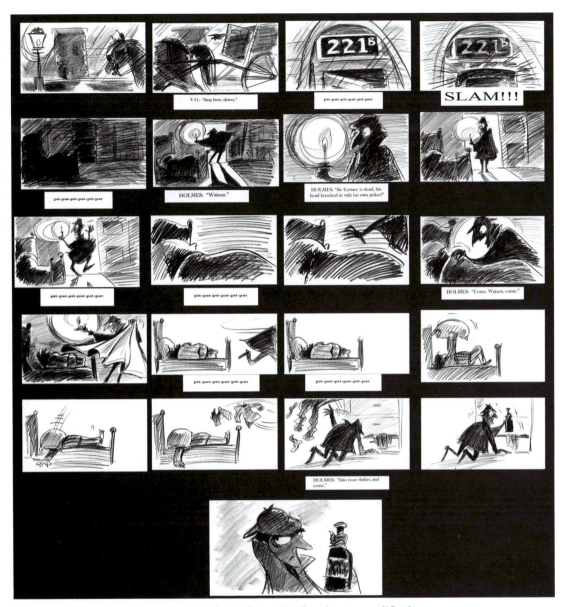

**[Fig. 15-6] The rough boards show how the script has been modified. Holmes' reaction to Watson's disinterest adds a pause that was not indicated in the script. Written sound effects give a rough idea of the timing even though this won't be finalized until the boards are cut into the story reel.**

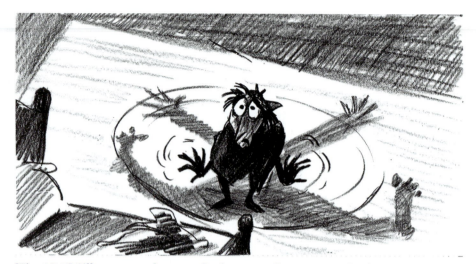

**[Fig. 15-7] Silhouette values worked very well to convey the farcical action in this absurd interpretation of the classic Sherlock Holmes story.**

Before the *pitch*, I'll draw rough character designs for Holmes and Watson or paste up action model sheets to show at the same time as the storyboards. I will frequently pitch all the artwork to another artist beforehand to see if everything is *reading* well. When I am confident that the sequence is ready to show, I pitch the boards and character artwork to the (hopefully) appreciative audience. Chapter 18 lists things to do and not to do during a storyboard pitch. Wish me luck.

Exercise: Try thumbnailing the script from *The Adventure of the Abbey Grange* in a different manner and mood than I have done. After you have finished, design rough model sheets for Holmes and Watson based on your storyboard sketches. Can you make these familiar characters seem new and different?

16

# Diamond in the Rough Model Sheet: Refining Character Designs

"Creativity is allowing yourself to make mistakes. Art is knowing which ones to keep."

—Scott Adams, creator of "Dilbert"

Your characters' bodies, typical expressions, actions, and emotions will become easier to draw as storyboarding progresses. Surface details will be eliminated or simplified and body shapes will change as you draw the character in different attitudes. Story-board drawings are the most practical way to see which design elements help and which ones hinder the character's ability to act. A character's appearance may change dramatically from the original rough design after a few sequences are boarded. You should wind up with an appealing design that you are comfortable working with. A character that easily conveys emotions with its face and body is known as a *good actor*.

This process of simplifying animation design is known as *evolution*.

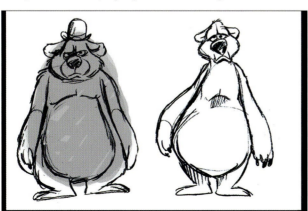

[Fig. 16-1] Papa Bear's design evolves in many of this book's illustrations. This process also occurs on actual films.

Character designs are developed concurrently with the storyboards and may be pitched at the same session. It is a good idea to have designs for CGI characters roughed out as early as possible since they will need time to be modeled and rigged.

With proper planning you will have the final rigs ready to go just as your *story reel* or *animatic* is finalized and production animation begins. Hand-drawn animation may continue 'evolving' the characters well after animation has started. It's not uncommon for hand-drawn characters' appearance to change between the beginning of the picture and the end, though good *cleanup* can prevent this from becoming obvious to the viewer.

Model sheets exist to standardize the character's appearance and suggest typical poses. They provide valuable guidelines but are not set in stone.

Pre-existing characters from another medium, such as toy design or comic books, sometimes appear in animated films. These characters often have 'approved' model sheets containing a limited number of official poses. Sometimes the animator is not allowed to distort the design at any time lest the animation be considered *off-model*. The creators of the character have not necessarily worked with animation before and may not know how it is produced. It can sometimes be difficult to convince them that squashing or stretching the volume of the character gives the animation a feeling of weight and solidity.

**[Fig. 16-2] Non-animators will sometimes have trouble understanding how animation is produced. Illustration by John Van Vliet, reproduced from the 1989 AVAILABLE LIGHT calendar by permission of John Van Vliet.**

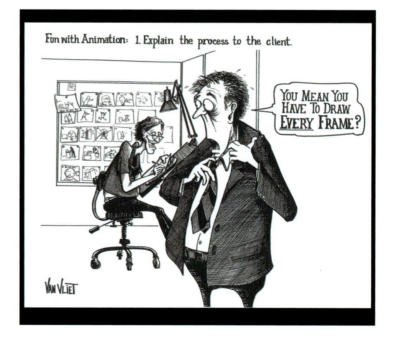

The distortion may be for only a few frames but that will not matter. I have known of clients who viewed an entire film one frame at a time and demanded that 'off-model' frames showing squash or stretch on the character be edited out.

It's easier to standardize poses and facial expressions in computer animation than in hand-drawn cartoons. Computer-generated characters, like hand-drawn ones, indicate weight and volume through distortion. If they do not ever distort there will be a floating, weightless quality to the animation and their movement will be unconvincing. Do not let your characters become too stiff. Be sure that the designs are able to distort enough to indicate weight. A mobile face and body can portray emotions and thoughts without dialogue.

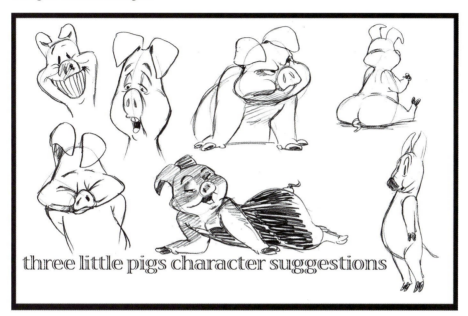

**[Fig. 16-3] Animated characters will distort to indicate their weight and volume. Eliminating all distortion causes the action to appear stiff, wooden, and weightless.**

We have already seen an example of a flawed design where one character's arms were too short to fit around another character's body in Chapter 6, Figure 6-2. While it is possible to temporarily lengthen the arms or vary the body width of a hand-drawn character to enable it to perform an action, CGI designs should be tested for mobility at the very beginning of the design process since it is expensive and inconvenient to redesign a CGI or puppet character when you are far into production. New controls are often added on feature productions when the animators need to have a character do something that the original rig does not allow it to do. A short film may not have the time or budget for this.

The most common mistake made by beginning designers is to assume that their first character design is also the final one. In some instances, the artist goes directly to *cleanup* without investigating the character's construction or the actions it must perform in the film. Sometimes a character has only a few poses on its model sheet. Lack of planning in character design will lead to problems down the line as surely as it does in story.

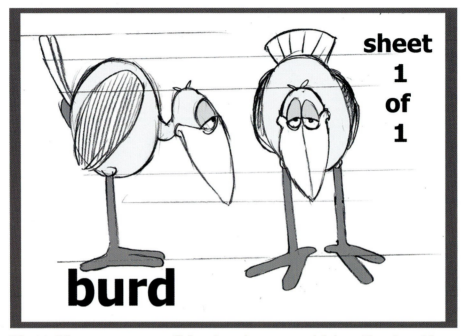

[Fig. 16-4] Two poses are not sufficient for a character model sheet. How does this character move? How does it open its mouth? Does it have one? This model sheet does not say.

Animated characters go through a long process of refinement and revision as a normal part of the design process. Design experimentation is particularly important in the early stages of computer animation. It is essential to eliminate design flaws before they are incorporated into the finished models. Several tools are used to accomplish this, including construction model sheets, test animation, and *maquettes,* or sculptures of the characters. Maquettes and their construction are discussed in Chapter 21.

# Tying It Down: Standardizing Your Design

An animated film may use materials from professional illustrators, cartoonists, or fine artists as inspiration for character designs. The look of the characters in ALADDIN was influenced by the work of theater caricaturist Al Hirschfeld. Gerald Scarfe produced conceptual drawings for all of HERCULES' characters, and TREASURE PLANET used the work of the Brandywine school of artists, such as Howard Pyle, as the basis for the art direction and character designs.

A storyboard artist does not need to take final character design into consideration when working on rough boards. But the character designer must be sure that the animated actors work with each other and with the backgrounds in a consistent style so that they are all in the same *universe,* as discussed in Chapter 6.

Storyboard drawings that convey character emotions or motions particularly well will be copied onto 'model suggestion' sheets. These are given to the designers along with any reference material that the directors and art directors have assembled as inspiration for the look of the picture. Sometimes a lead designer will go over each rough design and unify the styles, as Gerald Scarfe did for HERCULES' characters.

*Construction models* are drawn once the basic design is approved. A construction model shows the primary shapes that are used to create the character and standardizes its proportions. Figure 16-5 shows a simple construction model for Baby Bear.

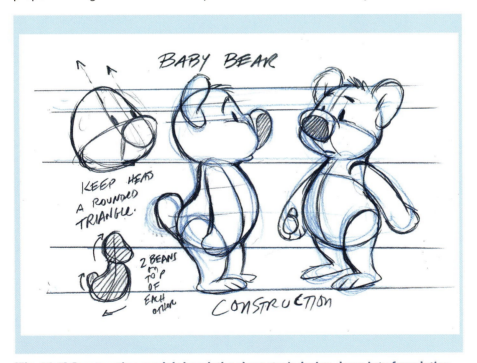

[Fig. 16-5] Construction models break the character's design down into foundation shapes.

The figures are usually constructed in profile since it is easiest to set proportions in this view. *Give all your characters names*, and write the names on all of the model sheets. A name is an important directing and compositional aid whether you have one or more than one character in a film.

Body construction is done by *drawing through the design*, or showing the trunk and legs through the transparent clothing level. The body may also be constructed first and the clothes added separately. In the next figure, two profile drawings have been done of the same girl, one with and one without the clothing.

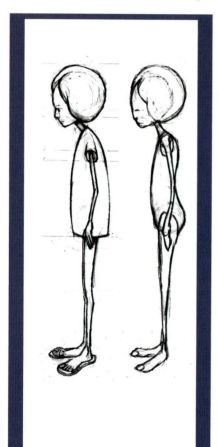

**[Fig. 16-6] Character construction is easiest in profile. Two drawings are provided in this example. The first shows Diane's standard appearance; the other indicates the construction of the body underneath her loose dress. Reproduced by permission of Jim Downer.**

Draw the body through the clothes even if it never shows in the finished animation. Underlying shapes will influence external surfaces. The body shapes the clothing, unless you are designing a corseted or armored character.

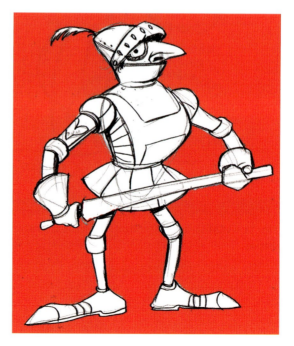

**[Fig. 16-7] Stiff outer garments will influence the shape and mobility of an organic character. Otherwise, the form of the body will determine the surface shapes.**

It's a good idea to experiment with the *proportions* of the character's body at this time. Try lengthening the legs and shortening the body, or try working with a longer torso and shorter legs. One design can have many variants. Your main concern is to design a character that is able to perform the actions required in the film, but it's also good to incorporate an interesting variety of proportions and shapes into your creation. Once you are satisfied with the proportions of the face and the body, you will finalize the character model sheets by standardizing these proportions on drawings of the character in static and typical action poses. This is known as *tying down* the design.

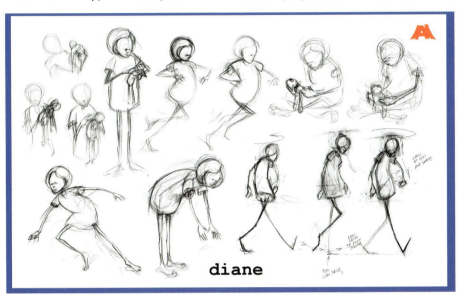

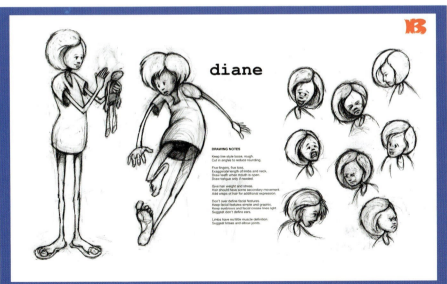

[Fig. 16-8] **Experiment with the character's proportions (A) before tying it down in the final design (B). The original character roughs can inspire many variants. Your final design may combine the legs from one sketch with the head and body from another. Work for proportions and design elements that please you. Reproduced by permission of Jim Downer.**

Since the character will usually need to turn in space and work in many different angles, the next stage is to draw *turnarounds* that will show the character in the same neutral pose from front, back, and three-quarter views as if it was rotating on a turntable. Horizontal guidelines are drawn on the profile sketch to indicate the top of the head and the bottom of the feet. Additional lines are drawn at the chin, shoulder, hip, knee, and wrist line where necessary. It then becomes easier to rotate the figure from profile to front and back views, and then create a three-quarter view that will usually be the most flattering angle to the design. Diane's height is measured in whole 'heads' so it is most important to standardize the distance between the crown of the head and the chin and measure body proportions by drawing 'head silhouettes' alongside the figures, as shown in Figure 16-9.

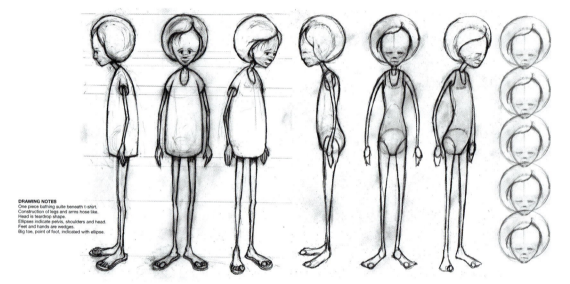

DRAWING NOTES
One piece bathing suite beneath t-shirt.
Construction of legs and arms hose like.
Head is teardrop shape.
Ellipses indicate pelvis, shoulders and head.
Feet and hands are wedges.
Big toe, point of foot, indicated with ellipse.

[Fig. 16-9] This turnaround shows Diane's volume and construction from several different angles. The new drawings are based on the proportions of the original profile drawing in Figure 16-6. Head heights are at the right side of the model sheet. Reproduced by permission of Jim Downer.

Character proportions are usually measured using the entire head and jaw, not just the ball of the cranium. Exceptions can be made if the head is very large or very small.

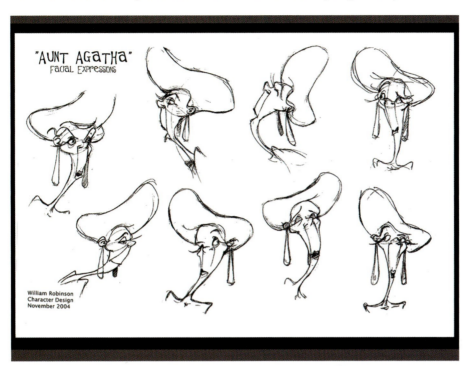

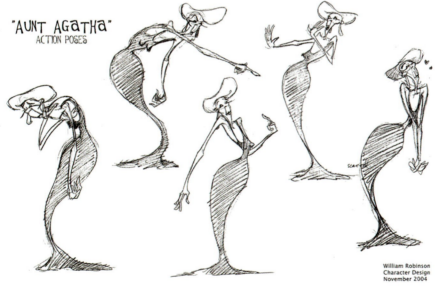

**[Fig. 16-10] Aunt Agatha's cranium is extremely small so her entire head is used to measure height and body proportions. Reproduced by permission of William Robinson.**

One dinosaur in the next figure uses its head and the other uses its body mass to measure the height and the length of their respective necks and tails. Use the simplest elements to measure proportions.

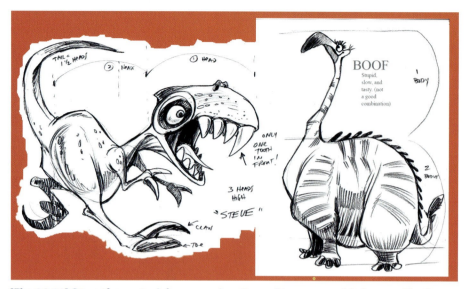

[Fig. 16-11] Steve the raptor's huge cranium is used to measure his face and body proportions. The Boofasaurus has a head that is too small to be used as a convenient measuring unit. Its body is used instead to measure its height and the length of its neck and tail.

No two size guides will be the same since each one is determined by the character's design. "Fred" is 4½ heads high. He has a small cranium so his height is measured with the entire head as shown in Figure 16-12. Fred's hair is a separate shape added after the head is constructed.

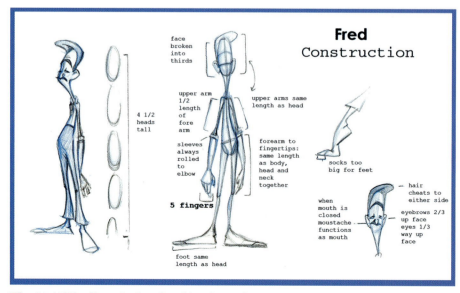

[Fig. 16-12] Fred's entire head and jaw is used to measure proportions for the rest of his body. Written notes and brackets are added to the model sheets. Hair shapes are added after the skull is constructed. Reproduced by permission of Brittney Lee.

Combined muzzle and skull shapes help measure a body, neck, and tail for a horizontal character such as a horse or a dog. The long skull may be measured in craniums. You may measure a horizontally-designed character's height with the combined cranium and muzzle, as shown in Figure 16-13. Notes are written to indicate the color of the inside of the mouth (which is usually shaded), and whether the character has a tongue or teeth. These features may not be obvious, particularly on a non-human character. Figure 16-13 shows a sheep that has a light-colored mouth. The entire head is shaded so that this feature reads better. The eyes are not indicated since they are not important (or the creature does not have them).

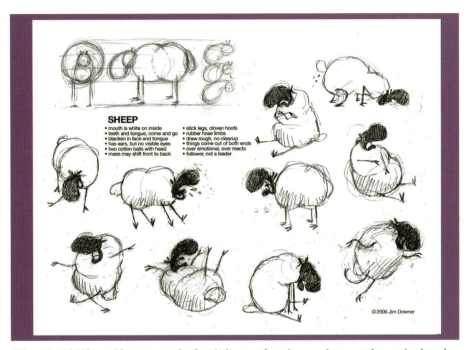

[Fig. 16-13] "Sheep" has a muzzle that is larger than its cranium, so the entire head is used to measure its height and body length. Reproduced by permission of Jim Downer.

Hair, hats, or long ears are indicated by a separate shape above the head after the skull is constructed underneath. Loose or flyaway hair is contained within a discrete shape so that it may be constructed in the round. Extensions from the skull or body are measured in whole or partial head heights added to the basic body and head construction after full turnarounds and head sizes of the basic body shapes have been completed, as shown with Diane in Figure 16-9 and Fred in Figure 16-12. Model sheets will also contain written notations that help the artist properly measure the limbs and identify small design details. Separate construction models are drawn for the head. The following figure shows identical head construction for two characters. Action poses show the range of Amma and Yuri's acting. Notes indicate the number of teeth, the appearance of eyes and eyelids, and other construction details. Amma sometimes uses extreme expressions, and this is indicated on the model sheet. Her twin brother Yuri is a more limited actor with heavier features. New drawings and new model sheets will supplement the originals once Amma and Yuri have been animated in a few scenes.

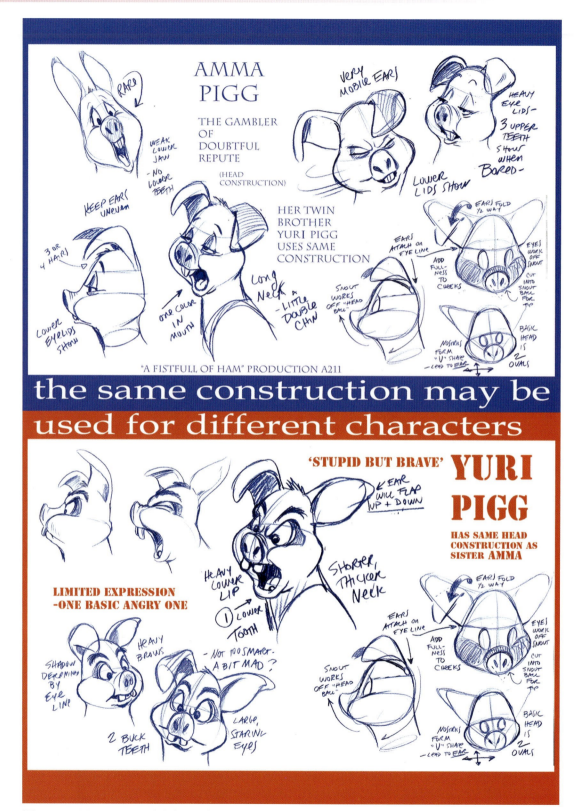

[Fig. 16-14] Separate model sheets for head construction and typical expressions are drawn for each character. The same construction may be used for two different characters but their body attitudes and dialogue mouth shapes may dramatically differ. Notes describe important details.

A model sheet for a CGI character will include typical facial expressions and more exaggerated ones that will be used to create blend shapes. Do not allow the restrictions of CGI to hobble your imagination. Exaggerate expressions if they are needed. They may become even more extreme than the drawing when transferred into the computer program, as shown in Figure 16-15.

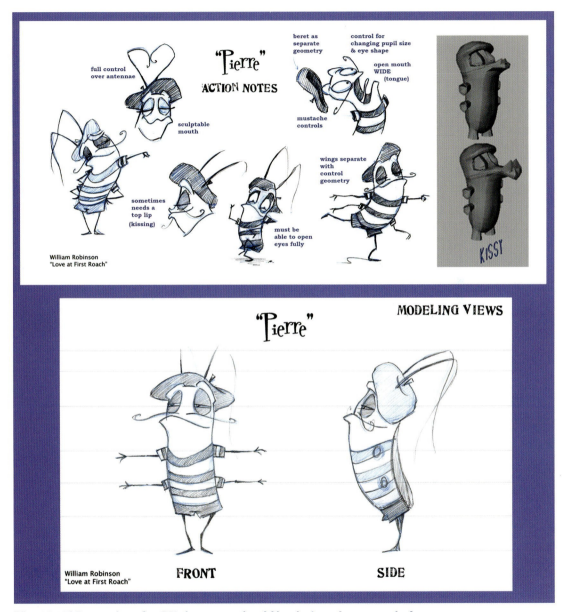

[Fig. 16-15] Expressions for CGI characters should be designed on paper before they are constructed on the computer. Blend shapes may be more extreme than the sketches. Reproduced by permission of William Robinson.

Hand-drawn animation is not as standardized as CGI and different animators may draw slight variants on the basic mouth and eye shapes. Teeth may pop on and off as needed for dialogue synch or strong expressions. (This can also be done in CGI by turning "false teeth" on or off as necessary.) If the teeth or tongue only show in certain expressions, write a short note on the model sheet and add an explanatory sketch if necessary. It is a good idea to always label tongues and the inside of mouths to prevent confusion. Leave nothing to chance.

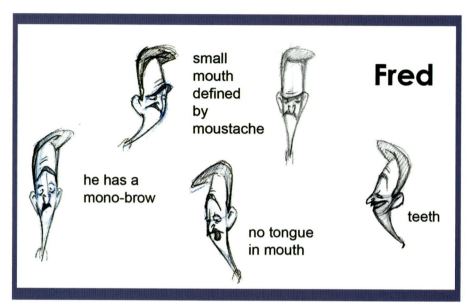

[Fig. 16-16] Model sheets for facial expressions serve as guides for dialogue animation. Teeth and tongues are labeled along with other features. Reproduced by permission of Brittney Lee.

I do not recommend making model sheets of 'standard' dialogue mouth shapes for animated characters. Mouth charts are mechanical aids developed to standardize the animation of dialogue. There are no standard mouth shapes in life or in good animation since no two people speak in precisely the same fashion. Mouth shapes may be underplayed or *cheated* and the body attitudes carry the action. There is no need for absolute fidelity to individual mouth shapes. Human actors do not enunciate every word equally, as you can see if you compare the acting of Humphrey Bogart with that of Woody Allen [Fig. 16-17]. Even in a still drawing the two men appear to be speaking different languages. Bogart's lines are slurred and *cheated*; Allen's mouth shapes are broader. Dialogue mouth shapes for the same character will vary depending on its mood and emotion. There's no standard way to animate dialogue, just as there's no one way to animate acting. Dialogue animation is conveyed by body language as well—indeed, the body attitudes are more important than the mouth shapes!

Dialogue 'action suggestion' model sheets are created after a test scene has been animated on a character, but they will always be *suggestions,* not absolutes. Each character will have its own particular way of moving and talking even when two designs are nearly identical, as demonstrated in Figure 16-14.

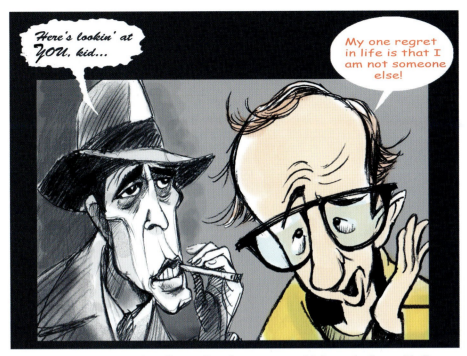

**[Fig. 16-17] No two people will say a line the same way. Dialogue is cheated in live action just as it is in animation.**

Blend shapes for CGI mouths should be extreme enough to allow you to modulate the forms in animation. You may need to break or distort the rig for extreme poses. The acting should determine the mouth shapes. Just be sure that your designs are able to act well. Dialogue is best conveyed by body attitudes and actions, with mouth shapes added afterward as secondary action.

# Your Cheatin' Part: Nonliteral Design

Animated characters may be *cheated* when in motion. Many hand-drawn characters are not really three dimensional at all. Mickey Mouse's ears are always seen from the same angle. Ariel from THE LITTLE MERMAID has a part in her hair that shows on one side of her head at a time. The part always faces the camera and her hair always frames her face. If Ariel was modeled in true 3D her hair would obscure most of her face in some angles. When these characters turn their heads, the ears and hair are "*cheated.*" Our eyes concentrate on Mickey's face while his ears shift slightly from one side of his head to the other without ever turning in space. Ariel's hair part pops from one side of her head to the other while she is moving rapidly. A slow movement would destroy the illusion.

Cheats will be indicated on the model sheets since they are an important part of the character's design. CGI designs may be more consistent than that of hand-drawn characters but animators may 'cheat' by breaking and distorting the rigs to exaggerate a pose or minimize a bad camera angle.

A graphically designed character might not actually turn in 3D space. In this instance the model sheets will indicate typical poses and suggest cheats that enable the animator to move it from one pose to the other. Mickey Mouse's ears are a famous example of a cheat. If a section of the design *pops* or *morphs* instead of turning in a conventional manner, this must be noted on the model sheet. The boy's face in Figure 16-18 will turn normally, but his hair part will pop from one side of his head to the other.

[Fig. 16-18] A hand-drawn "in the round" character may *cheat* certain views and not have all parts of the design move in three-dimensional spaces.

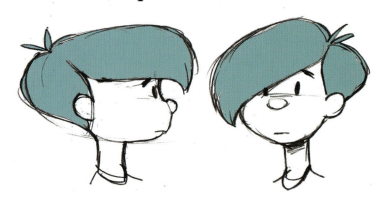

# cheat the hair part on head turn

Animated characters have 'good sides' and 'bad sides' much as human actors do. Not all characters look good from every angle. There is a famous story about animator Fred Moore, who redesigned Mickey Mouse in the 1930s so that he was more organic and expressive than the original design (which, according to legend, was sometimes drawn with the aid of a traced quarter for the head and body shapes, and a dime for the ears). Moore was considered the Mouse Expert, and so a couple of younger animators once asked him, "How would you animate a scene of Mickey Mouse in a down shot of the top of the back of his head?" Moore's answer was, "Why would you want to stage Mickey in that angle?" *Your character should be staged in the best possible angle, not the worst.* Model sheets will contain a straight-on front and rear view but these angles will often be more 'flattening' than 'flattering' to most characters.

[Fig. 16-19] A straight-on frontal view of a character will often flatten out the design. Important features may not show to best advantage.

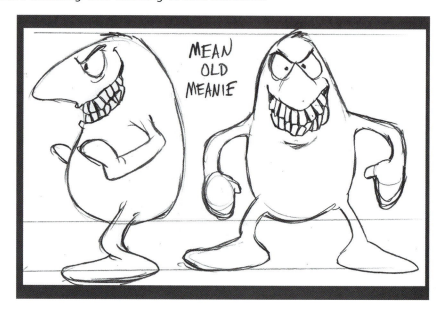

MEAN OLD MEANIE

Please refer to Chapter 10 for suggestions on how to stage your character effectively in a scene. A head may be turned into a three-quarter view while the body is shown from the front. Avoid staging characters directly from the rear, as shown in Figure 16-20. If you are working on a scene where layout has given you an unflattering angle on your character (as occasionally happens), cheat its pose into one that shows it to better advantage.

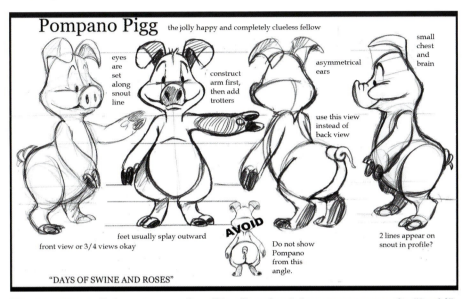

**[Fig. 16-20] Not all characters work well in all angles. It is customary to write "Avoid" on model sheet drawings that are used to determine construction or proportion but that do not read well in an actual scene. Straight rear or front views are usually cheated into three-quarter profiles since this is the best way to create depth of field on the character and avoid unflattering views.**

**Exercise:** Animate your character on paper in a 24-frame walk cycle. Work in profile or three-quarter views. Next, animate a short scene where the character acts and speaks in a three-quarter view. Use a *scratch* dialogue track and animate lip synch. Do not have it simply stand and talk. Your objective is to show an individual personality, not a mechanical action. The source of the dialogue is unimportant; you may use a line from an old movie, record it yourself, or use an actual line of dialogue from your picture if it is available. After the scene(s) are done, take your best extremes and breakdowns and paste them up on *action model* sheets. Then draw your character in new poses that show its acting and action range. Do not worry if these extreme poses or emotions are not called for in the picture. It pays to experiment since you'll get to know your character better. The test animation scenes will provide updated model drawings of the character since its appearance will *evolve* when it is animated for the first time. After you have completed the action models, rework your original construction and turnaround models if the character design has changed. It is not at all unusual to redo the model sheets after the design's animated trial run. This is animation *evolution* in action. The final design will be much stronger than the original.

Action sketches such as the ones in Figure 16-21 and 16-22 will indicate weak areas of the construction model.

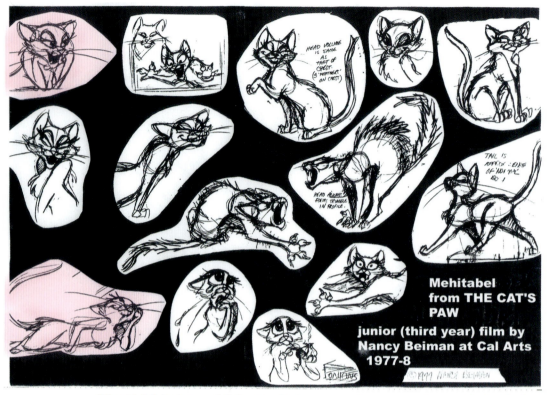

[Fig. 16-21] Action model sheets will show poses that may not be used in the final film. They are useful as indications of the character's range of motion and emotion. None of the original poses on this model sheet were used in my junior-year film, THE CAT'S PAW, but they helped me construct the character and showed her range of motion. The cat's evolution is apparent in some copies of actual animation drawings (shaded in pink) that were added after I'd completed a few scenes.

Action model sheets are used throughout the production to show typical character movement and attitudes. Label the sheets "Action Model Only" if the model varies from your final design. Sometimes a character's proportions and design don't change much at all.

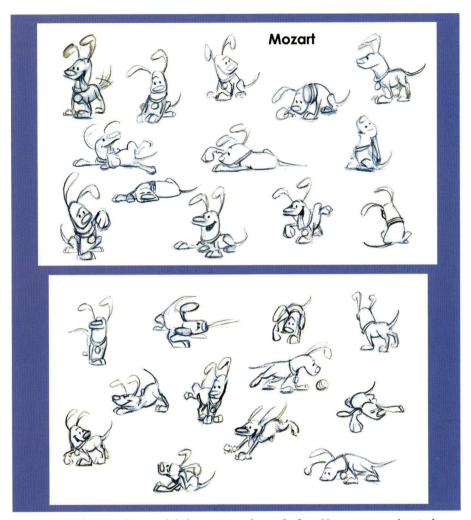

**[Fig. 16-22] These action model sheets were drawn before Mozart was animated. When he was animated, the dog's head and feet grew larger than planned on the original model sheets, but since the evolution was not obvious, the original models were not changed. Reproduced by permission of Brittney Lee.**

Draw final size comparison and construction models for the entire cast lineup after you have completed construction and action models for each character. Be sure to include important props. Figure 16-23 shows the rough character lineup that originally appeared in Chapter 7. One character, "C. Otter," is used as a standard of measurement. The taller characters are two 'otter heights' and the smallest character is one-half the height of C. Otter. Use simple fractions when making size comparisons; round off $\frac{15}{16}$ths to a whole head for simplicity's sake. Whole heads and quarters, halves, and thirds of heads are commonly used when measuring scale.

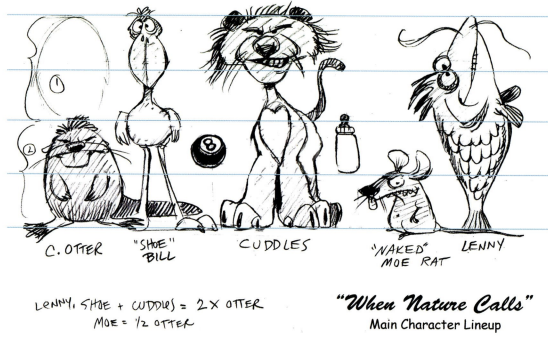

C. OTTER    "SHOE" BILL    CUDDLES    "NAKED" MOE RAT    LENNY

LENNY, SHOE + CUDDLES = 2 X OTTER
MOE = 1/2 OTTER

*"When Nature Calls"*
Main Character Lineup

[Fig. 16-23] Here is the original rough lineup and revisions for "When Nature Calls." The characters vary in size but can all fit on one model sheet. C. Otter is used as a unit of measure for the other characters. The tallest character is twice the size of the otter. Use simple measurements (one head height, or one-half or one-third of a head) rather than smaller increments when making size comparisons.

What happens if the size differences are so dramatic that a standard lineup is not possible (say, an elephant and a flea)? Compare the small character to a portion of the larger one on a 'close-up' model sheet. Here is an example of a small character, and smaller props, working with Diane from Figure 16-9. The doll and its props are too small to read well when placed next to Diane in a standard lineup, so the new model sheet scales the doll and the sewing materials to Diane's knee and foot. The girl's head and hand should also be drawn on the doll's model sheet as a size guide. A small character in a big picture will have most of its action staged in close-up or medium close-up because of the scale differences between it and the other characters.

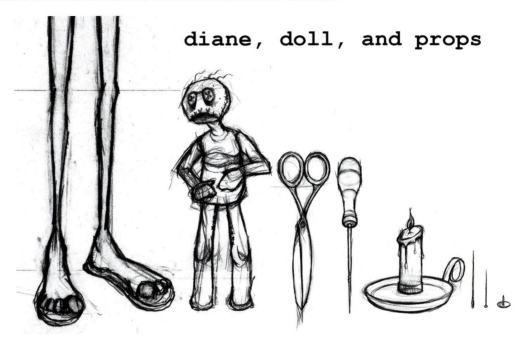

diane, doll, and props

[Fig. 16-24] A small character can be measured against a portion of a larger character's design on a close-up model sheet. The doll is as tall as Diane's knee. The props are scaled to the doll and Diane. Reproduced by permission of Jim Downer.

**Exercise:** When you have finalized the individual and size-comparison model sheets, draw action poses using two characters that appear together in the story. You may draw them separately or have both on the same page, whichever is easier for you. Keep the scale between the characters and silhouette value consistent with the other model sheets. Paste up the best of the combined poses on a new action model sheet. Work at your character designs until you are certain that they will work for you.

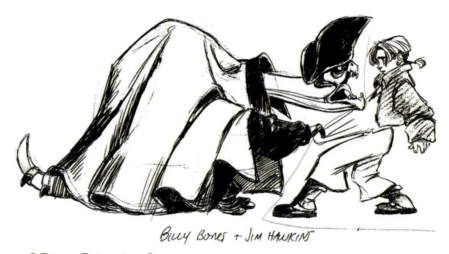

Buly Bones + Jim Hawkins

© Disney Enterprises, Inc.

[Fig. 16-25] I designed Billy Bones to work with John Ripa's design of Jim Hawkins in TREASURE PLANET. This size comparison was reworked several times after consultation with the directors. Used by permission of Disney Enterprises, Inc.

# 17

# Color My World: Art Direction and Storytelling

"Griselda woke up *feeling blue*. The *violet vault* sparkled with a billion *points of white* as the blotched banana of the moon rose behind the *gray ramparts* of the Castle Preposterous. Suddenly she espied Cyril and Cynthia gamboling through the forsythia. Griselda turned *green with envy* and then *rose* in a *red rage* since she'd never approved of gamboling.…"

—*"Purple Prose,"* excerpted from the unpublished romance novel *Love's Annoying Ache*

Color can convey symbolic meanings that add depth and resonance to characters and stories. An animated character can literally start out 'blue', then turn green and red in rapid succession. Color changes describe a character's emotional state even when they appear outside of a story context.

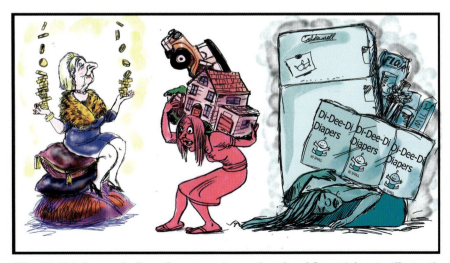

[Fig. 17-1] Color symbolizes the women's emotional and financial state. Illustration by Nancy Beiman for the film IN DEBT WE TRUST, reproduced by permission of Globalvision, Inc.

Some color symbols apply to settings rather than characters. It is possible to *see things in black and white, look at the world through rose-colored glasses, have a red-letter day, live in a golden age,* see something happen *once in a blue moon,* or find yourself in a *gray area.* Many animated films use color very creatively. Consider how color, or the absence of color, can help tell your story.

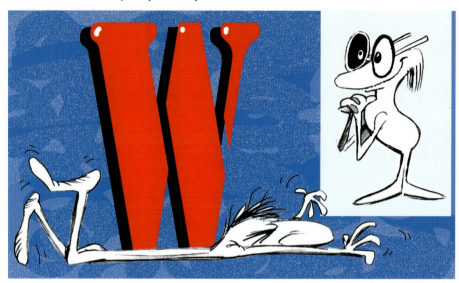

[Fig. 17-2] One character has a Red-Letter Day while another is in a gray area trying to see things in black and white. Stereotypical colors convey meaning whether used for characters or for backgrounds.

# Fishing for Complements

I recommend purchasing a rotating color wheel that allows you to compare and analyze *warm and cool, primary, complementary*, and *split complementary* colors. This will become an indispensable tool. Some wheels are specially designed for interior decorators and others are intended for use by Web artists. You may need to get more than one wheel, depending on your choice of medium.

A color reference library, or morgue, is a useful tool for the art director. I've used snippets of magazine photos that showed the color effect I wanted when pitching to clients. Keep your eyes open and your bookshelf and files updated with interesting books, pictures from magazines, stamps, postcards, and anything else that might provide good color reference for your project. I also like to get paint chips from a hardware store. These are helpfully filed by hue, often with four or five different values on each chip. Note the many shades of 'white' offered. Certain companies have published detailed guides offering advice on which color combinations work best with particular types of décor. Others suggest palettes for specific historical periods. Many interesting effects can be obtained with little effort by juxtaposing two or three paint chip samples and comparing the different values and hues.

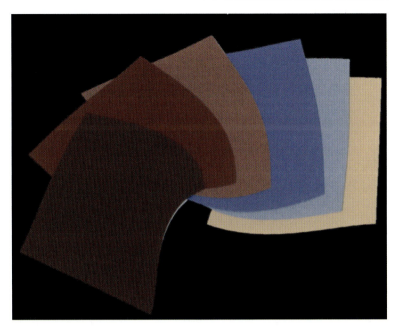

[Fig. 17-3] This color palette was based on paint chips obtained from a hardware store.

The Internet is the world's largest reference library. A good search engine will find even the most esoteric pictorial materials in a matter of seconds. These can inspire you and suggest new and different color combinations for your project. I recommend keeping a color morgue as well since not everything appears on the Internet!

You should also observe colors in nature and in the home environment. Color should not be an afterthought to your production design. The right colors can create an emotional mood that helps you tell your story more effectively.

Colors can stereotype as easily as character designs. A yellow sun shines in a bright blue sky, a gray thundercloud hovers over a wine-dark sea, white snowflakes tumble across a velvety blue background punctuated by yellow light shining from chill-gray cabin windows. It can be as much fun to work against stereotypes when planning your art direction as it was when planning the character designs.

Is a haunted house always moldy gray and black, illuminated by occasional stark flashes of white light? Maurice Noble used bright, cheery colors when he designed the 'ghost town' backgrounds for Chuck Jones' film CLAWS FOR ALARM. Sylves-

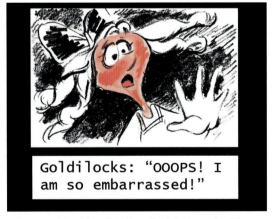

Goldilocks: "OOOPS! I am so embarrassed!"

[Fig. 17-4] Red is added to the black and white storyboard to convey Goldilocks' emotional mood.

ter Pussycat and Porky Pig stay in a 'haunted' hotel that boasts 'painted lady' late-Victorian detail and colors. Gingerbread carvings throw pink shadows on purple and green walls. The full moon casts brilliant yellow light outlined by tall, asymmetric French windows. There are no parallel lines in any of the rooms; everything is slightly askew and a little too brightly colored. This helps us understand Porky's ignorance of the dangerous situation. Porky sees a quaint old hotel. Sylvester knows better, as do we. Maurice Noble's unusual color palette and crisp art direction still look fresh today.

Warner Brothers Studio art director Maurice Noble said:

> "We had less to work with, [the cartoons] were spontaneous, and we had fun
> designing them. Chuck [Jones] gave me leeway and all of a sudden I was my own
> boss. I tried to be fresh in designing with color for each cartoon. I believe … that
> the graphic style was more fun to look at.… The graphics of animation stretch
> in *surprises* and that's what animation is all about.… The graphic style started
> because [the artists] began to realize that they could have more fun with it. It's like
> any other art medium.… What's the difference between a Picasso and a Van Gogh?
> I'm not comparing our talents to [theirs], but on the other hand maybe we *are* the
> modern artists. I do believe that animation is a fine art.… I think it still has a long
> way to go if we go back to graphics and forget the computer. When I give talks I
> always emphasize there is a difference between pushing a button and drawing.
> You can put down plenty of ideas quickly with a pencil."
>
> —Interview with Nancy Beiman, August 2000

# Saturation Point: Colors and Tonal Values

Color saturation, or intensity, is the equivalent of the gray and black values used on tonal storyboards.

Storyboards usually use shades of grey tone. Color is used as an accent. At times it will be necessary to do an entire storyboard in color. Everything depends on the story context.

A quick way of testing the readability of your color palette or background is to view it through narrowed or half-closed eyes as you did when testing the grayscale values on your storyboards. Lowering the light that reaches your eye also lowers the intensity of the color values. If the colors and objects now appear to merge, there is not enough contrast in your composition and you will have to change values or hues to make it read better. If certain areas are so contrasty they appear to 'pop off' the backgrounds, be sure that that is where you want the audience to look at first. A strong color accent in the wrong place can distract the viewer from the center of interest.

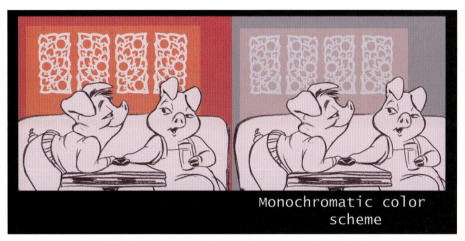

Monochromatic color
scheme

**[Fig. 17-5] The bright color accent on the wall distracts us from the characters in the foreground. Toning down the value of the background color corrects the problem.**

Ken O'Connor, the great Disney layout and story man, maintained that *tonal values were the most important elements of the scene even when the composition was in color rather than in black and white.* If the tonal values read well in grayscale, according to Ken, just about any color combination would work in the shot. Legibility is the most important thing, no matter what the medium. Viewing your color choices in grayscale will help you see whether the colors you have chosen for your backgrounds provide the same amount of contrast that their black-and-white equivalents would do.

Ken O'Connor would view his color compositions through a red gel filter to gray them down. Nowadays this comparison may be arranged with the click of a button. Let us see what happens when a color illustration is converted into gray tonal values using the 'grayscale' command in Adobe Photoshop. It is very important to use the *grayscale* and not the *desaturate* command when transforming your artwork. The gray tones that result from desaturation will not be accurate. Figure 17-6 shows color values that have been grayed out using the two different methods.

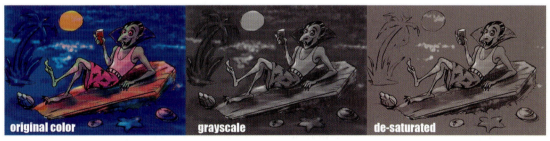

original color                    grayscale                    de-saturated

**[Fig. 17-6] This color image was put into grayscale and then changed with the desaturate command in Adobe Photoshop. Always use the grayscale command for accurate tonal values.**

If you get into the habit of viewing your color artwork in this fashion, your characters and background elements will read well in every scene. You can also test your compositions by viewing them in reverse (*flopped*) in a mirror, or turning them upside down.

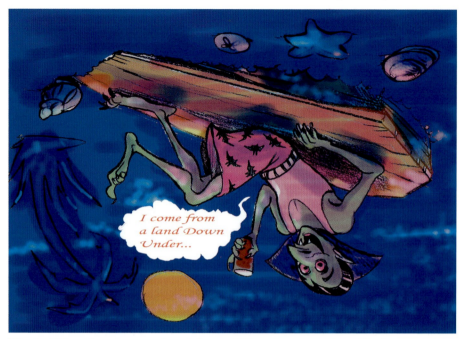

**[Fig. 17-7] Looking at your artwork from a different perspective will help you make your values and composition read better. Turn it upside down or mirror it so that you can view it as an abstract design.**

Color sources can be anywhere. The palette in Figure 17-8 was taken from an antique ceramic tile. The swatches are proportionately scaled to each color in the composition. These colors may be used in a completely different context. This figure shows them applied to a character rather than a background.

**[Fig. 17-8] An antique German ceramic tile and a small cat colored with a palette based on the tile (Nancy Beiman collection).**

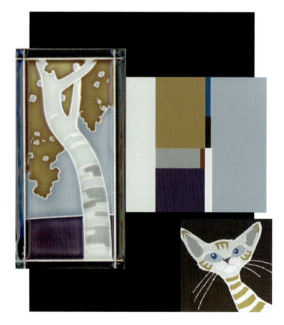

One of the signature-style goofs from the "Decade That Taste Forgot"—the 1970s—was the use of blazing-hot, fully-saturated, split-complementary colors in large areas. A violent repeated pattern was often applied in a contrasting and equally saturated color. Nothing appeared in moderation. There is a reason why some colors are called *loud*.

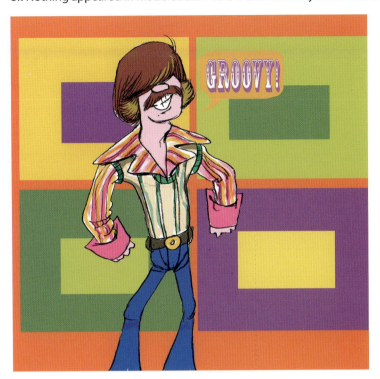

**[Fig. 17-9] This split-complementary color scheme uses four equally hot colors "screaming" at top volume.**

Hot, fully saturated colors can cancel each other out when liberally applied to characters or backgrounds. They work much better when used in small areas as accents. Oddly enough, the same hot, blazing 1970's palette we saw in Figure 17-9 *does* appear in the natural world, as shown in Figures 17-10 and 17-11.

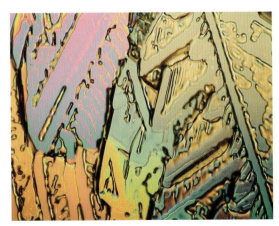

**[Fig. 17-10] Garish hues become attractive when values and saturation are modified. Urea photograph reproduced by permission of Alycia Yee.**

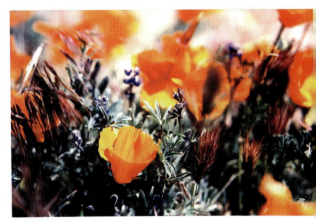

**[Fig. 17-11] Flowers use brilliant hues to attract insects. The flower's contrast with the duller stem attracts humans. California Poppies and Lupine photographed by Nancy Beiman.**

*Line is lighter than color.* Figure 17-12 shows the same character in final line and in its original CGI rendering. The rendered version reads as a solid shape; line reads as the outline of a positive space. The rendered animation will appear slower than the line version even if the animation timing does not change. *A line will always 'move' faster than a solid.*

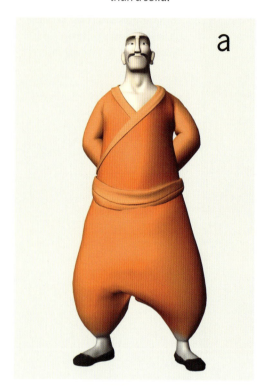 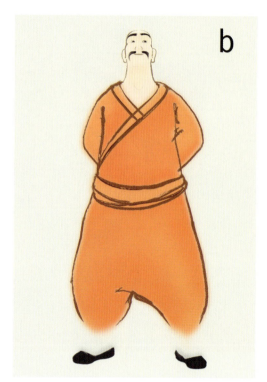

[Fig. 17-12] **Color reads as a solid shape while line will read faster. Reproduced by permission of Joseph Daniels and Jedidiah Mitchell.**

Colors can animate. They may advance or recede, as in Figure 17-13. We are shown two squares, one of which appears to have a larger center than the other.

[Fig. 17-13] **The two squares and their centers are exactly the same size, but our eye makes the central white square appear larger than the black one.**

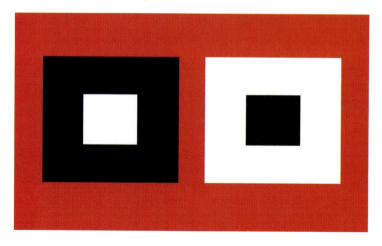

Advancing and receding colors used in combination may produce startling results when used on an animated character. In Figure 17-14 cool body hues contrast with the much lighter, warmer eye color so that the character's eyes appear to glow.

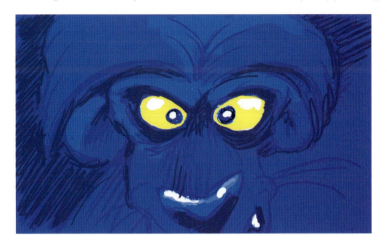

[Fig. 17-14] Color can be used to create glowing metallic effects or glowing eyes, with no need for special effects.

Colors may also appear to advance or recede in relation to another color. This contrast can actually create a feeling of motion in a still composition as we saw in Figure 17-13. Cooler hues can indicate early morning or late afternoon, while warmer ones suggest midday. Very close monochromatic values depict eventide, fog, or distance if they are cool and dark; bright sunlight if they are light and bright.

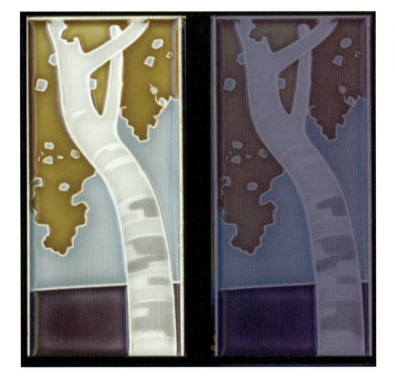

[Fig. 17-15] The changing time of day may be implied by color changes on the same background.

Color changes are often combined with the weather. How many climactic emotional or physical confrontations in animated films take place during a sudden thunderstorm?

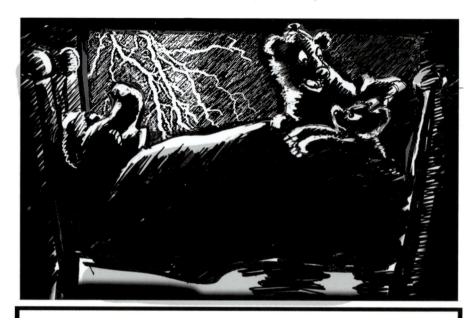

Mama Bear: "Yes, it is a bit melodramatic, and no, he isn't really dead."

[Fig. 17-16] No matter what the time of day, no matter what the season, violent emotional conflict in an animated film often coincides with the sudden arrival of a lightning-and-thunder-storm.

Figure 17-16 is an example of a cliché.  The emotional atmosphere need not be obvious to be effective.

Color adds another dimension to film and raises some interesting questions. How do you determine which color schemes work 'when' and 'where'? Take color cues from your story. A tale set in the Caribbean will use brighter and more intense colors than one set in Iceland—or will it? You'll start with nature, but then art takes over. The inspirational color for the Three Bears' house might be found in a piece of pottery or a fine silk scarf. Inspiration can come from anywhere. An icescape may use colors that are as fanciful as those in Maurice Noble's haunted house if they work within the context of the story. Can color indicate a change in emotional moods a bit more subtly than a lightning-and-thunder-storm? Yes, but it requires a script—one that is not written, but *painted*.

# Writing the Color: Color Scripts

> "As the light changed from red to green to yellow and back to red again, I sat there thinking about life. Was it nothing more than a bunch of honking and yelling? Sometimes it seemed that way."
>
> —Jack Handey, *Deep Thoughts*

A *color script* will be designed by the art director to indicate how the art direction changes during the time in which the film takes place. This color script will resemble a filmstrip of storyboard panels. Often, photocopies of storyboard panels are simply painted over.

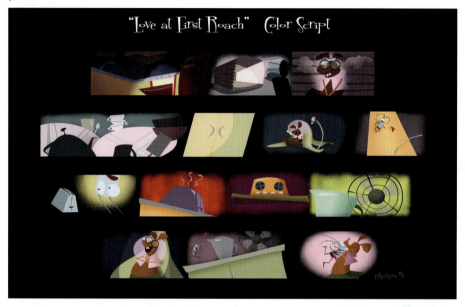

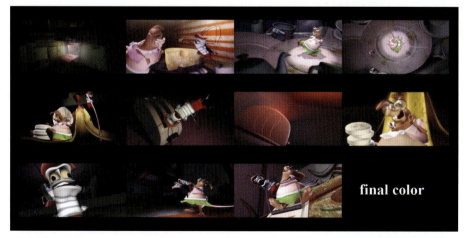

[Fig. 17-17] A color script shows how the color evolves from the first sequence of the film to the last. The art director determines the palettes and indicates transitional colors where necessary. Frames from the finished film show how the color keys were modified in production. Reproduced by permission of William Robinson.

The art director will determine which color dominates each sequence and indicate transitional colors that help maintain continuity when the scene shifts to a new location. Each sequence may have a different dominant color. A dominant color from an earlier sequence may appear with different values or in different proportions in a later one to maintain the visual flow. This is known as a *color bridge*. Color bridges link to other related colors. For example, a yellow-orange shape that is near a yellow-green one has the 'yellow' in common. The yellow hue creates motion within the composition since our eye will travel from one object to another via the 'bridge'. Our eye is attracted by contrasts in hue in the same way that tonal contrasts attract it in black-and-white storyboard drawings. This concept applies equally to still drawings and motion picture art direction.

**[Fig. 17-18] The eye can be directed around the frame by bridges; areas in the composition where the same color appears on two contiguous objects. Colors from the rainbow are repeated with variations on the characters in this still from SITA SINGS THE BLUES. Reproduced by permission of Nina Paley.**

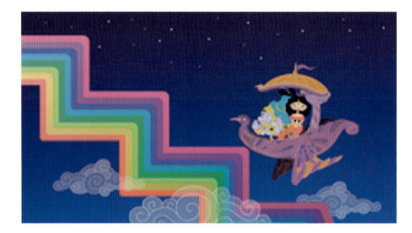

The art director will also create proportional color charts for each scene. Colors appear as simple blocks. The different sizes of the blocks indicate the proportion of the color that is used in the scene. Lighting color (especially important for CGI films) will also be indicated with a proportional grid, as shown in Figure 17-19.

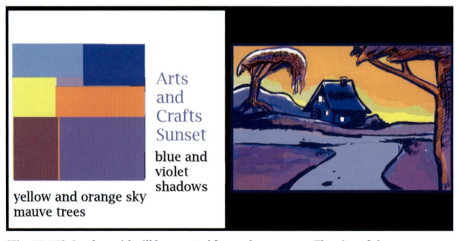

**[Fig. 17-19] A color grid will be created for each sequence. The size of the square indicates the proportion of the color in the overall composition. Lighting effects are indicated separately if a CGI production is being art directed.**

Color can be composed, like music. It can be harmonious or discordant, soft or loud. Color may be classical, romantic, jazzy, or modern. Use it creatively so that your visual compositions don't fall flat.

> Exercise: Create a small atmospheric sketch (4 × 6 inches) set in a specific location. The scene may take place indoors or outdoors. Draw simple background details, props, and one character. Construct a simple color script by creating four copies of the same sketch, each painted in color palettes that indicate different times of day. Start at dawn; have the second depict the scene at midday, the third at dusk, and the last one at midnight during a full moon. You may paint roughly and put the pigment directly on the drawings if you are working on paper, or you may use a computer graphics program to color the panels. Will your composition use different values of the same basic hues or will there be a complete color shift as time passes? Are your light sources from the sun and moon, electric lights, gas lamps, candles, firelight, or reflected light? What time of year do you wish to indicate? Summer light is very different from that of winter. Next, scan each of your designs and turn them into grayscale, black-and-white versions. Do the tonal values work well?

# O Tempora, O More or Less

Color can create a sense of place and time. An art director must research period styles and colors. Some color combinations are suggested by art that is contemporary with the film's setting. Historic painters are a terrific guide for period color. You'll find that contemporary artists from one country paint very different types of light. Palettes also vary from country to country and artists will reproduce the color of the local foliage and even the sky with great accuracy. Monet's hues are excellent representations of the colors of the 19th-century French countryside while Turner utilizes a grayer, equally accurate palette for his English landscapes.

You may also use the work of modern illustrators and painters as a guide for period films. Paintings and illustrations can give you the colors of a country or a culture from the distant past. Museums usually have brochures about their collection that contain color reproductions, or postcards of specific paintings. Old auction catalogues are a terrific and cheap reference source. They are sometimes available in secondhand bookstores. Anything and everything is grist for your color and design mill. You should never feel restricted by this material, but it provides great reference for possible color combinations and artistic styles.

Here's a little design secret: *A film that is set in a particular era need not use only contemporary material.* Any object, particularly architecture, dating from a period *earlier* than the movie's timeframe may be utilized in your background design and art direction. Oddly enough, some animated films that exclusively used then-contemporary design styles have dated more than films that contain a mixture of design elements from various time periods. Nothing dates faster than modernity.

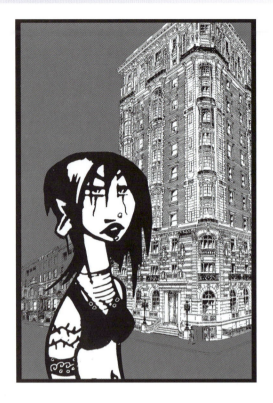

**[Fig. 17-20] A period piece may use elements from earlier time periods. This implies that settings grew over time and avoids the 'newly-minted look' that can occur when characters, backgrounds, and props all date to a brief historical period.**

TOY STORY contains many elements of a 1960s universe, such as period toys and Swedish Modern furniture, but its laser-shooting spaceman and themed restaurant (and video game in TOY STORY 2) date from the 1990s. The mixture of styles gives the TOY STORY films a period quality without making them appear dated. This is the same technique that Ken Anderson used for ONE HUNDRED AND ONE DALMATIANS (a discussion of this film's art direction appears in Chapter 9).

I do not recommend referencing artwork from other animated films since these may be familiar to your audience. Another art director has already researched the period and assembled color palettes and design elements from various sources. Find your own reference and adapt it so that your work does not slavishly copy the work of someone else. Specific cartoon or illustration styles should be viewed through the subjective lens of your own judgment and experience. Look through your own eyes, not someone else's. Artistic interpretation will make a style *yours*.

You now have rough character designs and color and atmospheric sketches that can be presented to an audience along with your storyboards. It is time to step up to the Pitch in Chapter 18.

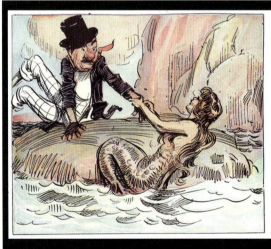
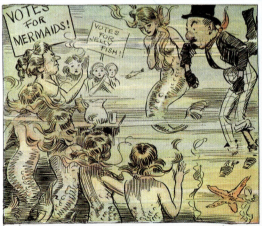

**[Fig. 17-21] A mixture of styles and period elements may be used for comic effect as shown in James Montgomery Flagg's comic strip NERVY NAT. Nat, a New York street tough from the 1850s, discusses 1912 political issues with some fifth-century mythological mermaids (Nancy Beiman collection).**

# Part Three

# Presentation

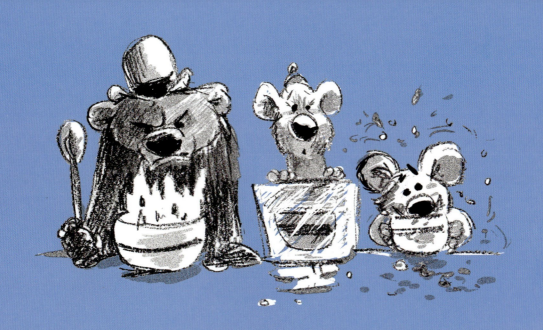

# 18

# Show and Tell: Presenting Your Storyboards

"You have to get the story point across in the first ten seconds of a pitch."

—Ollie Johnston (to author)

The day for the story pitch has arrived. Sometimes, it's the day after you get the hand-out! Your first consideration will always be 'readability' whether you have had one day or a month to finish your assignment. The boards are the most important part of the pitch but the quality of your presentation is nearly as important. A bad presentation will hurt a good storyboard. You're providing the acting and the timing for the action, so your commentary is 50 percent of the pitch and has to communicate as clearly as the boards do.

Your objective is to convey the story point clearly to the audience, in real time. Be prepared. *Number your panels* so that they do not get out of order. Be sure to pin the panels correctly beforehand. You won't have an opportunity to change the order during the pitch.

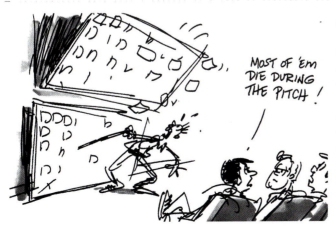

MOST OF 'EM DIE DURING THE PITCH!

**[Fig. 18-1] Number the storyboard drawings so that you are able to reassemble them in the correct order should a few fall off the boards. Drawing from *Son of Faster Cheaper* by Floyd Norman, reproduced by permission of Floyd Norman.**

*Memorize the dialogue and the action in each panel.* It is not good to stand and read dialogue off the small cards that are pinned under the panels. It's even worse if you forget it completely and freeze up or "die" in the middle of your pitch. Say the same dialogue that you have on the boards. *Use one sentence to describe the action in each panel.* If your panel shows Sherlock Holmes bursting through Watson's bedroom doorway, it's enough to state, "Holmes bursts the door open—Wham! Pit-pat-pit-pat," and let the drawing do the rest.

Do not use extraneous material. Stick to the story. Anecdotes, useless 'factoids', back story, and other stuff that doesn't matter will only slow down the pitch and bore or confuse your audience. Use simple descriptions of camera moves; don't give them a technical lecture.

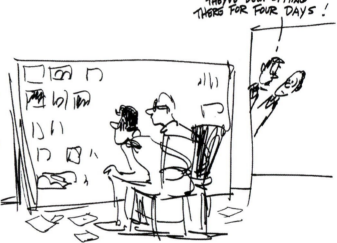

[Fig. 18-2] Know the action in each board and memorize the dialogue before the pitch. Be completely familiar with the material. Drawing from *Son of Faster Cheaper* by Floyd Norman, reproduced by permission of Floyd Norman.

*Make a joyful noise.* You should provide appropriate noises and sound effects where necessary. If you cannot reproduce the exact sound of a planet imploding, simply say "Bang!" Sound effects can add a lot to the presentation so it helps to be a bit of a hambone. Don't be nervous and don't worry about looking a little ridiculous—the audience should be concentrating on the boards. You are literally just a background noise.

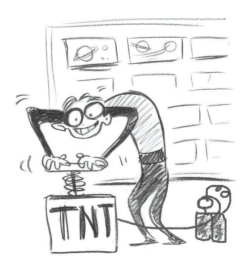

[Fig. 18-3] Provide any necessary sound effects with your own voice. Don't go overboard, but use whatever works in the context of the storyboard.

If your boards illustrate a musical composition, you can have it playing in the background while you offer a description of the action or simply play the music without commentary while you point to each panel of the boards. Don't be completely dependent on having the musical accompaniment during the pitch.

I've seen a story man recite his entire pitch with the aid of a puppet. Another one unrolled a ball of string around the story room and rewound it to a different knot as he made each point of his pitch. If you feel comfortable using additional materials and feel that it will help your pitch, use them—as long as they do not completely upstage your boards and your story.

*Rehearse the pitch.* Pitch the boards for other storyboard artists, for animators, for your mother, for total strangers, to be sure that everything reads well. You're too close to the thing to be able to judge it objectively, so a second or third opinion becomes necessary. I've received some excellent story suggestions from non-animators. After all, the ultimate audience for the project is ordinary people who are interested in hearing a story, not animation professionals. Rework and revise any inconsistencies or omissions before you go up before a highly critical professional audience. Be sure that all story points are reading clearly. You will probably change your boards more than once while rehearsing them. It's impossible to predict how directors and producers will react before you actually present the materials. If you are working with a *StoryHead*, they will have signed off on the boards before you pitch. If you are working alone, trying the boards out on an auditor who is not familiar with the material will help ensure that they read well to someone other than you. You will, with practice, be able to make your pitch easily and coherently.

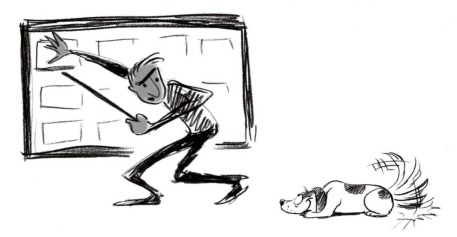

[Fig. 18-4] **Rehearse your pitch with the help of someone else. Be sure they are able to give you feedback so that you know when something isn't working as well as it should.**

*Show enthusiasm for the material.* If you don't think it is good, why should anyone else? Good story people are excellent actors. They keep the audience's attention focused on the story from the first frame to the last. Make the pitch entertaining enough to hold the audience's interest. Avoid ironic commentary on the artwork. Never make disparaging comments such as, "This isn't any good," or "I meant to do this instead of that." *Never apologize* and never tear down your own work—that's the director's job.

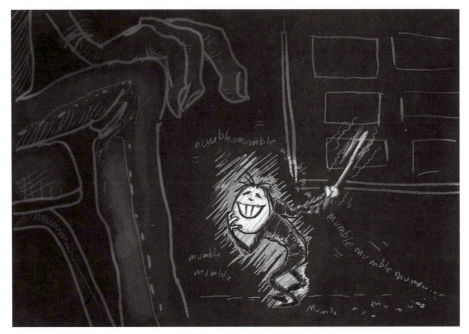

[Fig. 18-5] **Believe in your story. Don't point out weak spots in your own boards.**

Your panels should be pinned to large storyboards that are mounted on the wall or they may be pinned directly on the wall if the surface is suitable. They should not be displayed on a tabletop or handed around like playing cards (I've seen both). The storyboards should be a neutral color. Black, gray, cork, or off-white are common. Pin the drawings separately from the dialogue panels, since they may be rearranged. Get a simple pointer. A yardstick will do. Don't use your hands. Stand with your back to the board, a little to one side. Always face your audience. Make eye contact with them while doing the pitch. Never obscure the board by standing in front of it and never turn your back on the viewers. Your pointer will enable you to reach across the boards to pitch more distant panels without doing this.

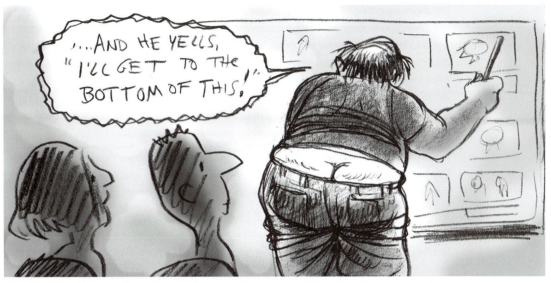

[Fig. 18-6] A pointer will enable you to pitch the boards without turning your back on the audience. Be sure that the boards are never obscured.

If you feel comfortable doing character voices, by all means do them. Story men will play women and story women will play men if they feel it will help the pitch. If you do not wish to do this, simply pitch the boards using your normal voice. Your inflection should help convey the action in the drawings. Don't mumble and don't read in a monotone. Speak clearly and loudly enough for the audience to hear you but not so loudly that you're audible next door. Keep a positive attitude. Smile. Act like you're enjoying yourself.

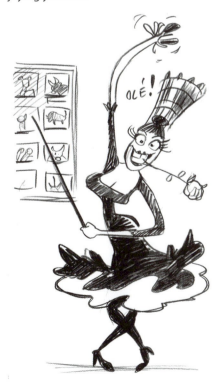

I have seen instances where story men and women got 'into character' with costume as well as voice talent. I was once only allowed to pitch my designs while wearing a huge felt high-cocked hat that I'd purchased as reference for the creature's costume! Use your judgment. Neat clothing is perfectly suitable for a story pitch.

[Fig. 18-7] You may want to do character voices for the different parts. Sometimes the character projection doesn't end there!

*Introduce yourself and your sequence at the beginning of the pitch.* A brief introduction will allow you to connect with the audience. If your sequence is part of a larger film it is good to let them know what comes just before your bit. Give them enough material so that they see how the sequence works in context, but don't try to tell the entire story. Ollie Johnston told me that the main story point had to be apparent to the audience in ten seconds or less. If you are pitching *beat boards*, state your *log line* first (the single sentence that sums up the meaning of the story as described in Chapter 4). The drawings and your brief commentary should be able to get the point across.

If you have character design sketches, pin these up on a separate board. It can help if you introduce the characters before beginning your pitch, especially if this is your *first pass* on the boards. Be sure to write the characters' names on all drawings.

It *is* polite to point. Don't smack the pointer up against the story panels. You are not mad at them—at least not yet—so don't work out your frustrations or nerves in this fashion. The noise will distract your audience from what is on the boards. Point to each panel in turn and *hold the pointer steady on the panel* while you say the dialogue and describe the action. Then *slide* the pointer to the next storyboard. Bouncing the pointer up and down on the panels is distracting and very counterproductive.

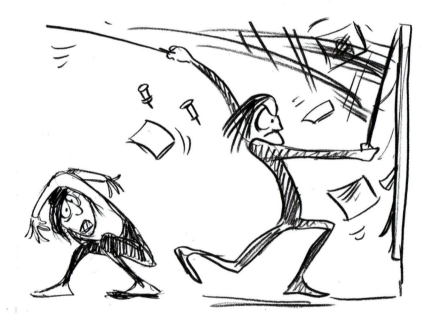

**[Fig. 18-8] Don't beat around, or on, the storyboard.**

*Work in real time.* You are giving your auditors a foretaste of what the finished film will be like. You will have to read brief explanations of some of the action occasionally since the film is not animated yet, but be sure to keep them *brief*. If you have to describe the action at length, chances are you did not draw enough storyboards to get the point over in the first place. It is better to speak too long than not long enough. Just be sure your audience is not nodding off (I've seen this happen during a dull presentation). Don't be pretentious. Keep your story points simple. Do not give convoluted explanations of the action and lengthy biographies of your characters. All that matters during the pitch is what is on the storyboard. If your story does not work, all the explanations in the world won't help you.

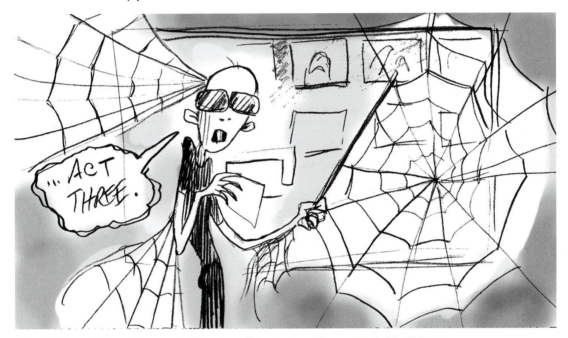

[Fig. 18-9] **Don't drag things out. If you're talking too much, you probably did not draw enough panels to convey the story. Your audience can, and will, lose interest.**

*Don't rush.* Take the necessary time to get the story point across. Don't run words to-gether trying to cram a lot of information into a short timeframe. Be sure to pace the story pitch. Speak in sentences, not paragraphs. Let the drawings carry half of the presentation.

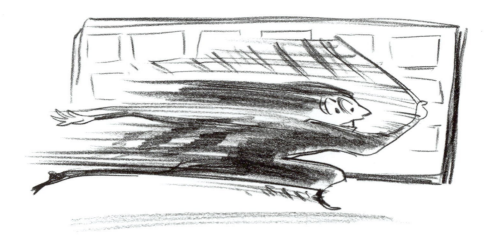

**[Fig. 18-10] Don't rush through at high speed.**

Director Jack Kinney wrote of a story man who got so 'into' his performance that he actually ran out the door while describing the character performing this action on his storyboard (The other artists locked the door behind him and went to lunch. They sensed that he was a showoff and reacted accordingly). Act, but don't overact. You will distract attention from the storyboard and you won't impress your audience.

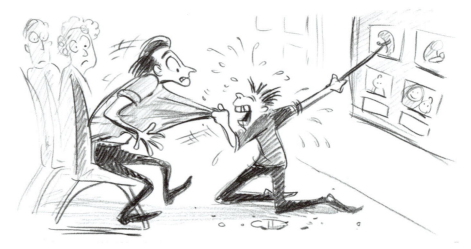

**[Fig. 18-11] Don't overdo things.**

After your pitch, you'll get down to the *real* work—*turning over* the boards and revising them!

# The More Things Change: The Turnover Session

Story people learn to welcome change. A *turnover session* is where you find out just how much change you and your boards can take. All storyboards are changed at least once. Never take these changes personally. Your only consideration should be that the story read in the clearest possible way.

Turnover sessions happen immediately after the pitch. The audience, which may consist of other story men and women, animators, the directors, and the art director, will make suggestions for additional action, revised staging, or new lines of dialogue. These suggestions, no matter how bizarre, are pinned up on an additional storyboard. If the directors like the changes, or do not like one of the existing panels, one or more panels of your board will be *turned over*. The deleted board(s) will be pinned so that their blank backs face the viewers, and the new drawing(s) will be pinned up on top of them. Sometimes the suggestions are drawn on new storyboards by the crew, but ordinary self-stick notes will often be used as well. The sketches will be very rough. If the changes are approved you will incorporate them into your reworked boards prior to the second pass, or pitch.

You may be asked to insert close-ups for a reaction shot or place your camera farther back to get more of the action into the frame. Someone may suggest an entirely new piece of acting or business that will lengthen the sequence. On occasion you will be told to *flop* a scene. This is not an indication of failure. Flopping a board means that the action will be staged as a mirror image. Sometimes entire sequences have their boards flopped. The advent of computers has made this a lot easier for the story people to do. In the old days, they just had to draw everything going the other way. Now, boards can be scanned and reversed automatically.

Plan to make at least two pitches for your boards. That is, if you are lucky. Some directors might make a few small changes or *tweaks* and get the boards *up on reels*, or shot and timed to a soundtrack in a *story reel*, before making a final decision on the staging. The boards might be sent back to you at a later date for reworking if the story changes. At the Walt Disney Studio, the boards were pitched "until they got it right or until they ran out of money," according to story man Floyd Norman. Constructive suggestions from your colleagues and friends will help foster a team feeling and make your boards stronger.

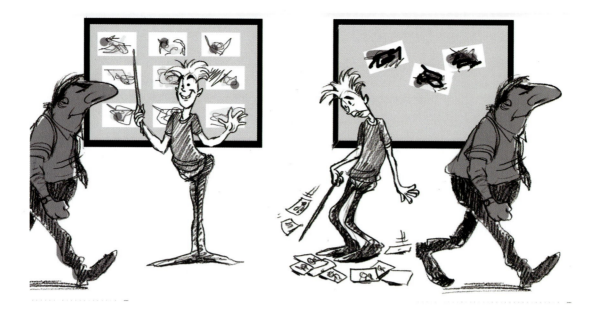

**[Fig. 18-12] An unsuccessful turnover session. Most won't be as dismissive as this, but some panels always wind up on the story room floor.**

The BBC reported that 3,000 adults who took a survey of most-feared incidents rated public speaking higher than financial ruin and death itself. If you prepare your pitch properly, you should acquit yourself well speaking in public and avoid the other two problems.

**[Fig. 18-13] Pitching a storyboard is rather like public speaking, but it need not be a dreaded occasion.**

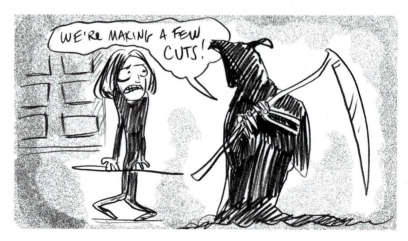

*"Dying is easy. Comedy is hard!"*

—attributed to Edmund Kean

# 19

# Talking Pictures: Assembling a Story Reel or Animatic with a Scratch Track

Congratulations! You have just pitched your boards and character concepts and had them approved—possibly with a few small *tweaks*.

After the turnover session a small removable sticker is placed in one corner of each storyboard drawing indicating the sequence, scene, and drawing number (Figure 19-1, top). Shorter films can have the scene and drawing numbers written directly on the boards (Figure 19-1, bottom).

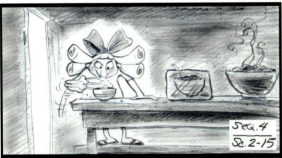

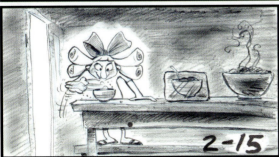

**[Fig. 19-1] When a sequence is approved, each storyboard panel is identified by a removable sticker listing the sequence, scene, and drawing number. Shorter films may eliminate the sequence numbers and write scene and frame numbers directly on the boards.**

Dialogue changes made during the turnover session are noted and incorporated into the recording script, which is finalized only after the storyboard is approved. When the script is ready the voice actors record the dialogue in individual or group sessions, depending on the project. The recording script is broken up into short numbered sections so that the actors do not read the entire script in one take. The editor and director then assemble the best takes from each section into the final track. Retakes of lines or portions of lines and additions to the original recording sessions are called *pickups*. If a character actor is not available for a session a dialogue *scratch track* may be recorded by another actor or the director and used as a placeholder until the pickup session is recorded. Scenes with scratch dialogue tracks will not be put into production since the synchronization will not be accurate for the animator.

At this stage the storyboards are transformed from still pictures into motion pictures in a process known as *getting it* (a sequence or project) *up on reels*. This term is used even though the story reel is now created with computers instead of animation cameras and reels of film.

The numbered storyboards are scanned into a computer editing program. Dialogue panels and screen directions are not scanned. The director(s) and editor assemble the boards into a *story reel* or *animatic* and time or *slug* each panel to the dialogue and a musical *scratch track*. Animated and live action film is edited to scratch tracks since the final scores are generally one of the last things that are completed on the production. (Song sequences are an exception to this rule.)

A *story reel* is constructed of scanned and timed storyboards. Camera moves may be shot but the drawings are not modified. Cross dissolves, fades, and simple camera moves, such as pans and rotations, created in the editing program replace the graphic symbols used during the storyboard pitch.

An *animatic* uses simple animation and special effects to add a cinematic feel to the storyboards. Techniques can vary from simply panning a character across a panel with the aid of a computer graphics program to animating character drawings, background layouts, and overlays to create a feeling of three-dimensional motions in the frame. Figure 19-2A and B show one storyboard that has been modified in a computer graphics program. Changes in layout, lighting, and character poses are used to convey the action in the scene.

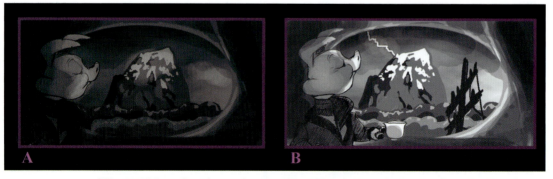

**[Fig. 19-2] An animatic may have action 'animate' in a single storyboard rather than progress on several separate panels. Simple character animation can time action more precisely than a still drawing.**

Complicated camera moves may be portrayed on one storyboard. Figure 19-3 shows the camera starting on the young cat in the doorway (field A). It then trucks up to the ceiling (field B) and rotates around the chandelier (field C) before descending toward a heroic feline statue on field D. The storyboard panel is larger than usual to allow for the camera moves, and the background detail is downplayed in the pass-through areas. The mood of the scene was fully established when this camera move was shot for the animatic.

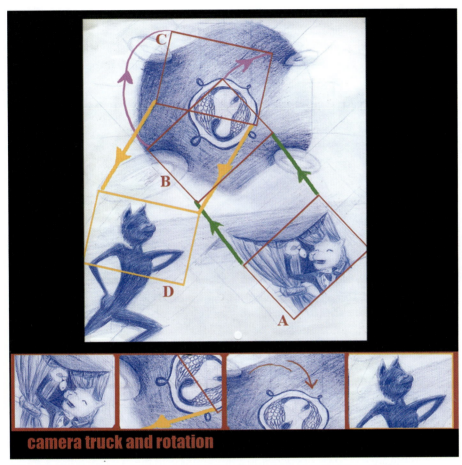

camera truck and rotation

[Fig 19-3] A complex camera move can be planned on one storyboard. This atmospheric establishing shot's background is detailed in areas where the camera lingers; less important sections are modeled with tonal values. Reproduced by permission of Sarah Kropiewnicki.

A scratch music track is often assembled from a variety of sources including classical and jazz music and soundtracks from other films. The scratch track sets a tempo for the editing and the action that will be retained in the final music track. Musical cues may cut abruptly during a change of pace in the action. The scratch track is only a timing device so the musical excerpts do not need to blend perfectly with one another.

Choose instrumental music with a tempo that matches the visual rhythm you wish to use for the film. Song lyrics sometimes help the action but can also compete with it. Music should reinforce the emotional mood of a scene. LOVE AT FIRST ROACH by William Robinson was originally timed to a 1930s jazz soundtrack. Its final track consisted of Parisian accordion tunes that helped turn a dirty kitchen into a romantic bistro. The two tracks shared a common tempo but created different emotional moods for the same visuals.

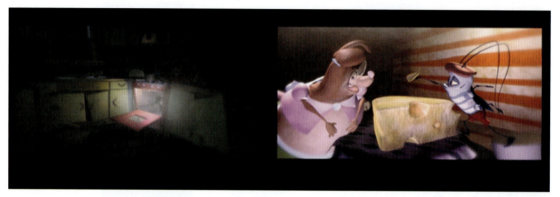

[Fig. 19-4] Parisian accordion music set the atmosphere better for this romantic date than the original jazz scratch track. Reproduced by permission of William Robinson.

A song sequence will usually have its final soundtrack recorded before storyboards begin. Dialogue is changeable. Songs are *locked down* when they are recorded. Even a scratch version of a song will have the same tempo as the final version. This is the reason why musical numbers are frequently the first feature film sequences to go into production.

Sound effects are usually recorded *wild* after the music and dialogue tracks are completed. These are *laid down,* or *slugged,* in a simple mix with the main soundtrack. Visual effects such as explosions and puffs of smoke are added to the reel with computer graphics programs if they are necessary for the story. If not, they are left for later and the storyboards carry the visuals alone.

*Previsualization,* also known as *previz,* adds a new string to the story artist's bow. Originally developed for live action, it has become an important part of CGI preproduction. Previz can be described as a CGI animatic created in the third and fourth dimensions with roughly modeled characters and backgrounds and in-depth camera moves. It closely resembles the *pop-throughs* shot by stop-motion animators using the finished puppets and sets. Previsualization artist Jean Pilotte describes the technique:

"3D implies volume and perspective in shades. The fourth dimension that *previz* brings is movement in time. A *leica* doesn't move like a real camera in space. So, the true *previz* is the one that moves the characters and the camera…. Once [it is] edited together [it] brings continuity of motion and camera planning to the [computer-animated film]"

*Previz* is an elaboration on the storyboard and not a substitute for it since it occurs at the end of preproduction after all story elements have been finalized. When the visual and audio materials are edited to the director's satisfaction the project is finally *up on reels*! And then the REAL work begins.

# This Is Only A Test: Refining Story Reels

*"If people don't want to go to the picture, nobody can stop them!"*

—Samuel Goldwyn

Screen your story reel or animatic for family and friends. Screen it for total strangers. You'll need a second and third and fourth opinion just as you did when you practiced pitching the storyboards, but now the film does the talking instead of you and it must stand or fall on its own merits. Stuff either works or it doesn't. (Don't tell the audience what they should be seeing. If they can't follow the story, it's your problem, not theirs.) Ask your viewers for their impressions after the screening. See if their interpretations coincide with yours. If not, ask for suggestions on how the material could be improved. Take notes. Revise the boards and story reel accordingly and screen it again for the same audience if possible. See if the problems are solved. Once everyone reads everything consistently, you're done—for now.

A feature film will 'screen and screen again' as the story is developed. Sequences may be added or dropped after different test audiences view the same material. Sometimes a secondary character may reveal its "star potential" and have its part expanded as a direct result of an audience's response during a test screening.

There is no blueprint, no one way to create an appealing story. I like to use the words of story man and layout artist Ken O'Connor as a guideline for story creation:

"We never achieved a formula. It was an interesting thing; I did [boards and layouts for] between 75 and 100 shorts, and you'd think that after a while you'd get the thing down to a routine, you know?… [B]ut [we] never succeeded at all. Every picture brings a whole new set of problems, and you simply can't make it like the last one, in my experience.… It's aggravating, but it's also very stimulating to me."

—Interview with Nancy Beiman, 1979

# 20

# Build a Better Mouse: Creating Cleanup Model Sheets

Animated characters have it rough. They're pushed, prodded, pulled into and out of shape on storyboards, forced to line up on size-comparison sheets, and put through their paces on action-model sheets. Their outlines are erased, redrawn, re-erased, reworked, reviewed, and redone. Their innards are exposed, their skeletons analyzed, and their clothes removed or left as transparent shapes over their naked bodies. But even the roughest animated character can clean up their act.

*Cleanup model sheets* standardize surface details, line quality, and the appearance of all characters. It is the Wardrobe, Makeup, and Hairstyling Department of animation. Inconsistencies in design such as cheats must also be labeled on the cleanups.

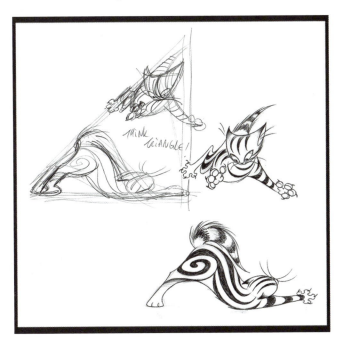

[Fig. 20-1] Animated characters can sometimes lose their appeal when the cleanup line is not handled with sensitivity. Cleanup drawings must retain the lively, animated quality of the rough. Reproduced by permission of Nina L. Haley.

Sometimes an animated character retains its rough, unpolished mannerisms and lines into the final color production. Color may be applied as a texture that moves continually as the figure animates. This shifting technique is called *boiling*. A rough line and boiling color on character and background can give a lively and vibrant quality to the images, creating a pleasing stylistic effect. Figure 20-2 shows two consecutive frames of a character that was designed to *boil* when animating.

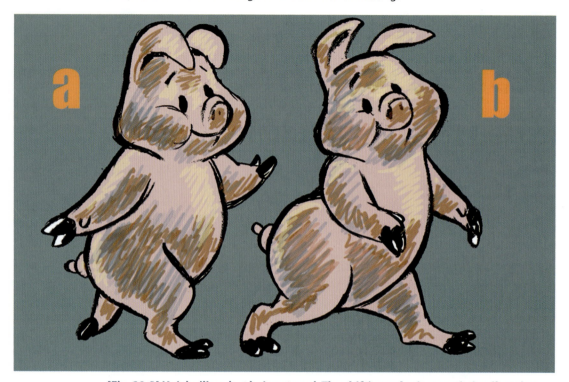

[Fig. 20-2] He's boiling, but he's not mad. The shifting color is an artistic effect that can create a pleasing complement to the rough outline of the character.

Boiling images and rough lines are not common in longer films since the constant variation may make the animation difficult to watch for long periods of time. Like all effects, boiling is best used in moderation.

Hand-drawn animated characters are typically cleaned up with the classic *wire line* that is thinly and evenly applied on all sections of the drawing. A *weighted* or thick-and-thin line is occasionally used on an entire character but more typically is restricted to outlines or limited areas of a design such as a female character's hair.

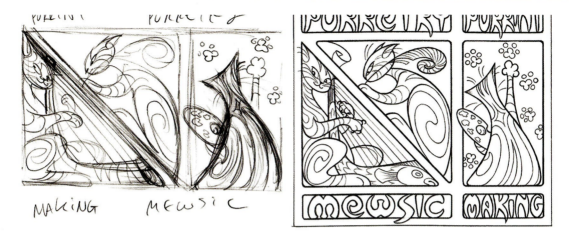

**[Fig. 20-3] The rough composition is very different from its final cleanup shown to the right. A weighted line gives a solid feeling to the cat's body outline. Interior lines are drawn with a wire line. Reproduced by permission of Nina L. Haley.**

Cleanups must retain the animation and life of the original drawing. If hand-drawn animation is *on model,* the assistant need only add details such as stripes, buttons, and flyaway hair that the animator or designer may not have included on the rough drawing. Rough animation that is fairly tight often has a lively, interesting quality that is maintained when the drawings are scanned and painted without cleanup.

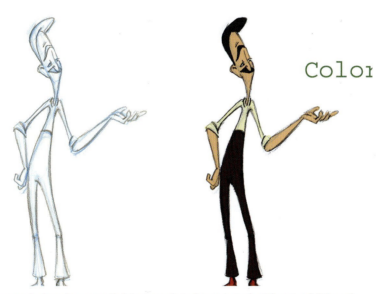

**[Fig. 20-4] This rough drawing was tight enough to be painted without additional cleanup. Note the non-photo-blue construction lines that drop out when the figure is scanned and painted by computer. Reprinted by permission of Brittney Lee.**

If a rough is extremely sketchy the cleanup artist may completely redraw the image, reducing or inflating incorrect volumes and adding details while standardizing the line weight and removing construction lines. The cleanup must retain the poses and composition of the rough sketch.

Most modern productions require the animator to draw *on model*, maintaining proper size relationships and volumes. A hand-drawn feature film is worked on by so many people for so long a time that the character's appearance may vary from sequence to sequence and even from scene to scene. Short films created by a few artists can run into similar difficulties if the character's design *evolves* as it is animated. Cleanup artists standardize the character according to the model sheets and maintain the consistency of the design throughout the picture. A Lead Key assistant will supervise a *crew* of cleanup artists on a feature production.

Certain computer graphics programs enable the artist to vectorize their drawings and clean up the line quickly. These programs can be a terrific aid in creating longer hand-drawn films, though they work best when the character is already *on model*; they won't correct shifting volumes or add missing costume details.

If your cleanup model differs from the original rough, or volumes are inconsistent, you should redraw the character's construction on a new sheet of paper in a pencil color that does not scan. Red is commonly used though non-photo blue is also permissible. Black line cleanup is drawn directly on top of the red sketch as shown in Figure 20-5.

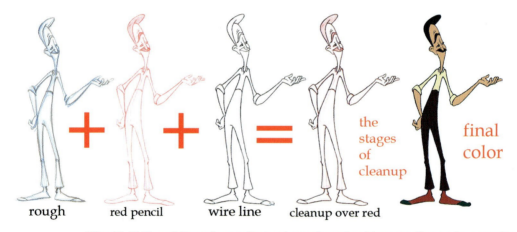

rough     red pencil     wire line     cleanup over red

the stages of cleanup

final color

[Fig. 20-5] "Rough" roughs are first redrawn in red or blue pencil to make sure that volume and details are consistent, then cleaned up with pencil or pen. Design reproduced by permission of Brittney Lee. Cleanup reproduced by permission of Nina L. Haley.

You may clean up on the same piece of paper as the red sketch (some computer pro-grams drop out red instead of non-photo blue) or put a new sheet of paper over the construction drawings and complete the cleanup with a mechanical pencil or pen. Check to see that all gaps in the lines are closed so that the "fill bucket" does not "leak" when the color models are painted on the computer.

Fortunately, animation paint programs now allow you to paint directly behind the roughs after they are scanned, eliminating the need for cleanup. This look can be very appealing if the animator has drawn important details on the roughs. My film YOUR FEET'S TOO BIG was animated rough and stayed that way in the final.

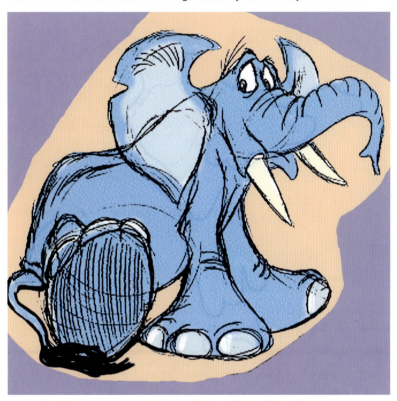

[Fig. 20-6] My rough animation for YOUR FEET'S TOO BIG was Xeroxed on cels and painted without benefit of cleanup. Today, I'd paint it on a computer in half the time at one-tenth of the cost.

A CGI character is constructed by importing concept drawings into the computer program and projecting the design into three dimensions via the modeling process. The character's modeling poses show the same pose in different angles. Cleanup helps maintain the integrity of small details in the design. Suzette the rat was designed on paper and drawn in action poses showing the range of motion that her CGI incarnation would need to perform.

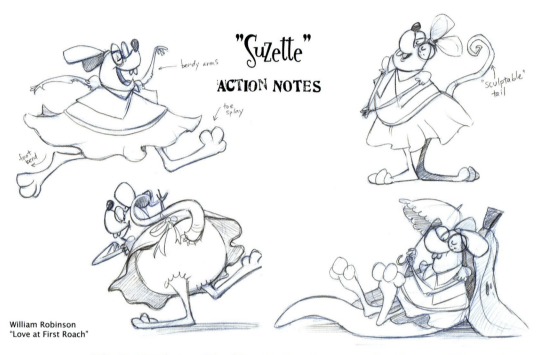

[Fig. 20-7] **Action models of Suzette show the range of motion her CGI incarnation must perform. Reproduced by permission of William Robinson.**

Figure 20-8 shows Suzette in modeling poses drawn after her model sheets were finalized. Her design was set before it went into the computer. Or was it?

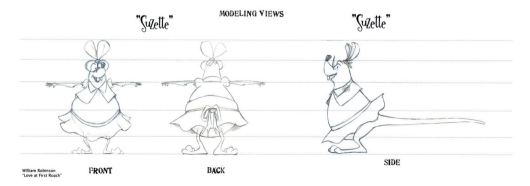

[Fig. 20-8] **Front, back, and side drawings of Suzette's modeling pose were imported into the computer. Reproduced by permission of William Robinson.**

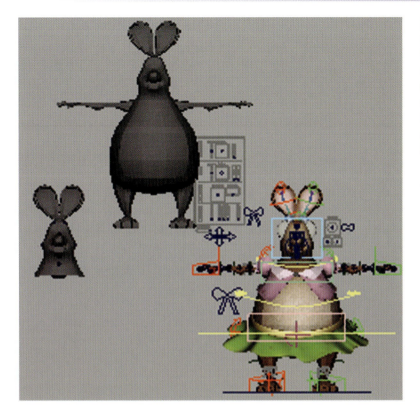

[Fig. 20-9] Suzette's arms were lengthened and her body proportions changed from the model drawings as she was modeled in CGI. Reproduced by permission of William Robinson.

Suzette's design was considerably modified after the drawings were imported into the computer. Her arms were lengthened so that they would be better able to hug her cockroach boyfriend Pierre. She got a nose job. Other details of her anatomy changed as she was modeled and rigged and transformed into a three-dimensional character.

The model drawings were the starting point for a character design that was finished in the computer. Only Suzette's clothing remained consistent with the original drawing, as shown in Figure 20-9.  Suzette appeared in a student film, so *evolution* of the character design at this stage was allowed and encouraged. A professional production will have the character design *locked down* on paper before it is imported into the computer. Full or partial character *maquettes* may be sculpted and digitized instead of sketches so that the CGI model will be identical to the original design. Maquette creation is discussed in Chapter 21.

CGI backgrounds and props are designed just like the characters. A CGI coffee shop will have floor plans drawn up and every table, bagel, and cup designed on paper before they are modeled.

A CGI character that is to be combined with live-action film is tested by digitally combining a 3D rendering of the character that was created in a 2D graphics program with one still frame from a live-action shoot. If there are design changes, another rendering is completed and re-composited until the look is finalized. Modeling, rigging, and texturing are the costliest parts of CGI animation, so testing the design in a less expensive format allows CGI designs to *evolve* before they are *locked down* for good.

CGI characters may be rendered with an outline that mimics the 'wire line' and eliminates interior shading so that the figures resemble painted or drawn animation. Special shaders can reproduce the look of brush or pen lines. An example of a CGI render in the style of Chinese brush painting is shown in the next two figures.

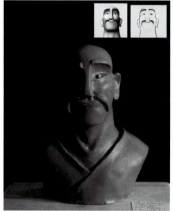 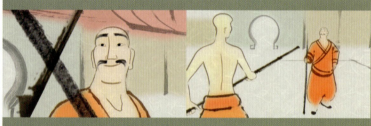

[Fig. 20-10, Fig. 20-11] This character was sculpted as a maquette, (Figure 20-10) then animated in CGI (Figure 20-11). The final render used the computer to create the look of Chinese brush paintings. Reproduced by permission of Joseph Daniels and Jedidiah Mitchell.

The artists emphasized the film's graphic look by using transparent color, flat lighting, and a digitized rice-paper background. Elaborate graphic effects can be animated more quickly on computer than by hand. *The machine need not create art that looks machine made!*

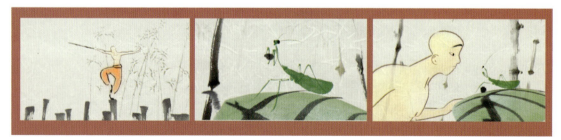

[Fig. 20-12] Backgrounds were painted conventionally, then scanned and modified in the computer. A rice-paper texture was applied digitally and the CGI-animated characters were rendered so that they resembled watercolor paintings. Reproduced by permission of Joseph Daniels and Jedidiah Mitchell.

*"Man has made many machines, complex and cunning, but which of them indeed rivals the workings of his heart?"*

—Pablo Casals

# 21

# Maquette Simple: Modeling Characters in Three Dimensions

*"Sculpture is really a drawing that you fall over in the dark."*

—Al Hirschfeld, THE LINE KING

Charles Philipon, editor of the French satirical magazines *La Caricature* and *Le Charivari*, commissioned the first *maquettes*, or three-dimensional models of a fanciful or imaginary figure. *La Caricature's* April 26, 1832 issue announced a "Celebrities" series of caricature portraits. Philipon stated that the political figures would first be portrayed *en maquette* and the drawings would be based on the clay sculptures. Staff illustrator Honoré Daumier was assigned to produce the artwork. He created more than 35 unbaked clay caricature *maquettes* of contemporary politicians that have survived to the present day. Legend has it that Daumier created the *maquettes* from life by sneaking lumps of clay into legislative sessions. More probably, he drew thumbnail sketches from life and then exaggerated the subject's features in clay. By using *maquettes* as models, Daumier was able to instill a lifelike, three-dimensional quality into his highly unflattering drawings. A lithograph that Daumier drew from one of his caricature busts appears in Figure 21-1.

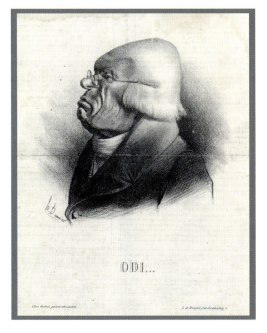

ODI...

**[Fig. 21-1] "Odi…" (Odier) was caricatured first in clay and then drawn by Honoré Daumier in May 1833 for Le Charivari's series of political portraits. (Nancy Beiman collection)**

Maquettes were first produced at the Walt Disney Studio in the 1930s to enable the animators to draw animated characters from any angle. A special Model Department was established at the request of Walt Disney by Joe Grant, a top caricaturist, character designer, and story man. Some maquettes for the Seven Dwarfs had movable wooden joints, but plaster or clay soon became the standard construction material. PINOC-CHIO's maquettes included full-sized functioning clocks for Geppetto's workshop and a life-sized wooden marionette of Pinocchio. A fully articulated wooden maquette of Bambi as a fawn had its construction based on traditional wooden artist's models.

The practice of creating character maquettes was revived for THE RESCUERS in 1972, and they have been sculpted for major characters in most subsequent films. Many CGI artists have continued the tradition by creating maquettes in clay or polymer plastic prior to modeling them on the computer.

Maquette production starts as character turnarounds and construction models are being finalized. Turnarounds provide a three-dimensional view of the character for the sculptor to work with.

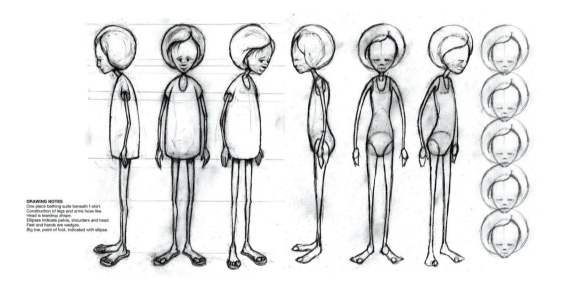

DRAWING NOTES
One piece bathing suite beneath t-shirt.
Construction of legs and arms hose like.
Head is teardrop shape.
Ellipses indicate pelvis, shoulders and head.
Feet and hands are wedges.
Big toe, point of foot, indicated with ellipse.

**[Fig. 21-2] Turnaround and construction models are essential tools for the maquette maker. Action poses show the personality and mobility of the character. Reproduced by permission of Jim Downer.**

The model sheets may change as the maquette *evolves* weak design features out. The maquette is baked and cast only when the final model sheets are approved.

Scale drawings for CGI characters have the arms spread out at a 45- or 90-degree angle, as shown in Figure 21-3. These drawings are then imported into the CGI program and used as modeling guides. A maquette for a CGI character will often be sculpted in a *modeling pose*, or a neutral stance. Maquettes may be scanned, digitized, and cleaned up in CGI so that the computer model is identical to the original design.

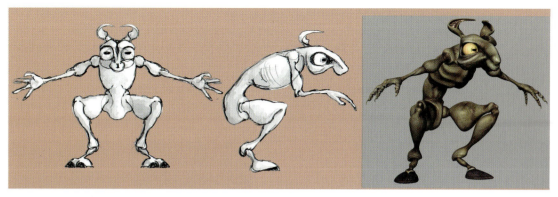

[Fig. 21-3] CGI figures use modeling poses that typically have the arms extended to the side of the figure. In this example the modeling pose is intentionally hunched, which will restrict and distort the character's body movements. Reproduced by permission of Nathaniel Hubbell.

The character designer next draws the character in the pose that is desired for the maquette. The drawing is the size of the actual maquette. Turnaround drawings and details of costumes or features may also be provided to the sculptor.

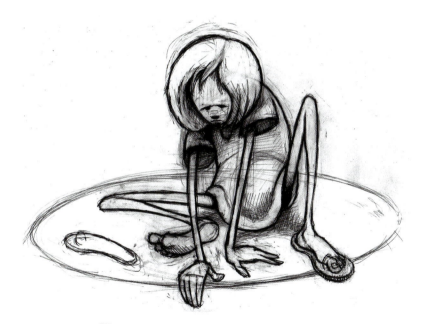

[Fig. 21-4]  A scale drawing of the character in an action pose is created as a guide for the sculptor. Reproduced by permission of Jim Downer.

The maquette drawing must be large enough to allow a wire armature to fit inside it and also leave room for the aluminum foil padding and clay or polymer "skin" that will be placed over the sculpture's wire "bones." A polymer figure must also be able to fit into an oven.

Next, twist medium gauge wire into a simple armature. Aluminum wire is used in Figure 21-5; steel in Figure 21-6. Steel wire is stronger and more appropriate for standing characters.

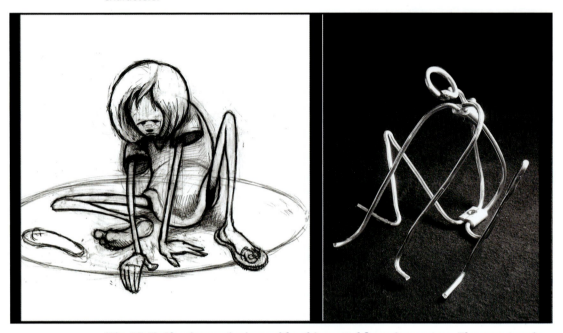

[Fig. 21-5] **Aluminum wire is used for this seated figure's armature. The armature is smaller than the maquette drawing. Reproduced by permission of Jim Downer.**

If you are sculpting a standing character *it is very important to attach the wire armature to a solid wooden base before proceeding further. Do not use plywood.* Secure the wire feet firmly to the base with staples, nails, or other metal attachments. You may drill holes in the wood and feed the wire feet through it, attaching it on the bottom of the base to secure the figure more firmly. Wires or wooden dowels may be camouflaged inside clothing or an object that the figure leans on for additional support, as shown in Figure 21-6.

A satisfactory base can be made from a piece of scrap wood obtained at a lumber yard or hardware store. If you are working with Plasticine or air-hardening clay that does not need to be baked, you may use plastic, plywood, or particle board bases without

**WARNING:** Polymer plastics such as Sculpey must be baked in a cool oven in order to 'set'. If your maquette sculpture is to be made of polymer plastic you ***must*** use only ***solid*** wood for the base. Do not use plywood, particle board, or any type of plastic as a base for polymer figurines. Use ***only*** aluminum foil to bulk up the armature, ***not*** paper, Styrofoam, or a rag, since these materials will release poisonous gases, burn, or melt during the baking process.

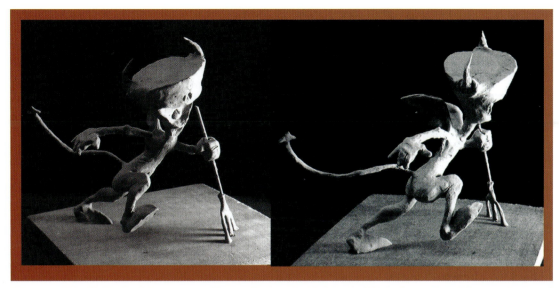

[Fig. 21-6] The little devil is supported by steel wires inside his pitchfork. Reproduced by permission of Jeremy A. Galante.

danger. The wire frame is then bulked out with aluminum foil. (*Do not use flammable materials. A list of what to avoid is provided in the previous box.*) Foil padding reduces the weight of the figure, conserves modeling material, and makes the resultant sculpture more resistant to breakage. The heat-conductive foil center bakes the maquette from the inside out and enables the polymer to set faster. The padding should be a ½ inch to ¾ of an inch smaller than the drawing so that the clay 'skin' may fit within its outline. A figure made of air-drying clay typically has its armature bulked out with strips of rag.

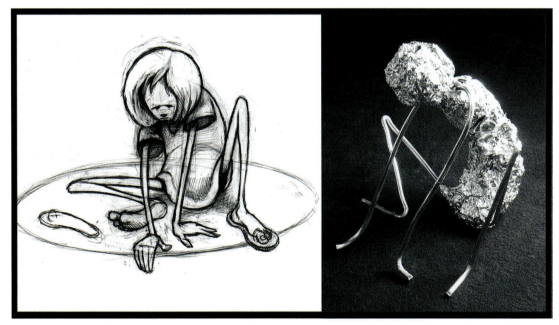

[Fig. 21-7] The wire armature is bulked up with aluminum foil padding. No plastic or paper padding should be used in a polymer sculpture. Reproduced by permission of Jim Downer.

The weight of the polymer plastic can cause it to sag slightly on the wire frame during baking. The material also will contract slightly as it cools. A foil center will maintain its shape and keep cracking and crazing to a minimum. Use enough foil to create a rough body shape for the character, but not so much that it completely fills the outline of the scale drawing. You must leave room for the 'skin'. Maquettes may be precisely proportioned by creating a wooden or cardboard negative outline of the scale drawing and ensuring that the finished maquette fits inside it. This technique is associated with "creature labs" and monster-movie model makers. A cartoon character maquette will usually be sculpted 'by eye' with frequent comparisons to the scale drawing(s) as modeling progresses.

Modeling material is applied after the armature is completed and attached to its wooden base. *It is very important to follow the directions on the box regarding time and temperature when baking polymer plastic. Low temperatures work best since they minimize cracking.* The polymer will be very hot and malleable after the figure is taken from the oven, typically after a 20-minute baking period.

Polymer plastic must be baked at a ***low temperature*** in a standard convection or radiant-heated oven. ***Never put polymer-plastic figures, with or without wire and aluminum armatures, in the microwave.*** Air bubbles in the polymer compound may explode, damaging the sculpture. Toxic chemicals may be released, damaging the sculptor. Read the directions on the polymer material's package and follow them to prevent serious consequences.

Once the maquette has been baked it should be allowed to cool overnight. When it is completely cool the sculpture and base are painted in one medium shade of gray water-based acrylic paint. *Do not use spray or oil paint on polymer compounds.* This neutral color allows values created by light and shadow to define the character's form in the same way that tonal values create contrast and depth in storyboard drawings.

Maquettes are used at several stages in hand-drawn animated film production. Animators use them to scale and distort characters. Art directors and background artists use them to determine how the quality of the light in the painted settings affects the characters. CGI lighting directors will literally use maquettes as models when creating the lighting for a sequence.

Figure 21-9 is an example of a polymer figure that I created in a sculpture class at the Walt Disney Studio. The maquette is designed to portray different emotions. It wears a cheerful expression on one side of its face and an alien, homicidal one on the other. The character's expression appeared to change when the light source was raised or lowered in relation to the sculpture. The planes of its head were carefully constructed to create shadows that created a more or less threatening appearance as the light source changed. I accomplished this by shining a strong light on the maquette while the sculpture was actually in progress and emphasizing or diminishing individual planes as required.

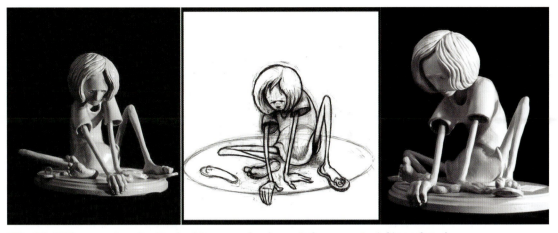

[Fig. 21-8] The armature is attached to a wooden base. Polymer material is sculpted over the armature in conformation with the scale drawing and the figure is baked. When it is cool and dry, the maquette and its base are painted with a medium-gray acrylic paint, which allows light and shadow to define three-dimensional forms. Decorative elements, such as patterns on clothing, are added at a later stage of production. Plasticine figures are not painted. Reproduced by permission of Jim Downer.

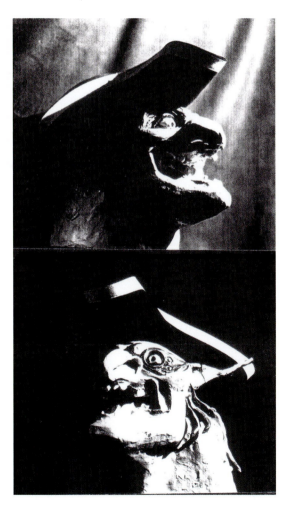

[Fig. 21-9] This maquette had two different expressions sculpted on either side of its face. The expressions were designed to intensify as the light source changed. Maquette sculpture by Nancy Beiman.

Not every character will work as a sculpture. A maquette has never been made for Mickey Mouse since his nose, ears, and other elements of his design do not turn in three-dimensional space. A "pure" graphic character does not need a three-dimensional representation. Simple, rounded characters such as the one in Figure 21-10 are usually animated without the use of maquettes.

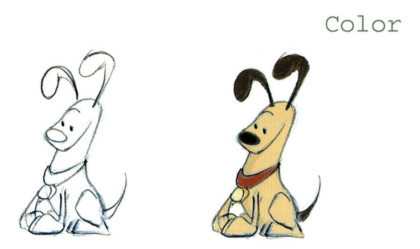

Color

[Fig. 21-10] A maquette was not considered necessary as an animation aid for "Mozart" since his design is very simple. Reproduced by permission of Brittney Lee.

A maquette helps you determine how your character's volumes turn in space and also enables you to "evolve" any lingering weaknesses or inconsistencies out of the character design before it is too late to change it further. A maquette is the last checkpoint on the long road an animated character must travel before it goes into production.

# 22

# Am I Blue?
# Creating Character
# Through Color

*"Colors, like features, follow the changes of the emotions."*

—Pablo Picasso

Color may be considered an independent element from character and background and can be used to convey an emotional meaning for both. In the early days of animation character color was interpreted very conservatively. It was considered desirable to have characters painted in rich, saturated hues that allowed them to read well over watercolor-wash backgrounds. Some films used color to emphasize a scene's emotional impact, usually by varying the lighting and tone on the backgrounds. These techniques sometimes became stereotypical. As we saw in Chapter 17, dramatic events in animated film often coincided with the sudden arrival of a thunderstorm!

More subtle shifts in color and graphic style were developed by experimental animators and breakaway studios such as UPA in the 1950s. Variably exposed backgrounds, pure line, and dramatic color changes were used to convey emotional impact in the UPA film ROOTY TOOT TOOT (1952), directed and designed by John Hubley. A crime suspect is painted in passionate red hues for most of the film. When her lawyer literally describes her in a different light, she appears virginally white in a flashback. A similar color variation is shown in Figure 22-1.

[Fig. 22-1] A character's color might depend on the context of the scene. This woman's color scheme changes from drawing (a) to drawing (b), showing how two different characters perceive her.

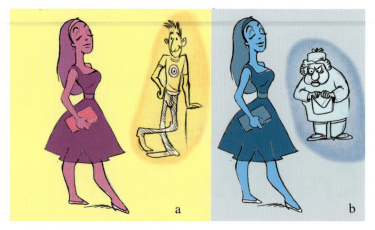

UPA films showed that character color did not need to be literal, 'realistic,' or consistent to be emotionally effective. Many cartoon animators have been influenced by this studio's technique over the years.

Oddly enough, CGI animators have more or less had to reinvent the color wheel. Many early computer-generated films attempted to copy live action and use a 'realistic' color palette for the characters, backgrounds, and lighting. There has been a shift away from this literal interpretation of color design that will continue to expand the artistic boundaries of this medium. A realistic or naturalistic color palette is not required in a CGI film, even one with 'realistic' characters, any more than it is required in other forms of animation. Computer graphics programs easily create textures and patterns that remain consistent on the character as it turns and distorts in space. Plaids and checks and elaborate textures are extremely hard to draw consistently by hand since they can *boil* or *crawl* around inside the character outline.

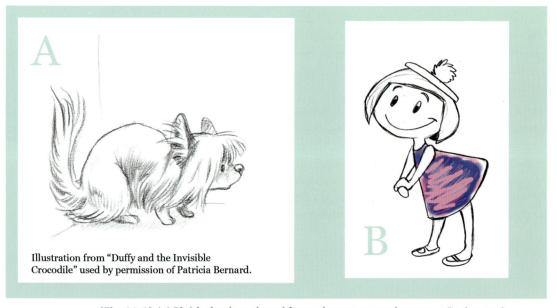

Illustration from "Duffy and the Invisible Crocodile" used by permission of Patricia Bernard.

[Fig. 22-2] (a) Plaid, checkered, and furry characters are known as "animator's nightmares" in hand-drawn film since they involve a lot of *pencil mileage* that might *crawl* or *boil* if not done perfectly. (b) In some cases boiling is used to create an artistic effect. The little girl's dress and the dog's fur will *boil* when they move since the scribbled color and line will not be applied in precisely the same manner on every frame.

Textural effects that once took teams of highly specialized artists months to create are now within the reach of any filmmaker with access to a good computer-graphics program. Characters and backgrounds may easily change color with the push of a button. Drop or contact shadows may now be mechanically created, speeding the production of hand-drawn animation and adding effects to CGI and stop-motion animation. The new media of the past 20 years have created enormous potential for creative color and textural design in all types of animation.

Color models can go a long way toward establishing your character's personality. You should experiment with a variety of color palettes on your characters just as you experimented with the proportions and look of the original design. Never assume that your first choice will be the last, or the best.

"Walt would love it. Marc said he was like a little kid opening up Christmas presents," says Alice Davis, whose husband Marc was one of the "Nine Old Men" of the Walt Disney Studio and also a versatile character designer.

The designers and color stylists had to appeal to a very demanding audience. Alice Davis explained how Marc Davis and designer Mary Blair would pitch concept art to Walt Disney. "You had better have something to have Walt going on when he finished with all the drawings, because he would want more. Mary would have lots of drawings taking one idea and showing different ways [it] could be used....Where a lot of guys would do two or three drawings, Marc and Mary would do twelve or more, giving Walt a variety to choose from. Marc said one day a young man came to [Walt] with one drawing and said, 'What do you think of this, Walt?' Walt looked at it and then turned and looked at him and smiled and said [sweetly], 'It's *very* difficult to choose between *one*.'"

—Interview with Nancy Beiman, August 2000

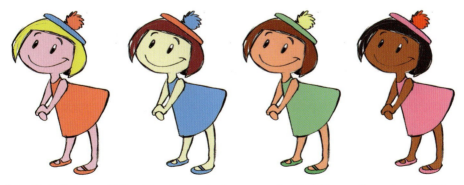

**[Fig. 22-3] "It's very difficult to choose between one."—Walt Disney. Experiment with different color combinations on characters; your first attempt may not be the last.**

*Color models* will change depending on the story and the mood of the character. It's customary to have different color models for each character showing standard hues by day and night. Costume changes will call for an additional series of models. A standard model such as the one shown here will give you something to start with.

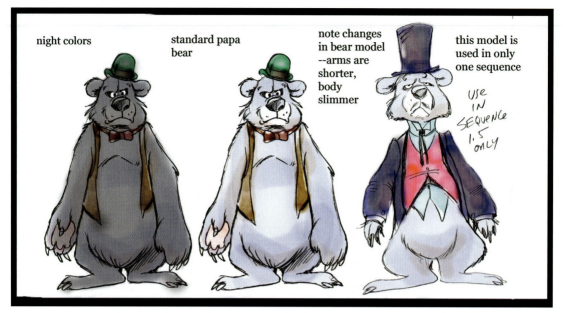

**[Fig. 22-4] Standard color models for Papa Bear indicate day and nighttime variations and a standard outfit. Costume changes will be indicated on new model sheets labeled with the relevant sequence number and name.**

The next figure shows The Three Bears in color. In this extreme case, each bear's color now indicates its species. Papa is a polar bear, Mama is a black bear, and Baby is a honey bear! A character's final colors will often "bear" no resemblance to the tonal values used for it on rough storyboard drawings.

**[Fig. 22-5] The Three Bears display colorful variants indicating their different origins. Dramatic character coloration will affect art direction for the entire film.**

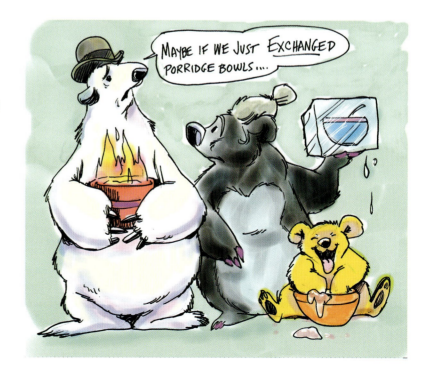

In the early days of color some studios designed character models first and modified them as needed after they were tested on film with the master backgrounds. In a modern production the character and background palettes are typically designed at the same time. This integrates dramatic palettes like the ones in Figure 22-6 into the film's *universe*. The characters will read well on their backgrounds since they were designed to work together. Color models are placed on the backgrounds to test readability and each is modified as needed.

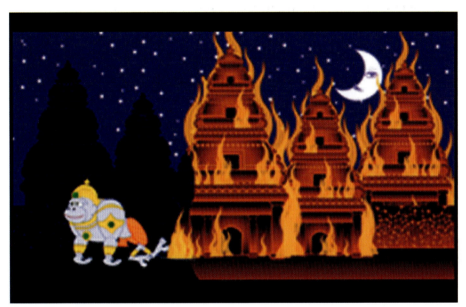

**[Fig. 22-6] Character colors are designed along with the backgrounds. Frame from SITA SINGS THE BLUES reproduced by permission of Nina Paley.**

# Creating Color in Context

*"I'm not crazy about reality, but it's still the only place to get a decent meal."*

—Groucho Marx

Color has a natural vocabulary since so much of our color inspiration is derived from nature. We have named colors after flowers (Rose Red), fruit (Orange and Lemon Yellow), plants (Grass Green), and birds (Peacock Blue). These are all natural, realistic colors. Geography contributes hues named for actual locations such as Copenhagen Blue, Prussian Blue, Sienna Brown, and Naples Yellow. Some colors are named after the artists who created them such as Van Dyke Brown, Matisse Blue, Hunter Green, and Titian Red. The color Magenta was named after the hue of the blood spilled on the battlefield of that name in 1839.

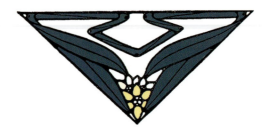

**[Fig. 22-7] Hunter Green was created by Roycroft artist Dard Hunter. Design from Pig Pen Pete (1914) (Nancy Beiman collection).**

But animated characters need *not* be rendered with natural colors! Maurice Noble said that it's desirable to *have fun* with the graphic potential of your characters, and that reality in design and color was optional. Animated characters may fly, change shape, or morph into something else at will. Why settle for conventional coloring?

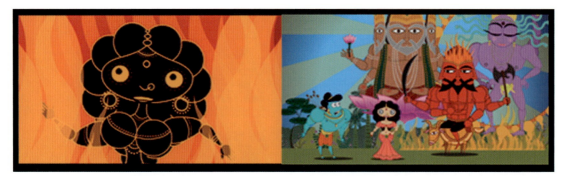

**[Fig. 22-7] SITA SINGS THE BLUES uses bright colors based on the art of India. The illusion of a burning figure is created with a silhouette. Reproduced by permission of Nina Paley.**

If we refer back to the graphically-colored characters in Figure 22-1, the entire palette changed along with the context. Can emotional qualities only be conveyed by dramatic color changes? As it turns out, we don't have to throw out the purple baby with the green bathwater. Changing the entire color palette of your character to reflect every emotional variant is technically similar to conjuring up a thunderstorm whenever the going gets tough in an animated cartoon. In other words, the technique can become a cliché or develop comic associations.

There is another, subtler way to convey emotional changeability through color.

Let us observe how a color variation on a *portion* of a character's design changes our perception of that character.

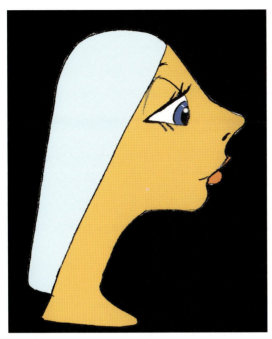

[**Fig. 22-9**] **The starting point of 'realistic color'.**

Figure 22-9 shows a simple character. The eye color is within the normal color range for this species. The eye and pupil create a nice, readable color combination that would work well for a project with 'realistic' art direction.

Figure 22-10 shows several different color variations on Figure 22-9. The first figure does not convey any emotional quality. But see how the remaining eye color combinations create the feeling of different emotions—and possibly different species—when the rest of the design does not differ in any other respect from the realistic original.

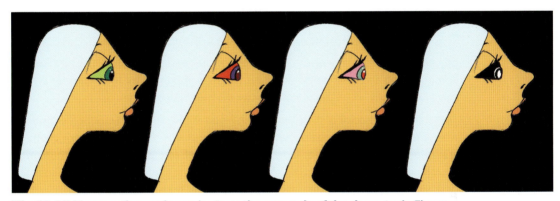

[**Fig. 22-10**] **Here are three color variants on the eyes only of the character in Figure 22-9. The skin and hair colors are unchanged. Strange or unusual eye colors appear to convey different emotional meanings based on our cultural perceptions.**

**Exercise:** Create a simple human character. Design him or her so that the eyes are prominent. Color the figure using hues that are found in nature. Now change only the *eye* and *pupil* color of this character, leaving all other colors consistent with your original. Create several examples since "it's difficult to choose between one." You need not use naturalistic color, but may try any combination that takes your fancy.

Color has different meanings in different cultures. In Eastern cultures, red is the color of joy and life. In Western culture, it symbolizes life, but it is also the color of rage, lust, and danger. I will be speaking of color from the Western perspective for simplicity's sake.

Following are some emotional associations that we typically assign to color. These perceptions are so strong that they read well even if the color appears outside of a story context.

RED: Life, love, rage, passion, danger, warning, speed, male sexuality, strength

ORANGE: Warmth, enthusiasm, optimism, happiness

PINK: Female sexuality, life, good health, youth, sentimentality, innocence, childishness

BLUE: Peace, water, unity, spirituality, happiness, stability; *also* coldness, depression. A *bluenose* is one definition of a prude. Male babies may wear blue clothing. A *blue-collar worker* is someone who works with their hands.

BLACK: Power, fashion, sexuality, sensuality, mystery; *also* evil, fear, death, unhappiness, the unknown

GREEN: Luck, nature, vigor; *also* lack of experience, illness, envy, bad fortune

YELLOW: Sunshine, joy, gold, inspiration, royalty, youth, hope; *also* dishonesty, cowardice, illness

PURPLE: Royalty, wisdom, richness, age, luxury; *also* arrogance, mourning, cruelty

WHITE: Purity, innocence, perfection, cleanliness; *also* coldness, death

GRAY: Boredom, blandness, sadness, illness; *also* simplicity, mystery

Color may be used against type. THE CORPSE BRIDE, a stop-motion film, used a funereal, monochromatic color scheme of grays, blacks, and purples for the living characters and a bright, fully-saturated riot of color for the ghosts in the Afterlife.

The changing eye color of the characters in Figure 22-10 creates an emotional context when there is no other variation between the figures. Will changing the color of other portions of a character's anatomy have the same effect? Many parts of the human body have symbolic meaning. We know that the eyes are "the windows of the soul." Here are some popular cultural associations for other body parts:

HANDS: *Open hand:* creativity, generosity, peace and friendship, supplication, prayer. *Fist:* Violence or strength. The *right* hand symbolizes good qualities while the *left* hand, and left side of the body generally, conveys a negative meaning. Gloves can also be symbolic.

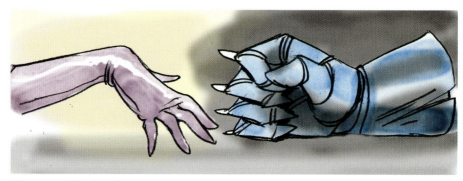

[Fig. 22-11] **The hand's covering can also convey a symbolic meaning.**

FEET: Life path, activity, agility. If *large*, they convey comedy or clumsiness. Caricatured characters are sometimes described as being designed in a *Bigfoot* style. Shoes are important indications of character. *Boots* symbolize violence, militarism, and fear. If the feet are *bare*, they may symbolize either poverty or freedom.

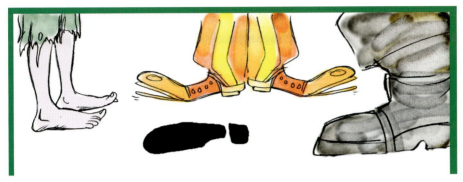

**[Fig. 22-12]**

HEART: Spirituality, love, the soul, sincerity, trust

**[Fig. 22-13]**

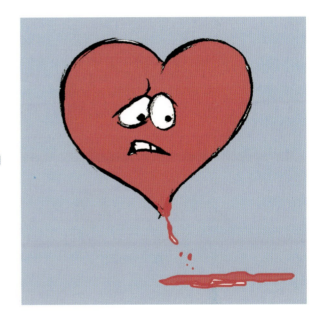

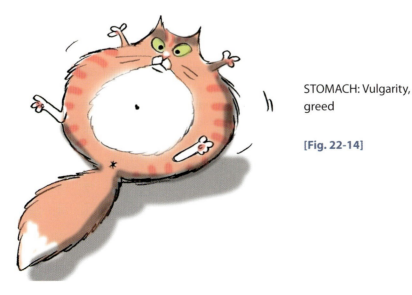

STOMACH: Vulgarity, greed

**[Fig. 22-14]**

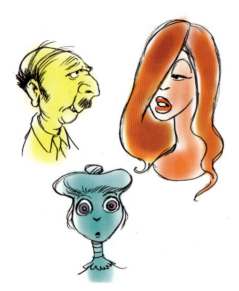

HAIR: Sensuality or vanity. If a man's hairline is *receding*, it can make him seem ineffectual (especially if it is combined with a comb-over). If hair is very *abundant*, it can convey a free or untamed personality. When *bound,* it signifies emotional restraint.

**[Fig. 22-15]**

When the color is changed on one section of the character design, the viewer associates the emotional qualities of the color with the symbolic meaning of the body part. One element will influence the perception of the other. In figure 22-16, the color Red is applied first to the character's nose. The next version changes the color of its entire face. Red is then applied to one of its hands, and lastly to one of its feet.

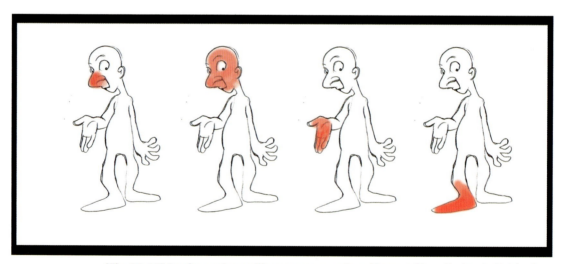

**[Fig. 22-16] A color variant will create an emotional impact if applied to individual body parts. You do not have to change the entire palette to convey meaning. The symbolism of the body part complements the color symbolism and helps refine the context. A different interpretation will arise with each change of hue and limb.**

*Red is the most emotional color* and conveys many meanings. A red nose can signify illness or drunkenness; a red face, anger or embarrassment; the third character has been caught red-handed; and a red foot may have been recently injured or simply be wearing mismatched socks! These are some stereotypical interpretations that come to mind when viewing character color variations outside of a story context.

**Exercise:** Redo this assignment with three new identical line drawings on white paper. On the first drawing, add color to one of your character's hands. Put the new color on one of its feet in the second drawing, and over its entire face in the third. Repeat the exercise with red, yellow, and green variants and see how your perception of the character changes.

Both exercises are inconclusive because some colors can suggest opposing emotions if the characters are not placed into any sort of context. If a prop is added to each of the drawings in Figure 22-16, our perception of the figure will dramatically change. A red hand may signify an accident with a paint can or the aftermath of an axe murder. A red nose may result from inebriation or a simple head cold, depending on whether the character is associated with a bottle or a box of tissues.

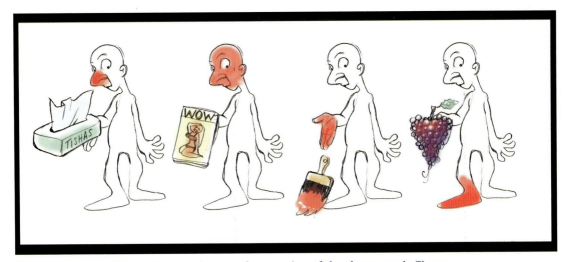

[Fig. 22-17] The addition of props changes the meaning of the characters in Figure 22-16. In some cases the emotion conveyed is now the opposite of that provided by the original image.

# It's a Setup: Testing Your Color Models

The last test for a character design is to place it over a background to see if it reads well. It is a good idea to establish color themes and color breakdowns similar to the ones described in Chapter 17 before creating character and background color models. A complementary or split-complementary color theme reads very clearly (an orange-toned character on a blue-themed background) but a monochromatic color palette works equally well if you set the color values in the same manner, as was used for black-and-white storyboard sketches in Chapter 10.

*Be sure to test all of the character color models in grayscale.* The value principle discussed in Chapter 17 applies equally to the backgrounds and the character models. Color values that work well in grayscale will read well no matter what combination of hues are used. Light values that are too close may 'run into' one another. Character models that are exclusively composed of dark values may not read when placed over dark backgrounds.

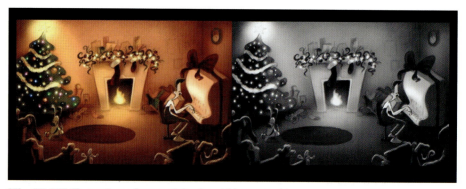

[Fig. 22-18] Character color models should be tested in grayscale and then checked again for readability by placing them and any relevant props on a typical background and putting the entire setup into grayscale. Reproduced by permission of Brittney Lee.

The human eye is drawn to the strongest color contrast in a scene, just as it was drawn to the greatest contrast between gray values on the storyboards. Generally you will have the greatest area of contrast appear on your characters with closer foreground and background values that do not distract from them. There are always exceptions to this rule. Character and background colors may both be modified after the grayscale test. You may need to adjust the intensity of the color values to improve the character's readability, and adjust it again if it does not read well when placed in a *setup* with the backgrounds, other characters, and props.

**Exercise:** Rework your designs one last time by adding one prop to each of the color sketches and placing them on top of a color background. Put the *setup* into grayscale. Modify the values if you have any difficulty reading anything in grayscale. These tests will put your character into context and then the story will truly begin.

*"It's not easy being green."*

—Kermit the Frog

# 23

# Screen and Screen Again: Preparing for Production

You have now officially ended Pre-production. The *film* is finished; the *animation* is about to begin. Story problems are dealt with in storyboard stage so that the picture won't need revisions after the animation is 40 percent completed (and there are films that have achieved this dubious distinction). Changes can and will still occur if you are on a commercial production. Sequences may be added or more likely dropped if directors and producers demand it. A well-run feature project will have some sequences in production while others are being revised, so that the film can be completed out of sequential order.

If you're working on a personal film, you have completed the boards and timed the story reel. You have prioritized the sequences so that the expendable "C's" go into production last and your major efforts go into the "A's and B's." The character models are finalized, rigged and modeled if necessary, and the art direction set.

Layout, the first stage of production, is the cinematography of animation. Good layout *pluses* the storyboard staging, choreographs the camera moves, adds depth and design to backgrounds, and sets the stage for the animated actors. After layout, it is *finally* time for the animators to create memorable performances that are based on storyboard 'rehearsals'. This book ends where most others begin.

I stated in the Introduction that animators were magicians. Like magicians, we work hard to make the impossible look easy. Our reward is a symphony of color, sound, and motion, and the pleasure of working in the most fascinating art form of the last hundred years. Best of all, in animation, the magic is real. It will come to you with practice. Good luck, and have fun!

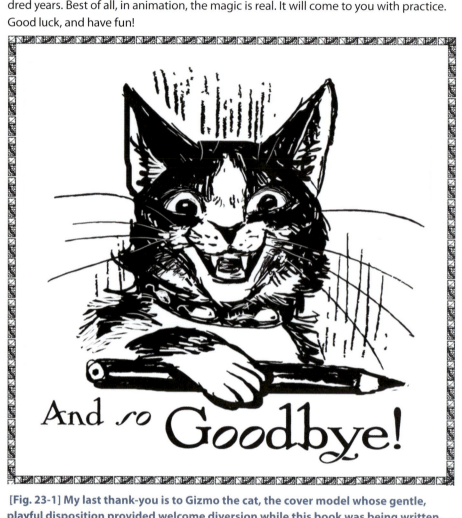

And so Goodbye!

[Fig. 23-1] My last thank-you is to Gizmo the cat, the cover model whose gentle, playful disposition provided welcome diversion while this book was being written.

# Further Reading:
# Books, Discs,
# and Websites

A single book cannot possibly show all art direction, character design, and storyboard styles. I recommend the following books, discs, and websites as good starting points for the aspiring preproduction artist's reference library. The first section lists websites of various artists. The second section lists books by character designers and writers, some of whom have generously allowed me to use their illustrations in this book. The third section consists of books on story and storyboard technique for feature and television productions.

Much of the best material on story and character design appears on "special-edition" DVDs of animated films, with new treasures released each year. Some recommended DVDs are listed in the fourth section. Artistic anatomy books appear in the last section.

## Artists' Websites

The Creative Talent Network is a collective of storyboard, animation, and design artists, many of whom are associated with major studios. An extensive gallery of character and inspirational art is displayed at http://www.creativetalentnetwork.com/.

Nina Paley, "America's Best-Loved Unknown Cartoonist," has an extensive gallery of her animation and comic art including *SITA SINGS THE BLUES* at http://www.ninapaley.com.

Nancy Beiman's website is at http://www.nancybeiman.com and more of her artwork can be viewed at the Creative Talent Network site.

John Van Vliet's cartoons about film and animation appeared in the famous "Available Light" calendars for over 20 years. His website is http://www.migrantfilmworker.com.

Bob Staake's animation designs can be viewed at http://www.bobstaake.com.

Brian P. McEntee was art director for *CATS DON'T DANCE*, *BEAUTY AND THE BEAST*, and *ICE AGE*. His futuristic novel *Eve* is featured on a cleverly animated website, http://www.evethenovel.com, that sells "DNA-spliced" household implements that appear in the book.

Peter De Sève's website has galleries of his character designs and illustrations at http://www.peterdeseve.com/.

Patrick Maté's caricatures can be viewed at http://patrickmate.blogspot.com.

Nina L. Haley draws cat-themed illustrations. Samples of her artwork can be seen at http://buttonheadcity.blogspot.com.

# Books by Animation Character Designers and Writers

Dean Yeagle is an animation character designer and *Playboy* cartoonist. His love-ly girls and comic illustrations have been collected in several books: *One Mandy Morning* and the *Scribblings* series, which are available at http://www.cagedbeagle.com/. Dean's design work can also be seen at http://www.bellefree.com.

David Chelsea's illustrations appear in *The New York Times*. His book *Perspective! For Comic Book Artists*, is recommended for every animation artist's library. He also wrote the graphic novels *David Chelsea in Love* and *Welcome to the Zone*.

Floyd Norman is "animation's editorial cartoonist" and a veteran story man for the Walt Disney Studio, Hanna-Barbera, Pixar, and Disney Publications. His books *Faster, Cheaper!* and *Son of Faster Cheaper* are available at http://www.afrokids.com along with his comic valentine to a certain former CEO, *How the Grinch Stole Disney*.

Michel Gagné's *Insanely Twisted Rabbits* and *Frenzied Fauna* are available at http://www.gagneint.com/ along with huge online galleries of his character designs.

Mark Newgarden's book *We All Die Alone* anthologizes his brilliant deconstructions of popular cartoon styles. EM! ® appears in *A Public Service Announcement* at http://www.laffpix.com.

Patricia Bernard is a best-selling Australian writer of travel, adult mystery, and chil-dren's books, several of which were illustrated by Nancy Beiman. Her website is at http://www.geocities.com/patriciabernard2001/.

Christopher Hart's series of character-design books are excellent guides to specific design styles. I contributed 12 pages to *How to Draw Animation*.

# Books on Scriptwriting and Visual Storytelling

*Dreamworlds* (published 2007) by art director Hans Bacher (MULAN) promises to become the standard text on animation art direction and screen design. Bacher's website is at http://its-a-wrap.blogspot.com/.

*The Art of Monsters Inc.* by John Lasseter and Pete Docter, *The Art of The Incredibles* by Mark Cotta Vaz, Brad Bird, and John Lasseter, and *The Art of Finding Nemo* by Mark Cotta Vaz (Chronicle Books LLC). All aspects of preproduction are extensively illustrated. Other books in this series are also highly recommended.

*Making Shapely Fiction* by Jerome Stern (W. W. Norton and Co., 2000) is a hugely entertaining guide to story construction that is useful for animators and creative writers.

*Layout and Character Design Made Absurdly Simple* by Brian LeMay (Sheridan College, privately printed, 1991) is a good guide to television animation layout and production design that also includes examples of television storyboards.

*Film Directing: Shot by Shot: Visualizing from Concept to Screen* (Michael Wiese Productions, 1991) is the basic textbook for cinematic editing and staging.

*How to Write for Animation* by Jeffrey Scott (The Overlook Press, 2002) is a guide to writing and pitching television series by an Emmy-award-winning author who also happens to be the grandson of The Three Stooges' Moe Howard!

*Sight, Sound, and Motion: Applied Media Aesthetics* by Professor Herbert Zettl (Wadsworth Publishing, 2004) is a detailed description of visual theory and applications that is useful for all storyboard artists.

*The Visual Story: Seeing the Structure of Film, TV, and New Media* by David Block (Focal Press, 2001) is an excellent guide to basic film language.

*Paper Dreams* and *Before the Animation Begins* by John Canemaker are out of print, but highly recommended.

*Animation from Pencils to Pixels* by Tony White (Focal Press, 2006) describes the preproduction and production of a single film.

# DVDs

SHREK (two-disc set) has three complete pitches of sequences that were later cut from the film. Uniquely, two camera views are included for each pitch: the audience's and that of each of the three story men who pitch the action, presentation, and acting boards. A large gallery of character and background designs shows how the look of the film evolved over time.

THE INCREDIBLES (two-disc set) has an excellent "making of" section on disc two that shows an animatic being assembled for the "100-Mile Dash" sequence. Rough and presentation boards, maquettes, model sheets, and color scripts are visible in some shots. Separate chapters discuss production and character design.

THE FANTASIA ANTHOLOGY (three-disc set) contains a complete rough story reel with soundtrack and cut-in animation for the unfinished "Invitation to the Dance" and story reels for "The Ride of the Valkyries" and "The Swan of Tuonela." There is a large gallery of story sketches and concept art from each sequence of both the original FANTASIA and FANTASIA CONTINUED and deleted scenes from "The Sorcerer's Apprentice" sequence

CINDERELLA and LADY AND THE TRAMP (two-disc sets) include story reels for sequences that were cut from the final films and galleries of preproduction artwork. *Cinderella* also contains a tribute to designer Mary Blair.

BAMBI (two-disc set) includes the original storyboard for what later became the "Bambi on the Ice" sequence and deleted boards showing the death of Bambi's mother. The director's voice-over is a skillfully edited and acted recreation of actual story meetings between Walt Disney and some of his key personnel. Extras include a fine gallery of Tyrus Wong's gorgeous color keys.

The WARNER BROTHERS GOLDEN COLLECTION's special features include rare storyboards, profiles of individual characters and artists, and 'schematics' or layout and art direction sketches. The entire series is highly recommended.

TREASURE PLANET (deluxe two-disc set) contains an interview with maquette sculptor Kent Melton describing his modeling technique.

THE CORPSE BRIDE'S extras describe the creation of maquettes and the armature and animation techniques utilized in the stop-motion production.

MUNRO is included in *Rembrandt Film's Greatest Hits*.

GORILLAZ' DEMON DAZE (two-disc set) contains the rough story reel for the "Feel Good" music video.

T.R.A.N.S.I.T by Piet Kroon is available on the 'Short 4-Seduction' DVD.

HOLLYWOOD CAMERA WORK: MASTER COURSE (six-disc set) contains virtual 'cranes' for Maya and two-dimensional blocking templates for Adobe Illustrator as well as comprehensive staging of live-action camera blocking using simple computer-generated human figures.

# Anatomy Books for the Artist

*Animal Painting and Anatomy* by W. Frank Calderon (Dover Publications) is still the best comparative-anatomy book in print.

*The Vilppu Drawing Manual* by Glen Vilppu (Vilppu Drawing Studio) is by an artist who regularly teaches at major animation studios. All of Vilppu's discs and tapes are recommended.

The books of George Bridgman are useful guides to simplified artistic anatomy. His style can get in the way but his principles of construction are excellent.

*Artistic Anatomy* by Dr. Paul Richer is an outstanding guide written and illustrated by a doctor who was also an artist. Kinesiology and the mechanics of movement are illustrated with near-photographic accuracy.

*Force: The Key to Capturing Life Through Drawing* by Mike Mattesi (Universe Star) is a good guide to gesture drawing that is an excellent supplement to Paul Richer's book.

**Appendix 1**

# Discussion with A. Kendall O'Connor

*Excerpts, February 15, 1979, © 1979, 2005 by Nancy Beiman*

Ken O'Connor worked as a story man, art director, and layout artist at the Walt Disney Studio. He began on short cartoons in 1935 and worked on most Disney films up until THE LITTLE MERMAID in 1989. This interview was conducted by Nancy Beiman at the California Institute of the Arts while she was a student in Ken O'Connor's layout and storyboard class.

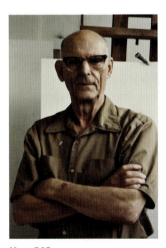

**Ken O'Connor, photographed in 1987 by Nancy Beiman.**

NANCY BEIMAN: When you were doing tonal studies, did you always have the color of the final background in mind?

KEN O'CONNOR: No, I'd say not. Not always.

NANCY BEIMAN: These layouts are highly rendered. You brought in one which was sketchier.

KEN O'CONNOR: Well, circumstances alter cases here all the time.... I think of the pure line effect, then the tone, then the color. It evolves that way sometimes; of course, there are no real hard-and-fast rules. Inspirational material—in this case Maxfield Parrish-like inspirational paintings—had been done before this was done. So you've got that in mind, you see. You know what shade of lavender you would reasonably use for the shadows, and you've seen the inspirational painting.

NANCY BEIMAN: I was wondering whether tonal rendering layouts was a general practice, or was it just done for the sheer pleasure of doing it?

KEN O'CONNOR: No, there was very little done for the sheer pleasure of doing it. There are a number of reasons for rendering, there's no simplistic answer…. This thing in line wouldn't impress a director anywhere near as impressively as a tonal version of the same landscape. And then, of course, the end product of layout is something for background. So the background man has to think in values, tonality; and you give him the best sendoff you can. If you hand the background man just a line drawing, he's got to do all the thinking of the values, the light scheme; where's the light coming from, where do you want the dramatic emphasis? We put in flashes of light and dark where we wanted it.

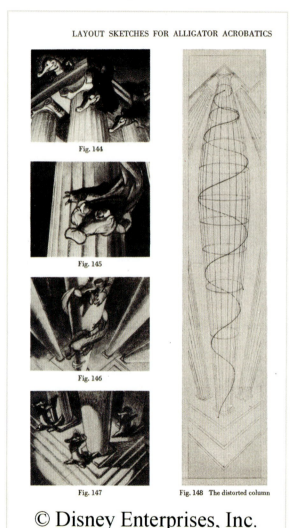

© Disney Enterprises, Inc.

**Storyboards and final layout by Ken O'Connor from "The Dance of the Hours" sequence from FANTASIA. Reproduced by permission of Disney Enterprises, Inc.**

You can see how your eye tends to go to [a certain area]. That's where the layout man wants you to go. Everything else is subservient. The tonality tells the background man to keep that in mind when painting. You bring one thing out, powerfully, and play that other down tonally.

NANCY BEIMAN: In animation, when you use reference material, the general guideline is to look at it once and never look at it again. Would you do the same thing when you were researching backgrounds?

KEN O'CONNOR: I would get every piece of reference I could lay my hands on before I started. Which frequently wasn't much time, I might say. I'd go to the library; go to other artists who kept scrapbooks; I'd go to my own collection at home. I keep a clip-file with maybe 200,000 clippings classified by subject, I imagine. I'd gather everything in like a big vacuum cleaner, almost regardless of exactly how valuable it would be —then I'd try to go through a period of absorbing it. … Then I'd regurgitate it as layouts.

NANCY BEIMAN: How long would this take you, on the average?

KEN O'CONNOR: Very variable—a matter of hours on a short film sometimes; a matter of months on a picture like PINOCCHIO or THE RESTLESS SEA. Before we did THE RESTLESS SEA, we sat down and read books for maybe two months. We were not up on such things as, for example, the differences between zooplankton and phytoplankton, or internal waves.

These things are not in the average man's vocabulary, you see. We had to study a great deal because this was to be authentic. Having got all the reference together, I would hang onto it right through the picture.… I'd often pass it on to the background men.… As far as I was concerned reference was a thing to be used the whole time.

NANCY BEIMAN: Would you caricature it?

KEN O'CONNOR: Yes, I'd try to make it appropriate to the picture. In this picture (FANTASIA) you can see that it is a very decorative style.… We warped everything toward the idyllic, romantic, classical, decorative mood in this particular sequence. We went in other directions depending on the mood of the picture.… There were certain key backgrounds painted from layouts which the other background men were expected to follow stylistically … we did a lot of conferring with the director, the head animator, and the background man as much as we could.

NANCY BEIMAN: Is it better to have more camera moves, or cut to a new shot?

KEN O'CONNOR: I think everything should be judged by what the scene calls for. I think there's probably a certain amount of ignorance today that's behind a lot of the lack of use of the camera. We studied live action very closely, and stole everything we could from it.… I'll give you an example. Alfred Hitchcock, in some of his suspense pictures, used what he called a "fluid camera." He kept it moving the whole time. It resulted in a flow to the picture that you don't get by "cut, cut, cut," you know. If you are building up toward a collision, or going to a battle, you build the tempo with shorter pans and faster cuts to get a staccato effect. It's like music; staccato versus legato. That's the way we thought of the thing.

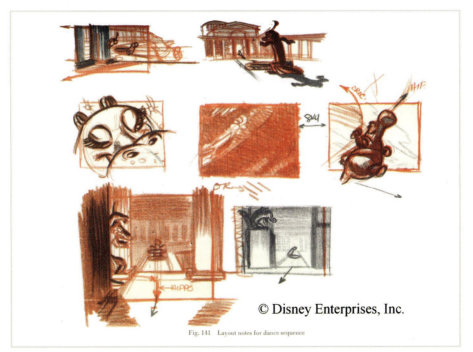

© Disney Enterprises, Inc.

Fig. 141   Layout notes for dance sequence

**Ken O'Connor's rough thumbnails for "The Dance of the Hours" sequence from FANTASIA. The shots were staged differently in the finished film. Reproduced by permission of Disney Enterprises, Inc.**

NANCY BEIMAN: How did they manage to get sequence directors to work together?

KEN O'CONNOR: Well … certain things tend to pull [a picture] together. One is model sheets, so the characters, at least, are consistent. Another is a good lead background painter who can see to it that the appearance of the thing doesn't suddenly jolt when you cut from one sequence to another. People respond to repetition, gradation of size and shapes, and airbrush gradations. These are things we know that people just love to see.

NANCY BEIMAN: Aren't curves also supposed to be something audiences respond to?

KEN O'CONNOR: Well, men respond to curves all the time. (Laughter.) Yes, if you play them off right—a curved line against a straight line, that's the strong thing.… Curves versus straights is a basic, and good, principle.… Different styles are good for study.

NANCY BEIMAN: You were talking about contrasts. A cartoon character, no matter how realistically animated, isn't real.

KEN O'CONNOR: Well, we've tried to get consistency. We've tried to make the backgrounds look like the characters, and the characters look like the backgrounds. I like experimentation and contrast too … there was a fashion for a while to take colored tissue paper and tear it up and use it for backgrounds. Frank Armitage used that in THE RESTLESS SEA.… It all depends on how much you want to convey the idea of the third dimension. Characters are, at Disney, normally animated in the round. They seem to be round, so the idea has been to try to make the background seem to have depth too. If you get it sketchy and flat, it won't achieve that. It might achieve something else, and I'm all for checking that out. Originally they used watercolor washes in pastel colors so that the character would kick out. Then they got more depth into the thing. Poster colors can really make the background go back.… I started the switch on THE MOOSE HUNT. We painted the characters in flat colors and then painted the rocks, and trees, and bushes in … poster technique. With the right values it did go back.…

It's always been a two-way stretch to try to make the characters and the background so rendered that they seem like one picture on the screen, and not like two disparate objects; the second direction of the two-way stretch is [that the] character must read and be seen as separate from the background. The primary thing is to have the character legible. This can be done by line design and color and sometimes by texture contrasts.

In other words, if you have a large, smooth character, you can put a lot of little texture things in the background for contrast.… Separating characters from backgrounds [while relating to them at the same time] has always been the big struggle.

NANCY BEIMAN: Do color key artists have a background in front of them so that they can relate characters to the background?

KEN O'CONNOR: No, color key starts at the story sketch stage. The color [modelist] has frequently seen the storyboards and so has a general idea of the color and tonality of the *probable* backgrounds. Background painting is frequently one of the last functions to happen [on a film]. The character is one of the first, so they have to get some sort of a model early on.

NANCY BEIMAN: When you have nighttime and daytime sequences in the same picture, do you design characters with colors that would fit in with practically any type of lighting?

KEN O'CONNOR: Some of the characters are naturally difficult. Pluto is difficult because he's sort of an intermediate, middle-value tan. This is the sort of color you're liable to use in a background quite a bit; so you want contrast. You've got to push the background down or up relative to his value. Some characters have built-in contrasts. A penguin, for example; put it on a dark background, only the light will show up, and vice versa. You can get contrasts within the character. You know that part of it is going to read, whatever you put it over. That could be important.

[Character colorists in the model department] would design what they thought would make a good character. A king, lion, whatever, would be designed for itself. Later they frequently had to be adjusted for color to go with the backgrounds that showed up. But they had good basic design and good tonality.

NANCY BEIMAN: There's a design principle which states that dark colors are "slower" than light ones.

KEN O'CONNOR: Yes, the "heavy" is heavy in the value sense as well as in the mind.

NANCY BEIMAN: How useful are inspirational paintings?

KEN O'CONNOR: There's an evolution that has to go on. When you do thumbnails [for storyboard] you find out that these [artists] are not concerned with, for instance, screen directions. We would change things around. These [sketches] are not too specific. They just have the atmosphere and feeling which they thought would be good [for the picture]. Almost none of [the sketches] have survived.

NANCY BEIMAN: Are there problems that are common to both short and feature films? Was there any difference other than that of scale?

KEN O'CONNOR: Nancy, you're full of questions like a dog is full of fleas.… Well, a lot of difference was time.… And there were essential differences in tempo. Short films had to be finished in six or seven minutes, so the story man had to gear his mind up to a rapid tempo and so did everybody else. Features have more opportunity for pacing—slow, fast, and climactic drops, rises, and dramatics and so on.

[Short-film] tempo is fast underneath, and scenes had to be shorter. Action was faster and we tried to get as much quality as we could into them, but due to time and budget they were necessarily simplified.

NANCY BEIMAN: I was wondering if you could comment on some of the early "Silly Symphonies," some of which had rather slow pacing.

KEN O'CONNOR: This was probably because they were geared to the music. But "Silly Symphonies" were different from the Mickey or Donald cartoons. They were into prettiness, beauty, and that stuff. They were more into the look of things rather than the story, such as the Plutos and Ducks and so on were.

NANCY BEIMAN: Would you do as much research for a short film as for a feature?

KEN O'CONNOR: Oh yes, I would do as much research on everything as I had time for, and that means getting data from every available source.

NANCY BEIMAN: On the shorts, what kind of story construction worked best for you?

KEN O'CONNOR: Normally the simplest story was the best.… This sometimes affected the features such as DUMBO, where the story is very simple.… Simplicity in story didn't mean that our settings or our drawings were simple necessarily. THE UGLY DUCKLING was a simple story … but we had a really complex forest and pond and all the hunter eyes there.… I didn't lay that out but wish I had.

We had shots down to eight frames in length in SNOW WHITE AND THE SEVEN DWARFS, where she's running through the forest and the trees came at her. Simple things were done here because there's no point in putting massive [detail] behind an 8-frame scene. It would never be seen. Contrariwise, if you had a 15-foot scene you would try to elaborate the background so that the eye didn't have to look at a blank wall for that length of time. Circumstances alter cases.

NANCY BEIMAN: Could you talk about some of the short films you worked on?

KEN O'CONNOR: Oh boy, that's like picking out of the Sears Catalog! Well, I liked CLOCK CLEANERS, because we got violent angle shots. There were some who felt that perhaps the layout man put in angle shots just for the sake of putting in angle shots! However, the picture called for it.

NANCY BEIMAN:  What characters did you work with?

KEN O'CONNOR: I worked with all the characters. I was with Freddy Spencer right from the very beginning when he was first developing the Duck, before the Duck became cute.

NANCY BEIMAN: Would you try for a different feel for each series, to get them to differentiate from each other? Would you do a different background for the Goof and the Duck?

KEN O'CONNOR: You fit the setting into the story each time. In MOVING DAY (1936) the story largely dictated the set [as well as] the action. The story man didn't necessarily have to work the [backgrounds] out thoroughly, but the layout person did.…

Silhouette value was something that [director] David Hand was very strong on, and it was particularly important to make the characters legible so that Walt could read them.

NANCY BEIMAN: If you were doing an atmospheric thing wouldn't you have to sacrifice some silhouette value to get the proper effect?

KEN O'CONNOR: Sometimes in a sinister or mysterious film you'd play silhouette down and it would be hard to see because that was part of the story … you'd see mysterious, dark figures moving through patches of light. Dramatics controls everything. But in a normal cartoon, we made things very clear and very plain.… [The characters] had to show up as strongly as we could make them, and silhouette value was [stressed] by the layout person and animator particularly.

I know of no law that is invariable. I think every rule is made to be broken. But you have to work on general average, and in general average you'll come out ahead by stressing silhouette value. When we have quick action, the audience has to figure things out very fast. [In life-drawing class Don Graham would say,] "Now black it in." Doing this to your drawings was oddly revealing because you'd [sometimes] find that you just had a blob that didn't express anything. It's very good training … and not only for animated cartoons.

**"Circumstances alter cases."**

**"Now, that's better than a poke in the eye with a sharp stick!"**

**"That's clear as mud!"**

—Ken O'Connor

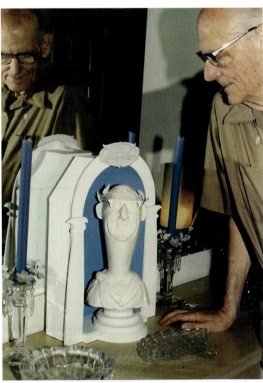

**Ken O'Connor with self-caricature bust, 1987. Photo by Nancy Beiman.**

HAIL GLUTEUS MAXIMUS

# Appendix 2

# Caricature Discussion with T. Hee

*FEBRUARY 23, 1979 (edited), © 1979, 2006 by Nancy Beiman*

T. Hee was a noted caricaturist at the MGM, Warner Brothers, and Walt Disney Studios. T. worked in story and character design on films such as MOTHER GOOSE GOES HOLLYWOOD, THE RELUCTANT DRAGON, and NOAH'S ARK, and was sequence director on "The Dance of the Hours" sequence of FANTASIA and PINOCCHIO's sequences with the Fox and Cat. He created storyboards for UPA cartoons including MR. FUDGET'S BUDGET, THE OOMPAHS, and GERALD McBOING BOING on PLANET MOO. The interview was recorded at the California Institute of the Arts when I was a student in T. Hee's caricature class. We never learned his real name.

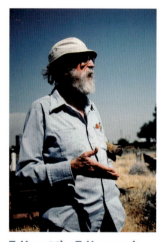

**T. Hee at the T. Hee ranch, 1982. Photo by John Van Vliet, reproduced by permission of John Van Vliet.**

NANCY BEIMAN: It's very interesting. This is the only art form that you need a machine to view it with.

T.HEE: One frame at a time. Consequently, you see the motion. [But] you can create motion through *design*.

[You can] express a situation through a variety of little actions … or one tremendous action carrying right through. [Edgar Allan] Poe used to say as he began to write a story, that "it wrote itself." I talk to animators who are like this. They start a scene, and as they start working with it, this character takes over and becomes the one who leads him or her to the final action. Each one of us sees things completely differently.

NANCY BEIMAN: Would it be good for [an animator] to have a set of guidelines, the way Japanese art has?

T.HEE: I think that each one of these [woodblock] artists had their own interpretations of what they were seeing. And this is the same thing that should be evident with people in an art school. Why *be* exactly like someone else? Create your own art that has a strong sense of identity. This is the only way that you can progress. If you try to copy and imitate you will find that somebody else who is *creative* will keep pulling ahead [of you]. If you're copy-

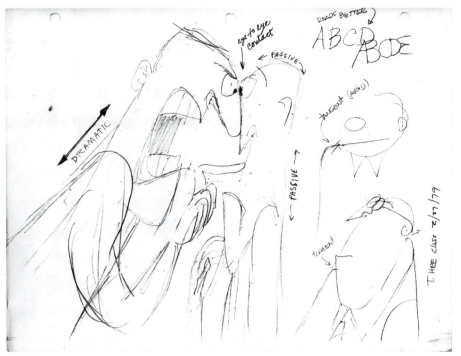

**A drawing by T. Hee depicting motion in design. Certain parts of the figure read 'faster' or 'slower' than others. The eye is led around the composition in the direction indicated by the arrows and captions. The composition and pose of the figures conveys a sense of motion in a single drawing (Nancy Beiman collection).**

ing and trying to do what somebody else did you will find that you are always two or three steps behind this other person.

NANCY BEIMAN: You once said that you can always tell when a drawing had been taken from life and when it had been thought up out of your head. How would you be able to do that?

T. HEE: You had an assignment where you made caricatures of each other using clay. They have a life because they were 'of' somebody who existed. Just to make a caricature without any kind of relationship to something that exists, that has life and action and vitality, will ensure that it will not have that liveliness.

NANCY BEIMAN: How do you design something that doesn't exist? Say, something that has no relation to anything on this planet. It's totally alien. Do you have to try to relate it to something that you are familiar with?

T. HEE: I think most everything is related to something else. There isn't anything that is original all by itself. No one describes those Martians, and so forth, exactly the same.

If you think long enough about a certain thing, it will make a picture in your mind.… The fact that you try to capture something that is real is better than having something that you made up. It will help you to give it life. Life aspects are the factors that make things on the screen appear convincing.

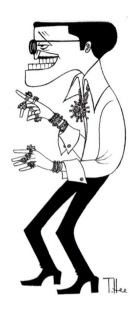

**Sammy Davis Junior caricatured by T. Hee (Nancy Beiman collection).**

To make a caricature of *anybody* is one hell of a challenge. I think you have to forget yourself, forget everything, and think in terms of what this person has that makes them different from everyone else that you've seen. You have to look at that person and look at another person and see how they contrast.

It's difficult to make a caricature of somebody unless you *know* them. So to get back from reality and work from that base is, I think, the only way to do caricatures. Look at dogs or animals and people in the zoo and really study them. I think studying the differences and uniqueness of each individual creature that exists is the way to do it.

NANCY BEIMAN: Would you find that it is harder to caricature someone when they are aware of you? Would you rather hide in the corner so they wouldn't see you and be off guard?

T. HEE: No, I think that it's better if they are busy doing what they're doing. They're not pretending to be something that they're not. Try to get them as they are. *You're being caricatured right now.* (General giggles from class.)

T. HEE: You got a whole million questions?

NANCY BEIMAN: No, only about four.

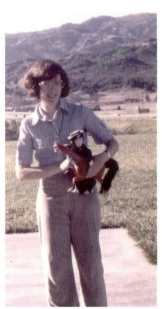

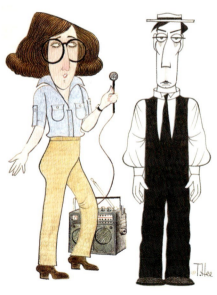

IMPROBABLE INTERVIEW # 1980
Caricatures of Nancy Beiman interviewing Buster Keaton, by T. Hee. Photo at left was taken by Enrique May the same day this interview and caricature were created

**Caricature of Nancy Beiman interviewing Buster Keaton, by T. Hee. T. told me later that "I drew both of you from life, only about 50 years apart!" The photograph was taken by Enrique May, at T. Hee's request, on the same day that T. drew the roughs for my caricature (Nancy Beiman collection).**

T. HEE: Okay, I came out with four answers this morning.

NANCY BEIMAN: You have been talking all morning about a different way of seeing that a creative person must develop. Is this something that you are born with or can you train yourself to look at something objectively?

T. HEE: I think it's something you are either born with *or* you can train yourself to do. If you could train your brain to record little details, well, it would be just a delightful thing. You can do it by going into a store and looking at the … textures of materials and how things are put together. Put colors together and see how they work, or go look at bark on trees to see how one is different from another. Start training yourself to observe things. That's why I think that little kids have it made—little tiny ones, about two feet tall—they fall down in the grass and experiment. They're tasting and really getting close to the earth. When we grow up we lose all sense of that; we look in windows as we go down the street [and we are] straightening ties or pulling a skirt down. We don't look up and see what's up there with those buildings.…

I think that everything you've ever seen or ever done or heard as a child is still there with you. It's not something that you're going to destroy. Your contemporary approach can open up your mind to recall these things and become involved in more things.

I believe very strongly that if someone is going to draw a horse they must go look at a horse; touch the horse … and get in back of a horse [but far enough back so that you don't get kicked] and get *on* a horse. Then you know what a horse is! But you cannot draw a horse by simply taking a look at one that goes down a street. You have to really study it and apply every bit of creativity you have within you to capture that horse.….

I am for learning everything you can about the human form. But you will never do all your animation [or design] based exactly on the training you received [in life-drawing class]. You have to observe from life.

You have guidelines, but if you were to take an animal and give it human characteristics—put clothes on it, turn it into a fat man or a skinny guy—it becomes a caricature. You don't have to make it too realistic.… Your best action will come from a caricature body. If the legs are short, you are confined to a certain kind of action. But if it's a high-waisted thing with long legs, then you've got something else. Go to some extremes to change what would be considered "normal" placement of proportions on the body. Unless you are going to be doing "lifelike" animation you should be getting into this offbeat type of thing. I think you can get away with all kinds of exaggerations. People will accept your 'giraffe walk' because they don't know the basis for the movements. Most animated animals are hu-

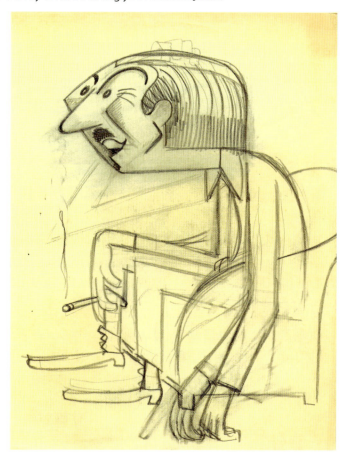

**Caricature of Walt Disney (circa 1940) by T. Hee (Nancy Beiman collection).**

man beings in animal skins.

NANCY BEIMAN: I'd like to talk to you about inanimate objects. If you are caricaturing your backgrounds and they are *not* moving, but one "inanimate object" is moving in the foreground, would it have a different design quality from the rest?

T. HEE: I think I would give them the same degree of caricature so that they would be related to one another. The one doing all the activity looks like everyone else but acts differently. If it looks different from the articles on the wall, there will be no correlation between the objects in the scene. There should be a marriage between the objects in the background and foreground.

NANCY BEIMAN: Cartoon characters tend to be stereotypes. Pretty girl. Handsome hero. Characters that are going to be nice, "look" nice.

T.HEE: Well, designs come from an expression of the character. It can't be pinned down. "All villains have to be big and strong. " I don't think so. I think they are stereotypes. The easiest way out is to make them big and mean.

There are degrees of nicety and villainy that you can play with. Once I was working with Frank Capra. He and his associate, Joe Sisten, were talking about a villainous character. They said you could not really laugh at a villain unless you liked him. So what they tried to do was have a bit of action happen to the villain that … made him seem a human being, not all bad. Then, whatever he did after that, you could laugh at.… If you make him all bad and show no aspect of weakness or likeability, then you've got a dead character.…

Of course, if you have all funny villains, you wind up with Dom DeLuise characters, a Mel Brooks picture. There have to be gradations of villainy and heroics.

I think that we are intrigued by villainy. The villains are usually the important people in the picture. They make drama happen. If you don't have drama, you don't have much of a story.

You get to know the characters and realize who they are by spelling out their characters, a little bit at a time, by their actions. Charlie Chaplin was the guy who was trapped with a villain in a snowbound cabin in THE GOLD RUSH. The villain fantasizes about Charlie turning into a chicken. He was at risk of being decimated and done away with. He was the hero dealing with this crazy madman.

NANCY BEIMAN: The villain in that picture wasn't really that mean.

T. HEE: *But he could be at any minute!*

NANCY BEIMAN: Chaplin was also the guy who had a millionaire friend who liked him when he was drunk but couldn't stand him when he was sober.

T. HEE: You cannot say, "This is what makes a villain; this is what makes a hero!" There are all kinds of gradations!

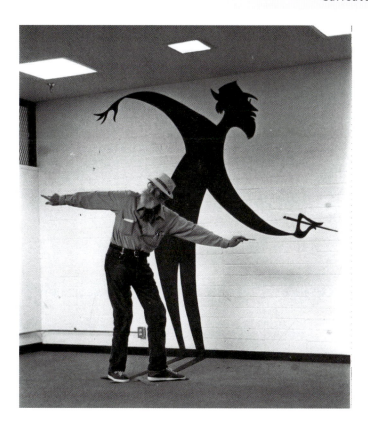

**T. Hee at Cal Arts, early 1980s. Caricature by Ralph Eggleston; photograph by David Fulp. Reproduced by permission of David Fulp.**

# Appendix 3

# Interview with Ken Anderson

*by Nancy Beiman (edited), © 1979, 2006 by Nancy Beiman*

Ken Anderson worked in story and development on many Disney features. His art direction credits include ONE HUNDRED AND ONE DALMATIANS, THE SWORD IN THE STONE, THE JUNGLE BOOK, and THE RESCUERS.

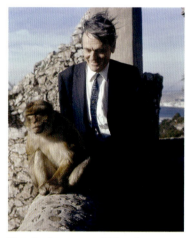

**Ken Anderson and friend. Reproduced by permission of Cyndy Bohanovsky.**

NANCY BEIMAN: Ken O'Connor's been bringing in a lot of stuff that you did. You seem to have done practically everything! My main questions will be about story, since we don't have a lot of information on how to recognize when a story has good potential for animation.

KEN ANDERSON: You don't mind if I ramble a little bit?

NANCY BEIMAN: No.

KEN ANDERSON: In the last 15 or 20 years the emphasis has been [in the right place] on animation. There is a tendency to specialize. [But] there is no reason why a good animator can't also be a good story man. I have to go back to the beginning to make my point a little more clear. We were all animators.

We were interested in animation as an art form and also as a way of expressing ourselves. And we were, or are, more or less, all frustrated actors. We feel acting, and we also feel art and design, and try to put that over [in the films]. Every one of the animators in the early days was also an idea man. Some of the animators were more interested in telling stories than others were. I believe that everyone who is involved in animation should also be involved in story. Which is what intrigues me with your question; it's a bit unusual, because it seems to me that that [ability] has been lost sight of in the industry.

There is no way that I've ever heard of that is a 'sure thing' in constructing a story. But there are a few guidelines that I learned, not things that I knew instinctively. I had to learn them through experience.

If you are considering making an animated feature, you must remember that the animation medium is predominately a pantomime medium. The most important thing in it is body language and expressiveness, put over by the way the characters move. This should not be overwhelmed by an excess of dialogue. The moment that this happens, you have an audio, or radio, medium and you really don't need the pantomimic gestures to put it over. The virtue of the medium as we know it today is that it is worldwide. Pantomime is understood everywhere, even though certain little gestures, in certain countries, mean the opposite. The basic movements of the human body—recoiling in fear, laughter, and so on—are all recognized universally, so pantomime has a very broad base of communication.

Walt said something that stuck in our minds. He said, "You don't write a Disney feature. Building a Disney feature is a lot like building a building, with building blocks. Our building blocks would be 'personalities'." It would be better for our purposes if those personalities were abrasive, or if there was some sort of conflict between the protagonist and the antagonist, because this gives you more room for entertainment and communication. In the early days we discovered that a true story line or "clothesline" for an animated feature would work best if the story line was extremely simple. If you could go from A to Z in as simple a direction as possible, you could hang more entertainment on that simple story line. It is very easy to explain why 'this' problem created 'that' problem and then 'that' problem all built and led, in consecutive order, to a finish. The extraneous things that were least entertaining and least helpful to the development of the story line would be gotten rid of. The better ones, we'd keep.

NANCY BEIMAN: Did you write the treatment first?

KEN ANDERSON: Oh yes. Your treatment—it's not a script, because we don't get too involved with dialogue, we just get involved in the 'clothesline'. We weren't trying to pass ourselves off as writers. We were writing a theme. If we can hang sequences on the clothesline, it's going to work. Simple stories are *defined*. This is the [type of story] that you should try to have. But it's not easy to come by.

NANCY BEIMAN: Nearly all animated films—I can think of very few exceptions—have been made from children's books. There is a lot of very good fantasy being written for adults. Has there ever been any attempt to develop something like that and would there be a potential for this type of story?

KEN ANDERSON: Yes, I think so. I'm sure there are many doors to be opened that can be opened. But we didn't consider SNOW WHITE AND THE SEVEN DWARFS to be a child's fantasy. Adults then weren't so afraid to be associated with things that children liked. During the past 20 years it seems that adults before the age of 50 don't want to be associated in any way with something that is perceived as 'childish', and after 50, there's no hope!

NANCY BEIMAN: Movies have become more diversified instead of appealing to a family audience.

I really would love to know how you go about taking a story sketch and breaking it down into camera angles. How do you know when one shot is going to work better than another?

KEN ANDERSON: I think that in order to plan the story sketch, you have to be primarily an animator, whether you are actually going to animate the scene or not. Unless it is a purely scenic shot where the animation is incidental, where there's some lovely establishing mood that has to be established. Otherwise you can't create something in story sketch if you are not thinking of animation. There is an ideal way, I think, of working. It involves thumbnailing *entire pictures*. I would go through breaking down sequences and scenes and how they would be animated. I'd do my own version of how the dialogue and staging would work best for particular actions. Thumbnails have to coordinate sound, picture, dialogue, and you have to be able to decide whether the script is useful. Nine times out of ten an animated feature cannot be written. It has to be visualized. The thumbnails could even be shot and timed. We would add scratch dialogue. And this became a "Bible." We'd do the whole picture, not just sequence by sequence. Each animator would be given a copy of this book [of thumbnails] for the whole picture before he came onto it. The animator would say, "I have a better way of doing this," and could substitute his own way of what the thumbnail action should be. Everyone should build the building if they can, and if theirs was better, it would become the version that was used.

NANCY BEIMAN: I sometimes have trouble distinguishing the thumbnails from story sketches. You use several different drawings for a scene where the storyboard might use only one.

KEN ANDERSON: It depends on who is doing the story sketch. In this case, it was Bill Peet. … He had a feeling for putting over scenes, too. Everything here is a re-evaluation. In most cases, there was no prior storyboard sketch for them. There was just writing. Bill's story sketches were undoubtedly a help.

NANCY BEIMAN: Would you work with inspirational drawings?

KEN ANDERSON: That's right. I also did some of them, and some of the storyboards, though more of those were done by Bill Peet. I took the storyboards and developed them a step further.

NANCY BEIMAN: So your cutting is determined by motion?

KEN ANDERSON: Yes, by putting over the idea of motion. I would make many, many sketches [for each scene in the sequence]. It wasn't just blind searching, because the minute you know what your story situation is, what you are trying to put over, you begin to have preferences: should it be real close, long shots, should you be looking down or up? Every part of your experience is used to interpret that particular instant of movement.

There are all sorts of reasons for angles—it might be a low angle if the viewpoint is Jiminy Cricket's. There are reasons for moving the camera. You maintain a mood with the camera angle and the station point.

NANCY BEIMAN: Were you influenced by live-action directors?

KEN ANDERSON: Absolutely. I used to go to the movies *all* the time and make sketches and drawings of how they put over certain things; [thumbnails of] staging in live-action pictures. Walt got hold of that, and one day we began to have classes on this very thing; cutting, staging, and storytelling with light. All the good pictures communicated with the audience. Today I find many pictures that have confused cutting—too fast, or with people going in different directions. They do that on purpose. They don't want you to know what's going on. They really don't want you to catch up with them until they can surprise you with the ending. It's a different way to put things over than my training.

NANCY BEIMAN: Have you ever tried to do this sort of cutting in animation?

KEN ANDERSON: Sure. I think there's no holds barred for anything that you can do to intrigue and entertain an audience. Obviously the new film held my attention or I wouldn't be talking about it. It was just hard to follow. We were afraid that if we did not let the audience know very clearly what story point we were trying to make, we could lose them for maybe a whole sequence.

NANCY BEIMAN: Is there a tendency to be a little over-obvious in the staging of animated cartoons?

KEN ANDERSON: I think so. Almost so that it becomes boring. But I think that no one is really equipped to do the cutting that is being done today unless they understand the staging that we were talking about earlier, which is very basic. If you understand how to communicate then you can deviate from it in the same way that knowing the scales on the piano enables you to play a complex piece of music. You can bang on a piano and make a lot of sounds that may not have any relevance to the people who are listening to you.

NANCY BEIMAN: You were sole character designer on the later Disney pictures. I notice in the thirties and forties, character designs seemed to be more of a group effort. Do you get better results when you have a group of people to bounce ideas off of?

KEN ANDERSON: Oh yeah. From the very beginning, every one of us overlapped into everything on the picture. It was a real delight. Everyone was involved in learning all the other facets of the production. Then you gravitated toward whatever your strengths were. Frank Thomas never gave up! He was a story man, an animator; he was interested in background painting and everything else, which is the way it was supposed to be. Ollie [Johnston] was the same. And I never got over animating, either! We interacted in every way. And some of us, because of the immensity of the project, found we had to level on something, because if you kept bouncing around you'd never get anything done. I found that I liked to level on the overall picture, the characters and the story situations. I gravitated on my own accord to the story department. I liked mood and locale also. But I kept animating scenes on my own just so I wouldn't forget how!

The day is coming when any person can make a film all by himself. And that is the optimum. But then if you have many artists, as in the great *ateliers*, each making their own painting or sculpture, the atmosphere is very invigorating. Many animators could work in one studio on their own projects. Think of the variety of films that will occur!

When writing for animation, if any one of us wrote the lines, and we knew which actor was going to play the part, we'd say, "This is what we want but we want it to come out of *you*. If you see a better way to say it, you should build on it." That is part of the building block process I referred to earlier. There's another thing to take from Walt: making a feature, to him, was like planting a seed. You want to have a plant with one beautiful bloom. You plant the seed and fertilize it, and prune it to make sure that the strength is not going to the wrong buds. You allow one beautiful bud to bloom and you've got your feature picture. But you don't stand around and admire it; you plant another seed.

NANCY BEIMAN: What sort of problems would be posed by work in short films as opposed to features?

KEN ANDERSON: The short film doesn't need to hold a person's attention for a long time so you can get away with a lot more; be a little offhand, less concerned with what is going to happen in subsequent sequences. It's a comparatively short piece of film and so its problems are extremely simplified. You can hang a short film on one character. You don't necessarily need two or three, although it's better to have at least one foil.

NANCY BEIMAN: Well, the advantage is that you don't have to make your point in a feature. The disadvantage of a short is that you have to make your point in six minutes or less.

KEN ANDERSON. That's true. It works both ways. You can concern yourself, if it is a musical short, primarily with entertainment. Some of the earliest Disney shorts were nothing more than movement to music.

NANCY BEIMAN: If you have a good story, how do you make a presentation out of it? Do you work your story sketch up immediately from thumbnails?

KEN ANDERSON: First of all, I will probably start visualizing the characters, making drawings so that I will have something to make little thumbnails from. It's almost the same as writing a book. But you can't write a story without characters and you can't get characters without the story! You have to have something to illustrate, and so I start fooling around with the characters. They keep changing—they keep getting better, as the story develops.

NANCY BEIMAN: Would you do a script treatment of the story after you had actually started drawing characters, or would you do them at the same time?

KEN ANDERSON: My script treatment would probably be done more or less coincidentally with the characters. Each one leads the other. As you find a simplified version that you are likely to work with, you are likely to see a flowering of certain portions of it. This gives you an impetus to move on to something else. One thing takes precedence for a while, then the other catches up, and so you finally arrive [at a finished story with characters set]. The written form is just a nice simplified version of a treatment. You should make it clear and very simple so that your story evolves through the relationship of the characters. Each entertainment situation will help the story progress.

NANCY BEIMAN: Do you occasionally find the story going in a different direction when you start doing your thumbnails?

KEN ANDERSON: It certainly has happened.

NANCY BEIMAN: Your script is not the final word?

KEN ANDERSON: Oh, no. The chances are that the script will be superseded by story-board, to the extent that when you get through, your original writer may not recognize the story that has turned into something quite different from what you started with. This is not so much an intention as a development. It grows so far away from the original that it demands new writing.

NANCY BEIMAN: Do you like to write original material as opposed to adapting something that has already been written?

KEN ANDERSON: I think that nowadays, you don't have to rely on a pre-sold story to a pre-sold audience. If you have a great story, if you can get it produced and distributed, you would easily succeed. Animated films can be made using a wholly different way to reach the audiences than they used in the past. I sure hope that this happens. I don't think we are at the 'end'.

NANCY BEIMAN: The color in modern films tends to be more garish than formerly. Older films used more muted tones. Violent colors are appropriate for a garish character like Medusa, but every character seems to be that way nowadays. Sometimes the characters do not seem to fit with the backgrounds.

KEN ANDERSON: In ONE HUNDRED AND ONE DALMATIANS, everyone suggested using muted grays on the backgrounds since this film took place in England. England is not a country that is associated with garish colors, considering the weather that they have. I found that [the limited palette] was a strength; it brought us full circle to SNOW WHITE AND THE SEVEN DWARFS, which had been designed in earth colors. BAMBI looked as good as it did because of the art of Tyrus Wong. Ty had a beautiful way of emphasizing a highlight in a forest and let it melt off into color tones so that you felt you were seeing a whole scene where only a part of it was actually painted.

Somebody has to have control over the color and style of each picture. Eyvind Earle's personal style of painting had a tremendous influence on SLEEPING BEAUTY; the characters were influenced by the backgrounds which were done first, with the strange angular design, and the characters came along later. And there was Mary Blair, who was just a natural colorist. Earle came to his color combinations mathematically.

NANCY BEIMAN: In character design, is it good to have a 'studio style' or to keep experimenting?

KEN ANDERSON: Inherently, for your own growth, and for the growth of the medium, it's wise to keep experimenting. We never tried to come up with a style. It's simply that certain shapes and forms are easier to move. Certain shapes make it easier to get expressions.

NANCY BEIMAN: What sort of reference do you use for character design? What if you were designing a mythological creature that you could not see in a zoo?

KEN ANDERSON: I research everything I can. For an actual creature, I get every photograph or book that I can find. I immerse myself in as much knowledge of the creature as I can, make it a part of me. Then I decide that some things have to adapt but I can make the adaptations based on what I know. The material leaves me better prepared to come up with something new. For mythological creatures: in the back of my mind I would think of an actor (say, Wallace Beery) when designing a particular dragon. So I was drawing dragons with that feeling of Wallace Beery. Shere Khan the tiger in the original THE JUNGLE BOOK was a terrifying menace. He doesn't appear until the last two sequences of the picture. We had to see why everyone else was afraid of him. I was stymied but had to come back with something. I thought of Basil Rathbone, but he was no longer around even at this time, so I used him as an inspiration. Shere Khan didn't even have to show up, he just *was*. I didn't try to draw him to look like a caricature of Basil Rathbone, but to have that quality of high-and-mightiness so that his appearance told you that he was this kind of creature. Walt looked at the drawings and said, "Oh, I know who that is, that's George Sanders." Milt Kahl, who loved it, developed the design much further but they were based on the sketches I did. So this is an example of a design that was based on a well-known person.

The vultures in [THE JUNGLE BOOK] were based on some of the animators! They wound up as the Beatles, but at the start, they were caricatures of the animation crew. Many times you are in danger of falling into the trap of caricaturing an actor or actress. What you really should do is create a new character that has the actors' attributes that help put over your story point. You never know where anything that influenced you is going to show up. And it will be subconscious, unless you are trying to do a conscious imitation of the style.

NANCY BEIMAN: How much do your character designs change by the time they reach the screen?

KEN ANDERSON: Generally, I'd say that they were pretty much right on. Most of the animators would better, or strengthen, the designs. But nobody ever gave anyone a command to stay right on that same model. We all believed Walt's tenet, which was "Everyone who has an input [into the film] must feel free to keep in-putting anything they can." If some animator made arbitrary changes, they would have to be prepared to defend it, explain why it was better. If they made changes, it was because they were generally stronger.

The thing I would like to impress you all with is this: we didn't have anyone to talk to. We had to learn all of this the hard way. *Nobody knew.*

# Glossary of Animation Preproduction Terms

**Action Model**  Model sheets depicting typical movements and expressions of an animated character.

**Animatic**  Filmed storyboards that also include simple animation, camera moves, or special effects, edited and precisely timed to a dialogue and/or music track.

**Animation**  An art form that brings life to inanimate objects. See also *2D Animation, Stop Motion,* and *CGI.*

**Art Director**  The designer of the production. The art director in an animated film will create settings, color palettes, lighting, character and prop styles, and may also design *layouts.*

**Atmospheric Sketches**  Experimental color sketches depicting moods or settings that may be used in the film.

**Barsheet**  A printed aid to the director indicating footage and frame counts and space to write music and sound cues beneath. They were used mainly in commercials to time the film and *slug* dialogue and music tracks. They have largely been replaced by computer editing programs.

**Beat**  See *Story Beat.*

**Beat Boards**  Storyboards showing only the main story points and major action of the picture; a visual *outline* of the story. They are also known as *outline boards.*

**"Bible"**  A pictorial guide to all aspects of the characters, props, and backgrounds. Television animation "Bibles" contain final clean model sheets for all characters, props, and backgrounds, brief story outlines, and written descriptions of the characters' personalities and attitudes. Feature "Bibles" may consist of reference and inspirational art assembled as style guidelines for character designers and layout artists. In television production, a "Bible" is also known as a *model pack.*

**Blue Sky**    Early stage of development where any idea is acceptable.

**Boarding**    Drawing storyboards for a film or sequence of a film; used as a verb (e.g., "I'm still *boarding* Sequence 6").

**Boil, Boiling**    Inconsistently applied color that moves independently of character or background motion. A color may *boil* inside a character's outline as an artistic effect in hand-drawn animation.

**CGI**    Computer-generated imagery, commonly referred to as '3D animation', although computer programs are also used for *2D* animation.

**Cheats, Cheating**    A technique that allows a stylized or graphic design to appear to move in three-dimensional spaces. Mickey Mouse's ears never turn, but are *cheated* as his body moves (e.g., "*Cheat* the hair part as her head turns"). *Cheats* are not meant to be seen by the viewer. See also *Morph*.

**Clean**    See *Tight*.

**Clean Up** (v.)    The act of standardizing the appearance of an animation drawing or image.

**Cleanups**    Model sheets, background, layout, or animation drawings that have had their line quality standardized and rough construction details removed.

**Color Keys**    Copies of panel(s) from the storyboard with characters and backgrounds rendered in color to set the palette, mood, and lighting for each sequence.

**Color Models**    Standardized color for animated characters and props. Each character may have several color models depicting its appearance at different times of day, changes of outfit or mood, or in changing seasons.

**Color Script**    A series of small *color keys* in a timeline showing all changes in the color palettes from the first sequence of the film to the last.

**Construction Model**    A simple breakdown of a character design into its component shapes. It enables an artist to move and judge proportions on an imaginary figure in two- or three-dimensional space.

**Crew**    The artists working on an animation production. A *story crew* works on storyboard, character design, and development.

**Dope Sheet**    See *Exposure Sheet*.

**Evolution**    In hand-drawn animation, the refinement and simplification of a character design if test animation indicates areas for improvement. CGI figures, once modeled and rigged, are *locked down* and are more difficult to *evolve*.

**Exposure Sheet**    A printed or digital graph depicting each frame of a scene, with specific layers assigned for animation. It also contains action and dialogue columns for timing and track breakdown. They are also known as *dope sheets* and are used in all types of animation.

**First Pass**    In animation, character design, and storyboard, the first pass is the initial presentation of the artwork to the story head or directors. It is usually experimental and always gets reworked.

**Flop**  To reverse the staging on a storyboard drawing; to mirror the action without making other changes in staging. *Flopping* a drawing is not the same as *turning it over.*

**Frame**  The fixed border of the screen or monitor; a set area where all animated action takes place. Or, an individual photograph from a strip of motion picture film. In storyboarding: synonymous with *Panel.*

**Handout**  A storyboard, animation, or design assignment.

**Lay Down, Laid Down**  Timing dialogue, music, or effects to a soundtrack. See also *Slugging.*

**Layouts**  The animated 'stage'. Layout develops from storyboard and includes backgrounds, camera angles and apertures, props, overlays, and rough character poses for each scene as a guide for the animators and background painters.

**Leica Reel**  A term originating in the Walt Disney Studio, which invented it. Storyboards shot and timed to dialogue and music. This is how animated film is edited. See also *Story Reel.*

**Linetest**  See *Pencil Test.*

**Locked Down**  Finished, without the possibility of further change.

**Log Line**  A single sentence that describes the story.

**Maquette**  In French, a model or mock-up. In animation, a three-dimensional sculpture of a character design. Maquettes enable artists to view a design in the round and help determine lighting on characters when combined with backgrounds.

**Master Background**  The animated equivalent of a live-action master shot. It establishes the setting, lighting, and scale of a sequence but may not be an actual production background.

**Model Pack**  See *"Bible"*

**Model Sheet**  A guide for the appearance and construction of an animated character or prop. Model sheets enable different artists to create the illusion of one performance by standardizing the character's appearance and suggesting typical actions. See also *Rough Model, On Model, Off Model, Action Model,* and *Cleanups.*

**Morph, Morphing**  A change in attitude or motion that is accomplished by modifying the character's entire design and 'growing' it into the next pose. This, unlike a *cheat,* is usually visible to the viewer.

**Off Model**  Character appearance that does not conform to the *model sheet.* Normal distortion is considered *on model.*

**On Model**  Character appearance that conforms to the *model sheet.*

**Outline**  A brief written description of the story.

**Outline Boards**  See *Beat Boards.*

**Panel**  An individual storyboard; synonymous with *frame.*

**Pencil Mileage**  Highly detailed and rendered artwork; or, a difficult design.

**Pencil Test**   Hand-drawn animation that is shot against *layouts* and used to refine timing and action before coloring and finishing the film. (Also known as *linetest*.)

**Pickup**   A line of dialogue that is recorded after the original session to incorporate script changes; or, a partial retake of a line.

**Pitch, Pitching**   The presentation of artwork to an audience in real time, with running commentary by the artist. *Pitching the boards* provides instant feedback on the *readability* of the story and the artwork.

**Placeholder**   A character design that is used for *rough boards* before its final appearance has been standardized.

**Plus-ing**   A creative interpretation or addition that improves the original story or design.

**Pop, Pop It**   A graphic shorthand used to turn a character in space without actual three-dimensional movements. If you are asked to *pop* something, the views will change abruptly with no in-between poses. Many characters will *pop* from three-quarter views to full face or profile. Persistence of vision creates the illusion of smooth motion.

**Post-production**   Compositing of pre-existing visual and audio elements to create a finished picture.

**Pre-production**   The conception, planning, and development of a film's story and characters. Pre-production artwork does not appear in the finished film.

**Presentation Boards**   Highly-rendered storyboards with detailed tonal work on characters and backgrounds; finished illustration rather than roughs. They may include a lot of *pencil mileage.*

**Previsuals, Previz**   The fourth-dimensional interpretation of a three-dimensional storyboard. *Previz* moves the camera through scenes and blocks character actions in real time using roughly-modeled CGI *placeholders.*

**Production**   Creation of artwork that appears in the finished film. This can include CGI models and rigs, animation tests, backgrounds and *layouts*, soundtracks, and finished color animation scenes.

**Push It, Pushing**   Exaggeration of a design, character pose, or story point.

**Readability**   Character designs, action, or storyboards that are staged in clear and understandable fashion are said to *read* well. Boards that do not read well are generally *turned over.* Story points that lack *readability* are generally done over.

**Rough Boards**   Quickly-drawn storyboards with basic tonal values designed only to tell the story. They may use *placeholder* characters that are not *on model.*

**Rough Models**   *Model sheets* that include standardized *construction models, action models,* and comparative sizes for the final design of the characters but do not include *cleanups.* The line quality will vary and details may not be finalized. Rough model sheets are used by animators to maintain the consistency of the character's construction in hand-drawn film. They also enable a CGI or puppet modeler to accurately reproduce the design in three dimensions.

**Roughs**   Drawings that retain construction lines and contain variable line quality are referred to as roughs. These may be retained in the final project, sometimes in conjunction with *boiling* color. See also *Cleanups*.

**Scratch Track**   A soundtrack that is not the final one for the picture. Scratch dialogue and music may be used as *placeholders* to time *story reels* and *animatics.*

**Screen Ratio**   The proportions of the screen where the finished project will be viewed. Storyboard panels can be designed to specific screen ratios, such as widescreen or Academy standard. *All storyboard panels in a production will have the same screen ratio.*

**Sequence**   A series of consecutive scenes related by setting, character, or story point.

**Setup**   A color test in which *color models* and props are placed over a background to check the *readability* and contrast.

**Slugging**   Indicating the timing for each storyboard panel prior to scanning or shooting a *story reel*; also, determining where dialogue and sound effects will appear. Formerly this was done on *bar sheets;* slugging is now usually done with computer editing programs or *exposure sheets.*

**Stop Motion**   Animation created by moving a jointed puppet or other object one frame at a time and photographing the movement in (very slow) real time. It is the only truly three-dimensional animation.

**Story Beat**   A major change in plot or action; a turning point.

**Storyboards**   A visual script for a motion picture. In animation, a guide for character performance, action, editing, and staging for the finished picture. (*Storyboard (v.)* The act of storyboarding a motion picture.

**Story Head**   The director of the story on a feature film. The Story Head (or Head of Story) assigns story *handouts,* reviews the storyboards before they are presented to the directors, and exercises artistic control over the *crew.* He or she will develop the story and *beat boards* with the writers and directors.

**Story Reel**   Filmed storyboards timed to a music and/or dialogue track. Animated films are edited here and not after camera, as in live action. Synonymous with *Leica reel.*

**Sweatbox**   Screening the *story reel*, *animatic,* or animation for a critical audience. The Walt Disney Studio was the first to sweatbox pencil tests and story reels and this is now common industry practice.

**Thumbnails**   Rough drawings or sketches, usually very small in size. (*Thumbnail (v.)* Illustrating a story point with small, sketchy drawings to determine staging.)

**Tied Down**   See *Tying Down.*

**Tight**   Very clean and close to the final model design; the opposite of *rough.*

**Treatment**   A written description of the story that is more involved than an *outline.* A treatment will include subplots and may include rough dialogue, but it is not as comprehensive as a script.

**Turnover Session**    A review session where directors and story artists make changes to the boards and story in real time after a pitch. Panels that are discarded or changed are literally turned over and repinned so that the blank back of the panel faces the audience. Panels may also be *flopped* during the turnover session. Changes can also be drawn on self-stick notes placed over the panels.

**Tweak**    A minor change or improvement to nearly-finished work.

**Two-dimensional (2D) Animation**    A common term for hand-drawn animation. It will also include various computer-graphic programs, cut-paper, sand animation, painting on glass, and other techniques lacking 'three-dimensional' appearance.

**Tying Down**    Finalizing, finishing, or standardizing a character model, storyboard sequence, or animated scene. After rough art is completed and approved, you will be asked to *tie it down*. See also *Locked Down*.

**Universe**    A consistent design element or technique that relates animated characters to one another and to the props and backgrounds, providing unification for an imaginary world.

**Up on Reels**    Storyboards assembled and timed on film or digital media with soundtrack. This may be a *scratch track* produced for a *story reel, Leica reel*, or *animatic* (e.g., "Sequences 1 through 5 are *up on reels,* and we're still *boarding* Sequence 6").

**Wild Track**    Sound recorded without a script, such as murmurs, chatter, exclamations, sound effects, or animal noises. These are usually added to the track near the end of production.

**Workbook**    An intermediate stage between *storyboard* and *layout* in which camera moves are designed to work with  *rough* feature boards. Workbook drawings are thumbnails for cinematic staging.

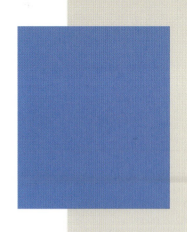

# Index

—